GLOBAL HINDU DIASPORA

Global Hindu Diaspora

Historical and Contemporary Perspectives

Edited by

KALPANA HIRALAL

MANOHAR
2016

First published 2016

ISBN 978-93-5098-153-5

Published by
Ajay Kumar Jain *for*
Manohar Publishers & Distributors
4753/23 Ansari Road, Daryaganj
New Delhi 110 002

Typeset by
Kohli Print
Delhi 110 051

Printed at
Salasar Imaging Systems
Delhi 110 035

Contents

Acknowledgements

I would like to express my sincere thanks to the following:

- The contributors in this volume for their very insightful papers and timeous submission of their proofs.
- This work is based on the research supported in part by the National Research Foundation of South Africa. Any opinion, finding and conclusion or recommendation expressed in this material is that of the author(s) and the NRF does not accept any liability in this regard.
- To Professor Pratap Kumar (Editor-in-Chief, *Nidan*) for granting permission to reproduce a few of the chapters in this volume (in a slightly altered form) which first appeared in *Nidan*, vol. 27 (1-2), July-December 2015.
- My family, in particular my husband, Sujit Roopnarain and my daughter, Priyanka, for their patience, love, support and encouragement.

October 2016 KALPANA HIRALAL

CHAPTER 1

Introduction

KALPANA HIRALAL

The term 'diaspora' means 'to scatter' in Greek. Traditionally diaspora was a term associated with the dispersion of Jewish people following their expulsion from the Holy Land and was often associated with pain, tragedy and loss and exile. However, over time the term diaspora has evolved to include a wide range of scattered groups (Vertovec 2000: 2-5). It has included people who have migrated because they were affected by 'push' and 'pull' factors, political persecution or others in search of new opportunities. Religion has become, over the decades, one of the most central categories of analysis in diaspora studies. The significant interconnections between religion and diaspora is succinctly noted by Ninian Smart (1999). According to Smart they provide insights into 'general patterns of religious transformation' in terms of religious beliefs and rituals and with the plurality of religion in the diasporas 'multiplicity is now commonplace' (Smart 1999: 421; cited in Vertovec 2000: 8). However, some scholars, like Robin Cohen (1997) are hesitant to describe religions as 'diasporas' but rather perceive it as 'cognate' to diasporas in that it 'can provide additional cement to bind a diasporic consciousness' (Cohen 1997: 189; cited in Vertovec 2000: 10). Vertovec argues that it is possible to talk of a 'Hindu diaspora', 'because, no matter where in the world they live, most Hindus tend to sacralize India and therefore have a special kind of relationship to a spiritual homeland' (ibid.: 10). James Clifford (1992) has written of 'traveling cultures' and has alluded to the transformative potential of religions in the diaspora in that time and space and travel 'displace conventional notions of culture and place' (Vertovec

2000: 9). Smart raises import questions on the transformative nature of religions through the example of Hinduism. He asks us to consider:

> themes such as caste, yoga, *bhakti* [devotion], pilgrimage, temple rituals, austerity (*tapasya*), wandering holy men, instruction in the scriptural traditions, regional variation, pundits, a strong sense of purity and impurity, household rituals, veneration of the cow, the practice of astrology, belief in reincarnation, the importance of acquiring merit, etc. These themes, which are woven together into the complicated fabric of Hinduism in India, do not all travel equally easily to new environments. The very act of going overseas implies something about purity and loss of caste, for instance. Though caste is not absent as a phenomenon in the diaspora, it is less rigidly observed. . . . (Smart 2009: 185).

Smart has alluded to the complexities and challenges of diasporic communities adapting to their new environment and its impact on religion. Well over a million Indians migrated as *girmitya* (agreement signers) from British India to various parts of the British colonies. They originated from diverse backgrounds in terms of their religion, caste, ethnic and language groups. The indentured labourers were not only confronted with the hardships of bonded labour but also in reconstructing their cultural and religious identities in the diaspora (Samaroo 2013: 316). Their way of practising and sustaining Hinduism in various parts of the globe often, varied. In Trinidad immigrants prayed under a tree, they gathered on a 'platform around a toolsi gatch (shrine adorned with tulsi or Indian basil) that housed their deity' (ibid: 320). Among the common deities found were Kali, Durga, Hanuman and Parmeshwari (ibid.). In Fiji lack of a structured family life and the dissipation of caste rules as a result of migration meant that religious practices were observed in a very simplistic form,

> A popularized ritualistic version of Hinduism with a focus on devotion and little intellectual content was practiced, rituals and ceremonies became the essence of the religion, and Brahmins derived their authority from a command of these rituals rather than religious learning. . . . In the barracks of indentured workers, the Ramayana was recited, and Ram Lila performances were staged. (Voigt-Graf 2010: 1112)

In the diaspora 'pioneering movements of the nineteenth century' has played an important role 'in helping the diaspora Hindus to adapt themselves to a new environment' (Smart 2009: 185). This is most noticeable in South Africa, Trinidad and Fiji at the turn of the century as the Arya Samaj movement in India sought to influence religiosity in these regions. The Samaj believed that migrants were being strayed from the path of Hinduism and they worked diligently to revive Hindu beliefs and principles. This took several forms: establishment of Hindi schools, propagation of Hindi language, the establishment of youth camps, and learned missionaries were invited from India 'who gave lucid explanations of Vedic thought and updated the local community on events in India' (Samaroo 2013: 319-20). In Trinidad among the leading Arya Samaj missionaries were Pandit Jaimini Mehta, Pandit Ayodhya Prasad (ibid.: 319-20).

In the diaspora *mandirs* (Hindu place of worship) took upon a special significance as "[M]eeting places where bonds between fellow worshippers could be forged, their deities praised, schools started, material and business arrangements sealed, and a sense of cultural self-maintained. The '*mandirs* and *kooties* (*kutia*, another name for temple) sustained the *jahaji* relationship, which had begun on the ships' (ibid.: 320).

In the diaspora, religious worship in the home has played an important role in sustaining the bonds of Hinduism. In their study, Mazumdar and Mazumdar (2009) have argued that the concept of 'home as a religious space' play a very significant role in assisting immigrants to reinforce, renew and reconnect with the past, the homeland, environments, and people,

> Hindus view their homes as sacred places. They transform their newly acquired secular residences or houses into what they consider to be appropriate space by consecrating these through enacting rituals and installing at sacred time their family gods. They also create an altar, which becomes a repository of religious objects and artifacts. Second, Hindus incorporate various forms of religious art into their homes. This art is symbolic and conveys important Hindu values by depicting gods, goddesses, and stories. . . . Third, Hindu families create gardens and work assiduously to obtain and grow particular flowers, plants, trees, and fruits they believe to be auspicious and use in

prayer. The garden appears to be an integral part of their 'home'. (Mazumdar and Mazumdar 2009: 264)

Regional variation of migrants also had an impact on the early development of Hinduism in the diaspora. For example, there were two main types of migration indentured and free migration. Indentured migrants, as alluded earlier, faced by labour bondage followed very simplistic religious practices. In the Caribbean, for example, the vast majority of immigrants originated from the Bhojpuri cultural area from present day Bihar and Uttar Pradesh and only a small proportion of indentured labourers came from Madras in south India. The Caribbean Hindus came from a region influenced by Sanatan Dharma,

> The Indians who would migrate to the Caribbean centuries later were predominantly rural people with little scholarly learning. Hence, this devotional trend in Hinduism became the most pronounced aspect of their religion. The general belief system of most religious groups that came to the Caribbean was 'Sanatanist', and the main form of religious expression was 'bhaktie' avoiding the heavily intellectual discourse that so characterizes Vedantic philosophy. (Samaroo 2013: 316)

Among the free Indians or 'passenger' Indians also known as unassisted immigrants who came at their own expense, their status enabled them to more easily establish contacts and links with India. They were primarily Gujarati speaking Hindus and Muslims. Free from bonded labour they often engaged in trade and semi-skilled work. Caste and kin networks plays an important role in their assimilation and adaptation in their new environment. In Fiji and in South Africa, for example, the formation of religious-cum-cultural organizations was common amongst them. In Fiji the Gujarati Samaj is one of the major organization for 6,000 Gujarati Hindus (Voigt-Graf 2010: 1113; Hiralal 2014).

Smart is correct to note that themes of the Hindu tradition 'do not all travel equally easily to new environments' (Smart 2009: 185). Migration bring its own challenges and complexities and immigrants' actions and identities are shaped and defined by the socio-economic, cultural and political stimuli of their environment. At times migrants are compelled to abandon certain traditional beliefs and practices and adopt new ones. Hence religious practices and beliefs are constantly being redefined, renegotiated and reshaped (Vertovec 2000: 22-35). For example, in Fiji there has 'been a major shift in ritual practices' (Voigt-Graf 2010: 1113). The Cobra Rock Temple at Labasa is an important place of pilgrimage to Indo-Fijians, Holi which was the major Hindu festival for early migrants was replaced by Diwali (festival of lights) (ibid.: 113). In Thailand the Chao Phya River has acquired the same status as the Ganges River for many Hindus (Suarez 1999: 156).

Hinduism in the twenty-first century is not without its challenges. In recent years the growing conversions of Hindus to other religions, the complexities of caste, the impact of AIDS, and the need to reinvigorate the youth in Hindu teachings are just some of the issues that it faces. What shape and form will Hinduism take in the twenty-first century? What will Hinduism look like in the future? These relevant questions are the subject of debate and deliberations amongst religious scholars, academics and politicians. This edited collection addresses some of these questions as well as the relationship between religion and diaspora within historical and contemporary perspectives. The contributors include scholars who come from various disciplines and seek to locate their analysis within different geographical contexts. In so doing, religion is not only problematized but one acquires a clearer understanding of its complex nature in the diaspora.

Usha Shukla maps out the lived human experiences of indentured Indians/*girmitiyas* of Hindu origin in the diaspora with special reference to South Africa. The paper highlights the challenges and constraints endured by the early Hindu immigrants and their descendants, at different historical periods and in the process highlight the importance and relevance of religion in their lives. The indentured communities in South Africa, unlike immigrants in the British Empire, did not attain political freedom with the dismantling of the British Empire but were subjugated people until the demise of apartheid in 1994. Despite their political adversity Hindu religion played an important role in their lives. The paper also highlights a growing sense of religious consciousness amongst South African Hindus in terms of blurring of linguistic, ethnic and caste divisions. The paper highlights the intersections of religion and identity in the diaspora.

Ramleela/Ramlila, a play that enacts episodes from the life of Lord Rama, is performed annually in more than 30 venues in the Caribbean island. This play and its significance in the lives of the indentured Indians to Trinidad and their descendants is explored in Kumar Mahabir's paper. Mahabir shows that Ramleela/Ramlila is more than just a religious play, it also contributes to the social fabric of the East Indian community. It engages youth in meaningful activities, it promotes Hindu ideals and moral values, it has challenged age-old conventions of caste, male supremacy, promotes religious tolerance and to some extent shapes the politics of the country. It has, withstood the vagaries of time, space and globalization. According to Kumar it is one of the institutions by which Hindus in Trinidad have used to reconstruct their community in the diaspora. Ramleela/Ramlila is not only the story of Rama, but Rama's narrative of exile, displacement, pain, suffering and his eventual return resonates with the narratives of indentured Indians who migrated overseas.

Vashti Singh's paper explores the interconnections between state religion and education. This paper provides a historical account of state educational policies in Trinidad and the formidable resistance by the Hindu community against the process of Anglicization. Singh highlights how the Hindu stance against Anglicization was aimed at protecting their cultural and religious identities. The educational issue provided Hindus with an opportunity to merge religion and politics. The Hindu religion became a driving force for political mobilization spurring locals to institutionalize Hinduism and to create a more homogenous culture which would stand above language and caste divisions and create a distinctive Hindu identity. Singh concludes that the early resistance to Anglicization has left a legacy in Trinidad among Hindus of shared heritage, cultural homogeneity and a resilient Hindu community.

Ruchi Agarwal focuses on the Hindu community in Thailand, a relatively under studied group in the diaspora. Agarwal assesses the transformations of Hinduism among diasporas and its impact in shaping and defining the Hindu identity. The paper draws on Ninian Smart's (1999) theory on the importance of studying religions and diasporas thereby providing an insight into how Hinduism evolved in Thailand over time and space. Historical trading links with India and Southeast Asia have played a pivotal role in the integration of Hinduism into this region and Thai society. The presence of Hindu gods and temples has thus enabled Indian migrants to assimilate and acclimatize easily into Thai society, making Thailand their home away from home. Interesting, too is how Hinduism has been incorporated into Thai Buddhism, shaping and defining the religious identities of local Thais. Agarwal concludes, that whilst Hinduism in Thailand have evolved and transformed over generations, some elements like customs, traditions and beliefs significant to Hinduism remain unchanged.

Gerelene Jagganath's paper examines notions of identity, belonging and homeland among a group of NRI's (non-resident Indians) living in Durban and their attempts at both integrating and preserving their cultural and religious/spiritual identity in South Africa. The paper addresses the challenges and constraints of immigrants in their efforts at creating a home and community away from home (India) and the practices and meanings they have developed in the local (South African) context. Based largely on qualitative methodology the study focuses more on the women participants or 'accompanying wives' (referred to as 'dependents' in migration discourse) but also includes male perspectives on some key issues raised such as identity, home and agency. Jagganath's focus on the 'accompanying' wives of the NRI's, shifts the migration lens away from the male migrant trajectory and the economics of migration. The paper concludes that transnational cultural barriers and diasporic religious presence gave rise to novel re-configurations of creating 'a home away from home'.

Both Sagie Narsiah and Namita Nimbalkar's papers add to scholarship on religion and environmentalism. Narsiah examines the Hindu response to climate change in South Africa. This paper examines the role of nature in Hinduism and argues that some of the very basic tenets of Hinduism such as *dharma* and *bhakti* (righteous living, non-violence) and devotion to god, have direct links to nature. These concepts can be invoked in responding to environmental issues currently facing the world today. Narsiah argues that religion has the potential to take the lead in providing an alternative rationale for the salvation of the Earth. Locating the discussion within the South African context, the paper concludes that Hindus need to be more actively involved in environmental issues and that they need to be part of an ecumenical movement to address these pertinent issues.

Namita Nimbalkar's paper seeks to show how religion can also influence how we perceive our roles with regards to protecting our environment. The paper provides the role religions can play in resolving the complex environmental concerns of today. The current environmental crisis is not only creating awareness amongst individuals and communities but also forcing one to relook at our most cherished religious beliefs and practices. The paper also examines Gandhi's approach to the environment. *Nimbalkar argues that the concept of* non-violence is also extended to include the responsibility which man should undertake to protect the biotic and abiotic world. Gandhi envisaged for a peaceful and just society, where man could cohabit in harmony and have reverence for all things living and non-living. The paper concludes that religion should engage with other disciplines (science, culture, politics, education, gender, public policy and economics) to seek comprehensive solutions to environmental problems.

Gail M. Presbey's review of Pedro Machado's *Oceans of Trade: South Asian Merchants, Africa and the Indian Ocean, c. 1750-1850,* (2014) highlights Machado's contribution in two important areas: departing from Eurocentric historical scholarship in the Indian Ocean trade and integrating race, gender and class as important categories of analysis, thereby incorporating the histories of marginalized groups. According to Presbey Machado provides an interesting account of the early Hindu Vaniya merchants in Kathiawar peninsula in Gujarat, India between 1750 and 1850 whose trading activities have been scantily recorded. Presbey's critique also raises important issues on religion, morality and trade in the Indian Ocean region.

Anand Singh's paper provides an interesting insight to the worship of Ganesha, its significance as a deity and its overall impact on the lives of Hindus in South Africa and globally. The paper highlights how Ganesha worship in South Africa evolved over time. Early indentured labourers, particularly those from North India, carried with them popular epic scriptures viz. the *Ramacaritamanas* (*Ramayana*) and the *Bhagavad Gita*. They kept their religion alive by gathering under shady trees reciting their hyms. Their deities were mainly Rama and Krishna, but other deities such as Ganesha did feature among them. However, over time, Ganesha has become a key deity in the lives of Hindus in South Africa and globally. Singh's paper raises pertinent issues around the seriousness and ambiguities of academic scholarship on Ganesha worship, the spread of Ganesha worship throughout Asia and the role that television can play in enhancing and reaffirming public belief in this deity. Singh's paper alludes to the interconnections of religion and identity and how it shapes and defines religious worship in the diaspora.

Kalpana Hiralal's paper provides a historical perspective on the role of missionaries in shaping and defining religious identity at the turn of the century in South Africa. Hiralal's paper on Pandit Vedalankar maps out the life and contributions of this remarkable religious leader. He was a man of extraordinary vision and infinite energy, he was totally dedicated to the cause of the Arya Samaj, these characteristics allowed him to make a significant contribution to Hinduism in South Africa. Yet in the vast corpus of literature on the historiography of Hinduism in South Africa his contributions have not been recorded. This paper using a biographical approach, documents the contributions of Pandit Vedalankar to Hinduism in South Africa. The paper maps out Vedalankar's efforts at promoting the Hindu religion and language in South Africa by giving it structure and clarity Ordinary Hindus could identify with its tenants and promote their religion within their home. He also promoted religious unity amongst the various Hindu ethnic groups. Vedalankar's contribution highlights the significant role early Hindu missionaries played in nurturing religiosity in the diaspora.

Collectively the above papers address key issues of Hinduism in the diaspora from historical and contemporary perspectives.

ACKNOWLEDGEMENT

A few of the chapters in this volume first appeared in *Nidan*, vol. 27 (1-2), July-December 2015. My sincere thanks to Professor Pratap Kumar (Editor-in-Chief, *Nidan*) for granting permission to reproduce these articles in slightly altered form in this collection.

REFERENCES

Clifford, James, 'Traveling Cultures', in L. Grossberg, C. Nelson and P.A. Treichler (eds), *Cultural Studies*, 96-116, New York: Routledge, 1992.

Cohen, Robin, *Global Diasporas: An Introduction*, London: UCL Press, 1997.

Hiralal, K., 'Forging a Gujarati Hindu Identity in South Africa: A History of Gujarati Hindu Organisations in South Africa 1900-1983', *Nidan*, 26 (2), 2014, pp. 60-82.

Mazumdar, Shampa and Sanjoy Mazumdar, 'Religion, Immigration, and Homemaking in Diaspora: Hindu Space in Southern California', *Journal of Environmental Psychology*, 29, 2009, pp. 256-66.

Samaroo, B., 'Hinduism', in Patrick Taylor and Case Federick I (eds), *The Encyclopedia of Caribbean Religions*, vol. 1, Urbana: University of Illinois Press, 2013, pp. 315-21.

Smart, Ninian, 'The Importance of Diasporas', in S. Shaked, D. Shulman and G.G. Strousma (eds.), *Gilgul: Essays on Transformation, Revolution and Permanence in the History of Religions*, Leiden: Brill, 1987, pp. 288-97; re-keyed in Shepherd, John J. (ed.), *Ninian Smart on World Religions*, vol. 2: *Traditions and the Challenges of Modernity*, Surrey: Ashgati, 2009, pp. 183-205.

——, 'The Importance of Diasporas', in Steven Vertovec and Robin Cohen (eds.), *Migration, Diasporas and Transnationalism*, Aldershot: Edward Elgar, 1999, pp. 420-9.

Suarez, T., *Early Mapping of Southeast Asia*, Periplus: Singapore, 1999.

Vertovec, S., 'Religion and Diaspora', paper presented at the conference on 'New Landscapes of Religion in the West', School of Geography and the Environment, University of Oxford, 27-29 September 2000, 1-45, accessed 18 November 2015 http://www.transcomm.ox.ac.uk/working %20papers/Vertovec01.PDF

Voigt-Graf, Carmen, 'Hindu Community of the Fiji Islands', in J. Gordon Melton and Martin Baumann (eds), *Religions of the World : A Comprehensive Encyclopedia of Beliefs and Practices*, vol. 3, Santa Barbara: ABC-CLIO, 2010, pp. 1111-13.

CHAPTER 2

Hindu South Africans and the Global Hindu Diaspora: Past Challenges and Future Prospects

USHA SHUKLA

INTRODUCTION: THEORETICAL AND METHODOLOGICAL APPROACH

This paper interrogates salient aspects of the indentured labour system which transported over a million Indian men and women between 1834 and 1917 to far-flung British and other European colonies as agricultural and general labourers, their lives in indenture and the emergence of their descendants in the diaspora. In tracing the processes and persons involved in the indenture or *girmit* (from agreement—hence *girmitiya* or indentured person) enterprise, dominant features will be highlighted to discover its real nature. Mauritius (1834), Guyana (1838), Trinidad (1845), South Africa (1860), Suriname (1873) and Fiji (1879) were the major destinations of the Indian poor who were recruited to turn the colonial lands into productive resources. The experiences of most of the *girmitiyas* were the same, although a destination such as Fiji (1879) shows greater counter-colonial spirit because of the higher degree of awareness that had by then emerged in the Indian political scene. The freedom struggle began in 1857, and the Indian National Congress (albeit spearheaded by English people) was founded in 1885. In the social and religious fields, the Brahmo Samaj (1830—Calcutta) and the Mahajan Sabha (1830—Madras), Prarthana Samaj (1867—Bombay) and Arya Samaj (1875—Bombay) contributed to the awareness (Parvatiya 1996: 192). The case of South African indentured Indians and their offspring differs from the other indentured communities, in that whilst India and the diaspora Indians attained political freedom or rights with the dismantling of the British Empire, South Africa and all its subjugated peoples including Indians only came out of the tyranny of Apartheid in 1994. This adds to the admirable quality of the Indian, including the Hindu South Africans' achievements, rightly attributed to the tenacity and faith of the *girmitiya* forefathers inspiring them. Hindu missionaries, social and political activists and associates of M.K. Gandhi also worked amongst them.

This paper deals with documented lives and experiences of a people who ventured out in good faith to seek a better life. They were, however, awarded much suffering and punitive measures; there cannot be a trade-off of their sufferings with the opportunities, which they used to their advantage at superhuman cost. Their historically lived experiences, as discussed below, will guide the theoretical approach. The migration of people throughout history was based on a variety of premises: Singh (2009: iii) mentions social, political and economic factors and discrimination by hegemonic groups of people as some of these. The migration of the Indian *girmitiyas* from 1834, whilst resorting under these heads to a certain extent, was not totally voluntary: The poorest of India's citizens were enlisted to tend the British plantations, because the exploitation of India's resources and people by the British had put these people in a state of 'high vulnerability' (Meer et al. 1980: 2), i.e. they had to seek a better life elsewhere. Methodological perspectives involved the examination of works, particularly of *girmitiya* descendants, and personal observation.

GIRMIT: OPPORTUNITIES OR *NARAK?*

An alternate source of labour was needed on account of the abolition of slavery, a scourge in the name of economic progress, exploited by the British and other colonial powers of the nineteenth century. This generated the myth in India that there were unlimited opportunities for economic advancement in the colonies for the starving, disease-ridden, landless and homeless Indians. To access this, they had to cross the Kala Pani (transportation or life imprisonment) and apply themselves to creating wealth, for both their employers and themselves. The system was thus a replacement for slavery, which was so pernicious and reprehensible that any comparison is truly odious. Indenture itself was no different from kidnapping and human trafficking. The Indians were lured into *girmit*, endured all the ordeals of a subordinate existence yet bequeathed to their descendants in the indenture Diaspora, the spirit of triumph and feeling of *Vasudhaiva Kutumbakam*—the world is a family—inspired by their religio-cultural traditions. They were not turned against life and humanity by adversity. Throughout the process of indenture, the official view was that indenture was an altruistic institution, as reflected in Queen Victoria's proclamation below, and the utterances of other members of the British Raj. However, the lived experiences of the *girmitiyas* record that it was a 'get rich at any cost' enterprise for the white farmers and real purgatory for the Indians, a situation which not even the Government of India, which was, after all, a mere representative of the British Crown, could ameliorate. Through values imbibed over centuries in India and moral strength gained through adversities, the *girmitiyas* embraced life in these foreign climes, emerging as economic and social victors in a milieu full of challenges and small mercies or opportunities.

A multitude of afflictions attended the lives of the *girmitiyas*: an objective assessment of the treatment they received at the hands of people in power over them, recruiting tactics and the true nature of the Raj and how it subjugated a vast nation deploying its citizens for its benefit will serve to explain how and why the *girmitiyas* with their evolved culture and world-view, could proclaim 'I am a Coolie', as Guianese poet Rajkumari Singh did (Bahadur 2014: xxi). It will also show why *girmitiya* descendants use words such as 'Odyssey' to describe their indenture experiences from the time of departure from India to the end of their lives, whereas some other *girmitiyas* use the term 'Narak' (Hell) for the same ordeal-filled journey.

In order to understand indenture one has to eschew a trade-off of the *girmitiyas*' sufferings against the so-called opportunities. Jain (2009: 7-8) cites Lal's words in a 2005 publication to reinforce this point: that indenture provided an opportunity and a challenge to thwart adversity with a mixture of adventure and fortitude. Lal, in his *Chalo Jahaji* (2000: xi) had already clarified that 'Scholars, many descendants of the *girmitiyas* themselves, are moving away from the morally charged indenture-as-slavery paradigm to look at the lived human experiences of indenture'.

There does not seem to be any trade-off here. The lived experiences of the indentured Indians before, during and after indenture and the factors behind these forms the focus of interest in this essay.

Both Lal (2000: x) writing about Fiji, and Bhawani Dayal (1947: 23) dealing with South Africa, use the Sanskrit word for Hell—Narak/Nurak (respectively) for the indentured life. This certainly implies that life in indenture was unbearable, and not like it was in India. The commonly propagated version of indenture makes the *girmitiyas* the beneficiaries of an altruistic and humane governing race, which it most certainly was not:

> All these factors (British land and agricultural policy in India) merely added to the plight of the peasantry who had already experienced poverty, unemployment and overcrowded conditions in a country permanently ravaged by disease, floods, famine, drought and the scourge of an over-expanding birthrate. . . . Emigration offered some hope to them of building the foundations of a better life for themselves and their offspring. (Henning 1993: 8)

The foregoing passage exemplifies the prevarication or equivocation often encountered when issues between rulers and the ruled arise. One has to isolate the facts behind the facades to discern 'morally charged' issues, to use Lal's phrase. From 1600 to 1857 the English East India Company gradually acquired influence over more and more territory in India whilst operating as a business with its Board of Directors in London. The Portuguese were in Western India for a longer time; and the French occupied Pondicherry, Mahe and Chandernagore contemporaneously with the British in India. The British crown only assumed control over India directly in 1857, after the First War of Independence (so-called Sepoy Mutiny). A few insights into the attitudes and atrocities of the colonial powers would help to appreciate their actions in India. In 1662, the Portugese 'gave' Bombay as dowry to Charles II of England when he married Catherine of Braganza. The English accepted this gift as a matter of course. The English government's dealing with their own kith and kin paints an intimidating picture of power in the wrong hands. The Scottish Highlanders who fought for Bonnie Prince Charlie against the English were 'banished and sold into indentured servitude' in Guiana after 1746 (Bahadur 2014: 183). In a hundred years' time they became adept at dealing with the indentured employees.

Moreover, the British colonists addressed their Indian workers in a very derogatory manner, yet they knew what they could get from them: 'I have never yet found a good honest workman make a frivolous complaint against his employer. On the other hand, the most worthless characters are the first to complain; men who have never worked in their own country and do not intend doing so here' (Henning 1993: 66).

It is clear that the plantocracy and the officials approved of silent perpetual working machines, whose working hours were extended at whim. Even complaining was fraught with danger. With no structures in place to really care for their welfare, the *girmitiyas* persevered with faith in God and the hope that adversities will eventually come to an end. The Natal *girmitiyas' mantra* to counteract hardships was to repeat the name of Lord Rama: *Rama ka naam liye ja, aur apna kam kiye ja*—Chant Rama's name and do your work (Shukla 2002: 123). The *girmitiyas* of other religious/linguistic groups used similar aphorisms. This is how they negotiated the *narak* of indenture. The *girmitiyas'* mute and meek acquiescence in their plight was, however, no justification for inflicting pain on them. It was unfortunate that generally the perpetrators were from the ruling race, and they broke their own elaborate rules of indenture with impunity, rules that were supposed to ensure fair treatment to the worker.

John Kelly (2001: 349) cites the British conception of 'Indianness' as natural 'coolies' rather than a civilized citizenry. He counters this by emphasizing that the *girmitiyas* used the paradigms of exile, battle against evil, victory and the obliteration of evil as a counter-colonial discourse. He states that they 'became not only *girmitiyas* but Indians who were Hindus in exile rather than coolies by nature'. In South Africa, the English attitude towards the indentured labourers was equally negative. Henning (1993: 103) writes that the Indians, particularly the freed Indians, were viewed as a 'sophisticated and active menace' to the Natal whites, especially as competitors in business and agriculture. The Colonial Secretary's office archive 2854/1906 records the following: 'The future of South Africa must forever be with the European races, governed by European ideas of government and peopled by a race of Europeans' (ibid.: 103).

As early as 1906, in colonial South Africa were discernible the seeds of apartheid, attempts at repatriation of Indians and all the injustices inflicted on them. Nor was Natal with its Indian population the only envisaged white enclave: Cecil John Rhodes, arch imperialist, politician and business magnate, expressed his plans for the Cape (and South Africa) thus around the same time: 'We have to treat the natives where they are in a state of barbarism, in a different way to ourselves. We are to be lords over them' (Xolela Mancu—*Sunday Times*, 22 March 2015, p. 19).

Rhodes used the word 'natives' to indicate the black African people of South Africa. The British in India and the colonies used the term 'coolie' more in the sense conveyed by Kelly above-natural 'coolies' (whatever that may be) rather than a civilized citizenry. Bahadur (2014: xix-xx) explains that despite the pejorative connotation applied to the weakest members of Indian society, in the Caribbean it became synonymous with 'exotic' and only later, with the rising of tension between Africans and Indians, a slur. In India and elsewhere, the term, applicable only to a very low class of menial workers, was, however, used by the English to include all Indians. In Natal the Coolie Commission reported: 'This word (coolie) in India is applied to the lowest class only, and it is regarded as a term of reproach in the nature of abuse. There is no doubt that the term is galling, and a source of annoyance. We would suggest that the term "Indian Immigrants" be substituted for that of "coolie" in all official documents' (Henning 1993: 47).

THE INDENTURE DIASPORA: ODYSSEY OR KALA PANI?

The Indian diaspora that evolved over 180 years presents a picture of successful communities with flourishing religious, social, political and business institutions and a vibrant cultural landscape. This diaspora and the *girmitiyas* comprised the different religious and linguistic groups of India. While *girmitiya*, Indian and Hindu are used interchangeably, the emphasis is on the Hindus as concern of the paper. The emergence of the Hindu *girmitiyas* from the *narak* of indenture was due largely to their faith in God and their strict adherence to ethical principles imbibed from their cultural and religious sources, some of which will be discussed below. Four hundred years prior to indenture, the Indian/Hindus had experienced the despair and humiliation of foreign domination and oppression. In those dark days '. . . for a nation bereft of its vitality, there was no alternative but to turn to the power and compassion of God' (R.C. Shukla in Shukla 2011: 149). Divine intervention was sought as a shield, and it gradually became a powerful weapon, with the rise of the Bhakti (devotional) movement in north India and the consolidation of Rama devotion. A closer association between Rama the God-King, also developed into a paradigm of exile and victory and return in terms of the *girmitiyas*' exertions and Rama's experiences.

The Indians did not leave on a journey to the colonies with any certainty of the future thereafter. They were recruited through false incentives and promises made by the recruiters or 'arkatis' from the 1830s. There was no 'sending' or 'receiving' agency at either end. This system lacked the humane elements of the supportive 'Kangani' system applied to recruits for Ceylon and Malaya, where officials of the villages oversaw the recruitment as well as the settlement of the workers in the work destinations (Hiralal 2009: 81), nor or the 'Maistry' system employed in Burma (Kumar 2000: 2).

The diaspora created by the *girmitiyas* is identifiable as settled communities with 'tourist' interest in the mother-country—India. The Indian or Hindu diaspora arose out of sincere motives on the part of the *girmitiyas* to work and serve the receiving countries. The ancient Hindu Diaspora of Southeast Asia in the early centuries of the first millennium, including Indonesia, Cambodia, Indo-China, and Malaya flourished under Hindu rulers and bequeathed magnificent monuments of religion and culture (Shukla 2011: 29). Parvatiya (1996: 11) mentions Hindu kings such as Surya Varman who were responsible for the gigantic temple complexes of Angkor (Siva) and Angkor Vat (Vishnu). The foregoing demonstrates that any Hindu conquest outside India was a cultural one.

Kelly (2001: 333) opines that 'Indian Diaspora' could be a multifaceted movement of Indians across the globe, including a 'highly self-conscious middle-class migration from India, especially into Anglo-North America in recent decades'. Kelly concedes, however, that the indenture system 'managed' by the British for the global distribution of 'coolies' is easier to locate in time and space. The phenomenon of NRIs in South Africa also demonstrates the differences between the *girmitiya* diaspora and the 'self-conscious' middle-class migration to South Africa since the 1990s. 'Self-conscious' is applied to Non-Resident Indians, skilled and confident, who went to the USA after the 1970s and South Africa after 1990.

For the Indian indentured workers or *girmitiyas*, their diaspora has become home for approximately 70 per cent of the immigrants and their descendants (Henning 1993: 23). The emergence of a stable, identifiable *girmitiya* diaspora was not due solely to choices made to settle in the colonies: the labour contracts provided for return passages (Law 14 of 1859, Clauses 24-8 passed by the Natal Colonial Government to govern terms of indenture – in Henning 1993: 9) and the *girmitiyas* themselves had not envisaged overstaying their *girmit* period. Why did so many of the *girmitiyas* not return? Were the British aware of these issues and yet recruited them?

THE LIVED EXPERIENCES OF *GIRMITIYAS*: ROLE ON RELIGION/CULTURE

If the return journey to India was fraught with doubts and fear, the onward journey to the plantations was not felicitous either: During the voyage they found themselves in purgatory without having sinned. The conditions on the ships were not conducive to human dignity, and women were subjected to lustful pursuit through cheap inducements such as sugar and biscuits (Bahadur 2014: 61) or forcibly overcome with leather straps. In those circumstances diaspora writers such as Lal (Fiji) and Bahadur (Guyana) use the phrase 'The Odyssey of Indenture'. Lal has a heading of a chapter of *Chalo Jahaji* (2000) and Bahadur part of the title—*Coolie Woman,* The Odyssey of Indenture (2014) using this appellation. Homer's hero Odysseus (Ulysses in Latin), having fought the war against Troy for ten years, continued on a ten-year voyage of adventure with his stalwart soldiers, as a means of evading the *ennui* of life in an uninspiring rocky little kingdom of Ithaca. This journey called the Odyssey, intended 'to strive, to seek, to find and not to yield' (Tennyson 1991: 47) had unforeseen hazards like the one-eyed giants, but also some romanticized adventures with the Sirens and the Lotus Eaters. The indentured labourers embraced their new homes as part of *Dharti Mata*—mother earth—which could provide for them who came to tend her. Today the Hindu diaspora made up of descendants of the *girmitiyas* has a religious, cultural and spiritual bond reinforced by shared histories. *Jahaji-bhai* (ship-brother) relations forged over 100-50 years ago created ties that persist between the descendants till today.

The human tragedy of *girmit* underlying the present-day progress and plenty was also exacerbated by the hard decision not to go back after the 5 or 10 years' contracts. Bahadur (2014: 49) shows some returning *girmitiyas* imploring the departing recruits not to leave India. There were also many cases of others who returned to the colonies! The moral lesson of the *Ramayana* denounced coveting other's property, country or person. Rama was their example of morality; he gave back conquered Lanka to the vanquished nation, saying 'the Golden Lanka does not appeal to me; the mother and the mother land are greater than heaven' (Sitaram 2004: 27). This underlines the battle for moral victory and non-covetousness. The flourishing Hindu culture in South Africa validates this. The foregoing contending forces made choices difficult. In addition to moral and ethical issues, some real impediments stood in the way: economic reasons being in the forefront.

Economic liberation was a key to a better life for some. Moreover, the funds required to finance returning on the expiry of the contractual guarantees was a serious deterrent. Henning (1993: 42) notes that 'It took a long time before either the Indian or colonial authorities would admit that most of those who returned had attained little benefit from them'. Women had to run the gauntlet of 'illiberal social and religious customs' (Bahadur 2014: 167) and a suffocating patriarchal environment in view of their being away from the watchful eyes of their families and communities in India. Mahatma Gandhi made a statement in *Young India* in 1926 that the returnees appeared to be 'social lepers, not even knowing the language of the people' (ibid.: 169). This was a bitter truth, coming from the pen of a Satyagrahi. To the men, ostracism from social circles or being denied *hookah paani* (hookah and water) was a great drawback. This was aggravated by their having come with a wife not married according to traditions. Some therefore abandoned their wife and children before reaching their villages (Bahadur 2014: 168). The women faced the greatest amount of calumny, coercion and cavilling at the hands of society.

Many people of Indian and European extraction were extremely concerned about the welfare of the *girmitiyas*, and pressurized the Government of India to terminate the system of indenture, much to the disgruntlement of the plantocracy. Gandhi, C.F. Andrews and Totaram Sanadhya were chief amongst them. The official view regarding the *girmitiyas* who were still alive, and their offspring, was that they must embrace their adopted homelands and not contemplate returning to India. Bhawani Dayal opposed repatriation, blaming the Government of India as much as that of South Africa for the *girmitiyas'* predicament. The South African government's desire to repatriate for racist reasons was anathema to Bhawani Dayal. Mahatma Gandhi was of the same view (Gandhi 1931: 13-14). Jawaharlal Nehru, first prime minister of India, was an aristocrat by nature and nurture, and had to deal with the realpolitik of India. It may seem churlish of him to have said *thethar log agaye* (The stubborn people have arrived) when the last batch of returnees arrived in 1955. This was heard in Guiana on 'all India Radio' (Bahadur 2014: 169). Whether Nehru expressed exasperation or disdain is not possible to determine. But Bahadur (ibid.: 169) feels irked by the fact that India could not graciously receive just

243 of her children, whereas she was dealing with millions of refugees. Jawaharlal Nehru espoused the cause of the liberation of South Africa from minority rule in forums such as the United Nations Organization. He often advised the South African Indians to identify with the majority in South Africa. The South African descendants of *girmitiyas* have no issues with such policy, as long as doors remain open for educational and cultural purposes.

One motivation for *girmitiyas* remaining in the colony should suffice to answer questions that may be posed by subsequent generations: Shri Prasad of Fiji in his poem *Girmit Ki Yaad* (Memories of Indenture) in Verma (2012: 137-8) proclaims that his forebears made sacrifices and toiled exceedingly hard to make Fiji productive. It is thus quite appropriate that they embraced Fiji as their homeland:

Hamne is desh ko sincha hai isliye apnaya hai.

We have cultivated this land, therefore we lay claim to it.

A few lines from poets of Trinidad, South Africa and Mauritius reflecting their tribute to the forebears serves to validate claims to the countries of their indenture. (All examples from Shukla 2011: 253, 257 and 260 respectively.)

Raviji of Trinidad in his *Ode To De Coolieman* says:

From all over Bihar and UP de arkatia fool up de poor coolie.
. . .
Bearing de pains they never squeal
Facing poverty they never steal.

Usha Shukla of South Africa pays tribute in *Pravasi Hindi*:

Bharat mata se laye sneha apaar
Dharm-sanskriti ke beej ka bhandaar
Kheton men eekha, man men raam naam
saath paalte, kabhi sahate ghor apman.

Bringing boundless love from Mother India, together with storehouses of religion and culture, they served and nutured both the sugar cane in the fields and Rama's name in their hearts, whilst also enduring the deepest affronts dealt by people in power.

Mooneeshwarlal Chintamunnee of Mauritius, paying tribute at the Kuli Ghaat where the *girmitiyas* disembarked since 1834, recounts the forefathers sacrifices and the legacy they left their progeny.

> *Dukha ke angaaron mein jalkar*
> *Tumane hamko sookhi banaya*
> *Zulm anyaya sahakar*
> *Jeene ka adhikar dilaya. . . .*

> You burnt in the furnace of suffering in order to make us comfortable,
> You endured atrocities and injustices to give us the right to live!.

The foregoing sentiments of *girmitiya* descendants speak volumes of their suffering, their labour and their love. They have recorded therein the pain and sacrifices of the *girmitiyas* who expressed them in their daily lives. We need to salute them for overcoming adversity and showing the coming generation how to survive the fire-ordeals (*agni pariksha*) of *girmit*.

THE PEASANTIZATION OF INDIA LEADING TO *GIRMIT*

It is unavoidable for questions to arise as to why and how citizens of a country with vast resources deserted their beloved motherland in search of material gain. Bhawani Dayal (1947: 6) provides glimpses of the mindset of the British, the real beneficiaries of indenture:

> In 1858 Queen Victoria made a proclamation with the concur-rence of the British Parliament, reassuring the people of India that Britain would rule India for the benefit of the Indian People. But the ink had scarcely dried on this proclamation when indentured slavery was revived.

This proclamation came soon after the transfer of political control over India by the English East India Company to the British Crown, pursuant to victory over the 1857 war of Independence. Thus all Indians were British subjects, whom the British treated with contempt and allowed the plantocracy and the colonial authorities to do the same. This transfer of power reinforced the British hold on

India, with the full might of the British Empire available to enforce the whims of the English from governors to the meanest officials. Queen Victoria assumed the title of Empress of India in 1876, and on 1 January 1877, Viceroy Lord Lytton held a Durbar in Delhi (which was not yet the capital—but the site of the defeat of India) to officially inform the subjects and celebrate the momentous occurrence. The official altruistic view of Queen Victoria was repeated at this ceremony by the Viceroy Lord Lytton, who 'mused on the "providential" nature of the British Raj, its intention to bring "progressive prosperity" . . .' (Misra 2008: 2). In his zeal to elevate Her Imperial Majesty's stature, Lord Lytton described her as 'worthy successor to the House of Tamerlaine' (ibid.). There was some irony in this: Tamerlaine, distantly related to the Mughals who ruled India from 1526 to 1857, was just a marauding bandit as far as his foray into India was concerned, spending only a few weeks in Delhi ransacking and plundering the city 400 years before. Lord Lytton aligned the British Crown with Tamerlaine, conveniently forgetting Bahadur Shah Zafar, the last Mughal ruler, whom the British deposed and exiled to Burma after the 1857 war. The British diligently and faithfully played the role of marauding bandits in India over two hundred years. 'Push' factors for emigration vary from one situation to another. Views of scholars tend towards the notion that the British emasculated the Indian populace and their homeland to make them vulnerable and pliant and available for their own benefit, either for labour or economic markets. Meer et al. (1980: 2) supra, refer to the exploitation of the vulnerability of the Indians by the British.

The period after the war of 1857 saw famine affect large parts of India. Movement of food grains was the immediate solution: however, J.P. Das (2009: ix) documents a case in Orissa where one-third of the population of the state was killed by famine, while Ravenshaw, the Commissioner told an enquiry that there was no famine, and the shortage was caused by hoarding. His answer stood in bleak contrast to what his own English (and Indian) subordinates reported about the dire situation. Misra (2008: 18) also shows how the British had peasantized India with their land and agricultural policies for their own advantage. Bhawani Dayal, son of indentured labourers in Natal is more forthright. In his book *Pravasi ki Atmakatha* (1947: 2) he writes that Indian Industry had been destroyed in order to make the factories of Lancashire and Manchester viable and prosperous. India's role was to supply the raw materials and markets for finished English goods.

The *girmitiyas* who were enlisted to make the British Empire and people wealthy had nothing tangible to call their own, particularly as a result of the peasantization or pauperization of the people. In spite of this deficiency, their spiritual culture and history enabled them to outlive the indenture system, the plantocracy and the Empire. John Kelly (2001: 331) creates the metaphor of the banyan tree (*bargad* or *vatavriksha*) which is sacred to the Hindus to explain the source of the *girmitiyas'* power and protection. He portrays the diaspora (including Fiji) as 'extensions of a vast cultural banyan tree with no hiatus because of the physical separation of Indians from the motherland' (ibid.). To Kelly, the *Ramayana* paradigm of banishment, exile and destruction of evil (Ravana represented by the plantocracy) are all seen as Hinduism in exile, waiting to return. In the *girmitiya* diaspora this metaphor acquired a life of its own, through Rama devotion. Shukla (2009: 72) reports thus: 'With the dawn of the twentieth century and the rise of social consciousness Rama's story provided the basis to negotiate social, political and economic rights'. Kelly (2001: 331) extends the banyan tree metaphor, suggesting that the destruction or termination of the indenture system was an 'inevitable result of the intervention of possibly divine forces raised by supplication for deliverance'. Whatever the objective validity of Kelly's metaphor of the banyan tree and the paradigm of exile, moral strength did ensue from these to fortify the *girmitiyas.* Jain's use of the word 'syntagm' for the paradigm of exile and return reduces it to a mere linguistic feature (Jain 2009: 8). Kelly has reported the elevation of Tulsidas's version of *Ramayana, The Ramcharitmanas,* as the Fifth Veda in Fiji (2001: 347). Kelly also notes that the *Ramayana,* wrapped in red cloth, is still used as scripture for administering 'oaths' in Fiji's courts (ibid.: 343). Faith in, and dependence on Divine Providence and ethical norms of Hinduism were integral to the *girmitiyas'* lives.

Whilst the *Ramcharitmanas* is couched in the Awadhi dialect of Hindi, the spirit of its teachings is embraced by all Hindus. In the diaspora, the verses such as the following are still used to denote adherence to sublime values:

1. Recognizing the entire creation as full of Sita and Rama, I make obeisance to them with joined palms (Balakanda 7.2)
2. It has always been the rule with the race of Raghu (Rama's ancestor) that one's plighted word must be redeemed even at the cost of one's life (Ayodhyakanda 27. 4).

As explained in this paper, the Rama ethos is pervasive in India, especially but not exclusively, amongst Hindus. The works of Father Kamil Bulcke, Justice Ismail, etc., bear testimony to its wide appeal. Currently, devotion to Rama is universal amongst Hindus; facilitated by the neo-Hindu movements.

CRIMINAL CONDUCT TOWARDS *GIRMITIYAS* BY BUREAUCRACY AND PLANTOCRACY

The recruiters (Indian and English) were both ruthless and unscrupulous, with a sense of contempt for the recruits and all the rules developed for indenture contracts which the recruits could not understand. Their primary concern was that the recruits did not abscond. Terms of the contracts were not explained, e.g. that criminal sanctions would be applied to enforce contractual obligations (Bhawani Dayal 1947: 18). Gandhi noted with displeasure and disbelief that criminal laws applied to civil matters (1970: 152). Gandhi cites Sir W.W. Hunter who opined that such legal anomalies made indenture akin to slavery.

An even more egregious subversion of legal process applied especially in Natal, is described by Henning (1993: 109). According to this aberration, 'it was almost impossible for the labourer to make a complaint without first being punished for having to make the complaint.' Henry Polak, reporting on the Protector of Indian Immigrants, said that the Protector, Mr. Pearson, had assumed all Indians to be guilty until proved innocent, and all employers innocent until proved guilty. The burden of proof lay on the illiterate labourers (ibid.). An official with the designation of Protector viewed his duties in a very unorthodox light, to say the least!

Criminal, offensive treatment of *girmitiyas* was more severe and barbaric against women. Bahadur (2014: 61) shares how women were harassed, raped and subjected to calumny thereafter if they complained. The plaintive voice of Kunti of Fiji reverberated throughout the Diaspora in 1913 when she revealed through the press in India attempts of plantation officials to sexually abuse her, and the ignominious attempts by the Government of India and Fiji (both British) to silence Kunti by attacking her character (ibid.: 156). Even by 1913 the plantocracy still needed *girmitiyas*—fresh victims who were desperate to grasp the frail and fragile, if not elusive, hope of a better life! But opposing voices in India succeeded in terminating the system in 1917, when it became impossible for Indian leaders in India to silently acquiesce in the brutalization of their fellow Indians (Lal 2000: 190). Indian women throughout the *girmitiya* diaspora were victims of sexual predators, and Kunti's voice was intended to expose these and protect the women. It was a call for deliverance, not some feminist or counter-colonial discourse. Victims of these crimes against the women were also their husbands and families. Husbands assaulted or even killed their wives for being 'polluted' by their assailants! (Bahadur 2014: 157). In Guiana Kumar Ranjisingh killed his wife Sunita for desertion; and Latchmin Mohabir survived a barbaric attack by her husband Subhash who died by ingesting pesticide (ibid.: 13). This environment of suspicion and victimhood was a result of the gross impunity with which the *girmitiya* women were preyed upon. Women in Hindu society were subject to the patriarchal system which did lead to abuse. However, their suffering in indenture was much worse.

The following gruesome anecdotes of criminal treatment of *girmitiyas* in Natal demonstrate that the ordeal suffered by people during the Crusades and the Inquisition were replicated in the nineteenth and twentieth century indenture diaspora in the name of Mammon. They exemplify the 'ordeals of indenture' well known to the descendants of *girmitiyas*. Henning recounts this case reported by H.S.L. Polak in his book *The Indians of South Africa: Helots*

Within the Empire and How They Were Treated, and also published by the *Times of Natal* (6 October 1908). 'A farmer Mr Armitage was fined twenty pounds by the magistrate for cutting off the right ear-lobe of his Indian employee. When reprimanded by the Court for treating an employee like a sheep, Armitage retorted that he regarded all indentured Indians as "no better than sheep"' (Henning 1993: 110).

Gandhi encountered the dark side of indenture shortly after commencing his attorney's practice in Durban. In the criminal case that was disturbingly brought to his attention at his legal practice, labourer Balasundram was brutally beaten by his employer, losing two front teeth. Poor and humble Balasundram removed his turban in deference to Gandhi, for which he was upbraided for his lack of self-respect. Gandhi found this occasion a beacon to serve the community, as well as to apply jurisprudence and moral authority. He did something which Balasundram would not have done unaided: he took him to a white doctor for examination and medical report, and then to the magistrate. Gandhi's concern was Balasundram's pain and injustice, not the colour of the authorities. As a result of Gandhi's intervention, Balasundram was transferred to another employer, a major victory (Gandhi 1970: 151-2). This was the beginning of Gandhi's role as 'protector' of the Indians in South Africa: he inspired them to defy unjust laws and demand their rights.

HINDU *GIRMITIYAS* AND DESCENDANTS IN SOUTH AFRICA: RELIGIO-CULTURAL ADVANCEMENT

The *girmitiyas*' religious practices were part of their existence, carried through all vicissitudes of indenture. Speaking of immigrant Hindus in the USA, Parmatma Saran (in Singh 2009: 65-7) opines that whilst the immigrants' social patterns 'do not fit' into the new host society, they nevertheless consider maintenance of their 'Indian heritage and identity' as very important. They encourage their children, through appropriate literature, to learn about their heritage. The Gandhi link represents political conscientization and reinforcement of their own religious beliefs. Another important link, particularly with the Hindi speakers, was Tulsidas's *Ramayana* or *Ramcharitmanas*. The *Ramcharitmanas* was as popular in Gandhi's province Gujarat as in Uttar Pradesh and Bihar. Gandhi came into contact with this scriptural work at the age of thirteen in 1882. He wrote, 'Today I consider the *Ramayana* of Tulsidas the foremost book on devotion' (1970: 42). By the convergence of various factors, children of India from different quarters of the vast motherland, met in South Africa, to be championed by Gandhi as a lawyer and leader, and also inspired and empowered by devotion to Rama through Tulsidas's *Ramcharitmanas*, the Telugu *Ranganatha* and *Bhaskar Ramayana*, the Tamil *Iramavataram* of Kamban, works of Swami Tyagaraja and innumerable regional and local compositions. Universal allegiance to Lord Siva, the Divine Mother in various manifestations, from the Devis of the Sanskrit scriptures, to the regional and localized mother forms, were all accorded equal reverence. Regional, linguistic or denominational differences did not create barriers: certain paradigms, ritual procedures, etc., provided common ground.

Whilst the spirit of Hinduism flowed from the same sources, the manifestations differed as a result of time and geographical separation. Early in the ninth century Shankaracharya (788-820 CE) had created a laager-like religious situation, to protect India from outside as well as unite and reinforce from within. Born in Kerala, Shankaracharya was one of the foremost spiritual luminaries of India; he gave the dispensation of the *Sanatana Dharma* (eternal religion) according to which worship of God in these five forms could be performed, making one manifestation primary and the others subsidiary: Vishnu, Shiva, Surya, Durga and Ganesha. This constituted the Smarta Hindu tradition. He further established seminaries or *maths* in the four quarters of India, viz., at Sringeri (south), Goverdhan (east), Sharada (west) and Jyoti (north). These are aligned to the four ancient spiritual centres of Rameshvaram, Puri, Dwarka and Badrinath respectively. Hindus from different regions followed this religious dispensation according to local conditions (Parvatiya 1996: 504-5, 873). There was a development of Vaishnava, Shaiva and Shakta denominations with conflicting claims, often manifesting in confrontation. Goswami Tulsidas reconciled Vaishnavism and Shaivism in the *Ramacharitmanas*, in order to introduce social and religious cohesion during Mughal rule.

Another vital element in the religious unity of Hinduism stemmed from the origin and growth of the Bhakti (devotional) movement in the Tamil country. Doniger (2010: 341) states that, having penetrated the other Dravidian languages from Tamil, 'It (Bhakti) swept over the subcontinent, fertilizing the worship of Krishna at Mathura and at Jagannath Puri'. Whilst this brought about a sharing of beliefs and practices, Doniger emphasizes that there was also a 'major linguistic shift from Sanskrit and the North Indian vernaculars . . . to Tamil . . . and its South Indian cousins'. Thus the unity was characterized by greater diversity which permitted spread of religious knowledge to the masses (ibid.). The discourse on 'Sanskrit' and the 'non-Sanskrit' traditions emanates from this.

Today the South African Hindu calendar of fasts and festivals shows about 40 different events for all the linguistic groups. The Tamil/Telugu new years are different. The Hindi and Telugu New Year come in Chaitra, followed two weeks later by the Tamil. The Gujarati New Year begins the day after Diwali (Deepavali). According to the Western Calendar, the Tamil Kavadis and Thai Pongal start the year. Major Tamil festivals besides these are Varalakshmi Vratam, Puratassi and Karthigai Deepam. The specific Hindi events are Makar Sankranti (same as Thai Pongal), Vasant Panchami, Holi, Naag Panchami and Vijaya Dashami. The Hindu sacred events common to all are Maha Shivaratri, Ramanavami, Hanuman Jayanti, Krishnashtami, Ganesha/Vinayaka Chaturthi, Navaratri with the worship of Saraswati, Lakshmi and Durga, and Diwali. The growing attendance at the major religious organizations and temples is blurring linguistic divisions—and many Hindus of a particular linguistic group attend temples traditionally identified with another group. The attendance at the Isipingo Mariammen Temple and the Mount Edgecombe Marriammen Temple and Emperuman Temple reflects all linguistic groups; the same applies to religious observances at Sathya Sai Organizations, ISKCON, Divine Life Society of South Africa, Sri Ramakrishna Centre of South Africa,

Chinmaya Mission and other organizations. Interlinguistic/inter-denominational marriages have enriched Hinduism in South Africa. For example, Kavady, a Tamil festival, has married couples from Tamil, Telugu, Hindi and other groups as adherents.

Maria Misra has titled her book on India's history since 1857, *Vishnu's Crowded Temple* (2008) discussed later. A similar situation in South Africa can be labelled 'God's Crowded Temples' in acknowledgement of the growing religious consciousness amongst South Africa's Hindus, manifesting in temple attendance and mass Hindu events such as recital of the *Hanuman Chalisa* over a whole day. Kumar (2000: 211) whilst asserting that all rituals have meaning writes: 'Thus, ritual is a most dominant form of Hindu religious orientation in South Africa and seems to be the most integrating force within the Hindu community'. Kumar also states (ibid.: 207) that the neo-Hindu movements also integrated ritual in practice of Hinduism. Temple worship, ritual and philosophy are thus integrated. The earliest temples built before the end of the nineteenth century hold a respected position amongst the proliferation of temples representing north and south Indian emphases. Some of these are Isipingo Rail Mariammen 1870, Mount Edgecombe Emperuman (Vishnu Temple) 1875 and Sri Gopalal Verulam Temple (north Indian) 1888, which was officially opened by Gandhi on 15 May 1913. The larger groups of Hindus, the Tamils and Hindis established cultural institutions early in the twentieth century (Kumar 2000: 101-4). Some of the Tamil bodies were Hindu Tamil Institute 1914 and the Young Mens' Vedic Society 1915. The Tamil Protective Association was formed in Pietermaritzburg in 1916 whereas in the old Transvaal the Pretoria Tamil Sangam was formed as early as 1905. The Hindi group formed Arya Yuvak Sabha in 1912. The Sanathan Dharma Sabha came into existence in 1942. The Andhra or Telugu Group formed their umbrella body, the Andhra Maha Sabha, in 1931. The multitude of linguistically or ethnically-based institutions did not detract from Hindu unity: the umbrella body of all Hindus in South Africa, the Hindu Maha Sabha was established on 31 May 1912, after considerable organizational work by Swami Shankaranand of India. The founding members were fully representative of all Hindu linguistic groups and denominations.

With the tremendous awareness of religion and culture amongst the *girmitiyas* and their descendants there was still one major avenue for proselytization of the Hindus. Education was provided by private or church organizations; state authorities only took cognizance of the need to educate the Indian children in 1910 when all the provinces came under the control of the Union of South Africa, a British Dominion. It was only after the Cape Town Agreement of 1927 that secular Western education was conceded for Indian children. Indians were hesitant to send children to the church or Natal government schools in the nineteenth century because they clung to their religion. The state did not deem it necessary to educate the children of temporary residents who did not pay taxes (Henning 1993: 165). In 1886 only 1702 Indian children attended school (ibid.: 165). Formal education commenced after the Cape Town Agreement, and underwent various metamorphoses resulting from political changes, under British rule and Nationalist Apartheid rule after 1948. The Department of Indian Affairs controlled Indian education in South Africa from 1965, followed by the South African Indian Council and for a decade, the Tri-cameral House of Delegates (from 1984). Thus whilst Hindus lived in amity with Indian Christians, Muslims and local African followers of traditional religion, they were wary of the Christian proselytizing missionaries.

Political policy changes impacted adversely on Hindu communities settled in areas such as Clairwood, Cato Manor, Puntans Hill, Springfield, Stella Hill and Westville. They were moved to newly-created Indian areas, and had to rebuild their temples and cultural institutions at their own cost once again. These institutions represented the life-blood of their religious/spiritual lives, and were erected through voluntary contributions. Apartheid's Group Areas Laws inflicted blows on some of the surviving *girmitiyas* and their children a century after the first indentured Indians arrived in South Africa. This was the price the Indians paid for the citizenship status reluctantly conferred on the Indians after all the attempts to repatriate them by the white authorities failed. Segregation was the only way the whites could tolerate the Indians in South Africa. The foregoing discussion on religion and education demonstrates the strong adherence to Hindu religious values, even at the cost of education when it was offered at the risk of conversion to Christianity. The Hindus' stance does not seem to have been misplaced chauvinism; even a Christian Indian Schoolmaster, J.S. Done, had rejected proselytization because 'Here the unadulterated Hindu philosophy would serve as well, would be readily embraced by all Hindu Indians' (ibid.: 157). The Hindus continued with their traditional domestic and temple rituals, as well as philosophical engagements. Shankaracharya's *Panchadevopasana* (worship of the five deities) served South African Hindus well; it provided a common cause in every aspect of their devotional ex-periences.

HINDU SOLIDARITY IN SOUTH AFRICA

During the reign of Akbar (1556-1605), Hindus from all parts of India joined forces to reclaim the birthplace of Lord Rama in Ayodhya which was appropriated by Babur and called the Babri Masjid (Shukla 2002: 61). Swami Balram Dhari of Coimbatore in south India mounted twenty armed campaigns to liberate the Janmasthan (birthplace) from mughal control. Sikh Guru Gobind Singh also joined Hindu forces headed by saint Baba Vaishnava Dasa in an effort to reclaim the Janmasthan (ibid.). The Prime Minister of India, P.V. Narasimha Rao described the demolition of the Babri Masjid on 6 December 1992 as 'the lesser evil' (Misra 2008: 420).

The continuation of a united Hindu ethos in South Africa was noted in 1960 when the century of the arrival of Indians in South Africa was observed. Nowbath (1960: 12) remarked that, despite different emphases on observances and religious practices, . . . 'North Indians and South Indians merged in their practices, their beliefs and their rituals, and saw in all their common heritage'. Over the years since, 'massification' of religious observances through the enormous participation in the Isipingo Mariammen, Mount Edgecombe Mariammen and Emperuman celebrations, ISKCON's Jagannatha Ratha Yatra (chariot festival) mass recitals of the *Hanuman Chalisa* (eulogy of 40 couplets to Hanuman, supreme devotee of Rama), the cosmic *108 Hanuman Chalisa* by Chinmaya Mission, and recitals by the Shri Vishnu Temple Society, and the Durban Diwali Festival organized by the South African Hindu Maha Sabha facilitate easy integration of all Hindus as well as the participation/observation by other religious groups. The traditional observance of the rituals based on the 'vernacular' customs, e.g. Draupadi Amman Festival or Firewalking, as well as the more important life-cycle rituals (birth, marriage, death) has made the inter-linguistic variations familiar to all, and assimilation into the north Indian tradition, especially of Firewalking, has occurred. According to Kumar (2000: 207), 'In South Africa, the Gujaratis, Hindis, Tamils and Telugus participate in it, and it is beginning to draw some European participants also'. This unity of the Hindu community is responsible for the strength it evinces, in its faith, its institutions and magnificent temples and statues, its elaborate and meticulously conducted public functions, as well as its combined show of resistance when under threat, from within the country or abroad. When South African cartoonist Zapiro of the *Sunday Times* depicted Lord Ganesha as the Board of Control in India, threatening and offering bribes to the Board of Cricket South Africa (*Sunday Times*, 27 October 2013), the South African Hindu Maha Sabha and the Hindu Dharma Sabha of South Africa, amongst others, took issue with misrepresenting of the deity Ganesha sacred to, and loved by every Hindu of the traditional faith. The Hindus also react to attempts by other sources locally or abroad who depict Hindu images and symbols in a disrespectful manner.

The South African Hindus are known to be peace-loving, secure in their faith and tolerant towards other religions and cultures. They welcome all to their functions and festivals; and feel elated by events such as the International Holi Festival of Colours. Their openness and receptiveness reaches an incredible level: they even accept new gods and goddesses, e.g. Santoshi Mata 'manifesting' in Uttar Pradesh, India in 1960. She became nationally popular after the Bollywood film *Jai Santoshi Ma* was screened in 1975. Her worship became popular even in South Africa because of her connection to Ganesha and the simple procedure of her *puja* (worship) (Doniger 2010: 677-8). Hinduism has seen hundreds of new saints and sages, *babas*, *avatars*, *swamis*, *avadhoots* and *paramhansas*, all contributing in varying degrees to the common weal.

Hanuman, the exemplary devotee/servant of Rama was mandated

to remain on earth to protect the *dharma* of Rama. His response to the mandate was 'As long as your Divine Tale will circulate on this earth, so long shall I stay on earth, carrying out your orders' (*Valmiki Ramayana*: Uttarakanda cviii 35-6). The *Valmiki Ramayana* was written by the sage Valmiki in Sanskrit in the fourth century BCE (Parvatiya 1996: 783). Goswami Tulsidas wrote his Awadhi Ramcharitmanas in the sixteenth century CE. These two versions are regarded as authoritative; hundreds of other versions in all Indian languages, and languages of Thailand, Malaysia, Indonesia and China also exist. The *Ramcharitmanas* is worshipped as scripture, with Rama and His servant Hanuman, the divine heroes of this work. The *girmitiyas*' descendants continue the practice, observing Rama's birth, Ramanavami, with much fervor. Paula Richman (2008: vol. 2.2) observed the week which is celebrated as Ramayana Week, preceding the birth of Rama, in 2008 at the Shree Ramayana Sabha in Overport, the Sree Venkatesvara Devasthanam and Cultural Centre in Chatsworth and the Durban Hindu Temple (one of the oldest temples) in Somtseu Road. Of the attendance at the Durban Hindu Temple, Richman writes: 'That the Temple holds its main Ram Navami ritual at noon on a week day and the temple still fills with people illustrates the draw it continues to exert on Hindus in Durban' (2008: 120).

The same ritual at Durban Hindu Temple twenty years earlier recorded by Shukla (2002: 147) showed the same degree of 'meticulous procedures, dedication and interest'.

Hindus throughout the globe, and certainly in the indenture diaspora, cherish and tenaciously perform all the traditional observances whether 'north' or 'south' Indian, whilst regional differences are celebrated for diversity. Yet Rama devotion, in the ancient Hindu diaspora of South/Southeast Asia, as well as the entire modern diaspora, is forever in the forefront. The Fijians accepted the *Ramcharitmanas* as the Fifth Veda (Kelly 2001: 350); it is also recognized by their courts as scripture (ibid.: 337-8). Further, Kelly (1991: 211) quotes Dharm Ram Chandra Sharma of Fiji, who said, 'The great Tulsi Ramayana (Ramacharitmanas) delivers the medicine of immortality to the foreign dwelling men and women'. Shukla (2001: 181) opines that to Trinidad the *Ramayana* is what the Vedas are to India. A comprehensive article on *Ramayana* in South Africa by Shukla was titled 'Ramayana as the Gateway to Hindu Religious Expression Among South African Hindi Speakers' (2013: 83-91). This study mentions 'Hindi speakers' because the specific *Ramayana*, the *Ramcharitmanas* of Goswami Tulsidas, is in Awadhi. Today the institutionalization of religion has brought this scripture to all Hindus, in the original and English transliterations and translations.

The *girmitiyas*' descendants in South Africa are becoming stronger in religion and spirituality. The worship of Hanuman, who has always been seen as inseparable from Rama, is gaining momentum in South Africa and worldwide. It would seem that Rama is being acknowledged more often as the Lord of Hanuman, although Hanuman would never have claimed priority for any reason whatsoever, over Sri Rama. Misra (2008: 449) explains how the once 'subaltern' Hanuman is achieving status akin to that of his Master. Thus, although Vishnu's temples are still crowded, the 'drawcard' may be Hanuman who Misra believes is 'awake' and 'his pervasive influence seems a highly promising cosmological development'. Hindus in South Africa and the diaspora express their adoration for, and reliance on Hanuman through chanting the *Ramcharitmanas* and the *Hanuman Chalisa*, observing his birth anniversary (Hanuman Jayanti), erecting temples and statues, and emulating his qualities. This is visible across the linguistic spectrum.

The *girmitiya* Hindus, including those in South Africa, exhibited traits that belied their lack of education. Religion and philosophy had become ingrained in them as cultural tradition. The notion of *sarva dharma sama bhava* (all religions are equal—as all rivers leading to the same ocean) reflected in Gandhi's ecumenism, did not attenuate his belief (faith) in Lord Rama. The *girmitiyas* lived in peaceful acceptance of all religions—although the Arya Samaj decried Hindu (male and female) participation in the Muslim Muharram or Tazia (Bhavani Dayal 1947: 184).

Hindu development, vis-à-vis caste and gender issues, has taken laudable steps towards equality. Caste had begun to be blurred through the Kala Pani syndrome, meaning loss of caste on leaving India, aided by the development of ship-brotherhood. Hindu women bore the full brunt of gender oppression from family and strangers alike. However, education and the influence of religion and culture are diminishing gender discrimination.

Today, the Hindu practices amongst *girmitiya* descendants may be different from those of the recently arrived NRIs; and also descendants of the passenger Indians of the nineteenth century, i.e. those immigrants who came from western India after 1890s to do business (Hiralal 2009: 81) The *girmitiya* Hindus had brought rural India's life-systems and these have survived to a great extent—observation of Pitra Paksha and Puratassi are examples. These have enriched Hindu thinking, encouraging consideration of interests beyond the self. Traditional stratification of religious groups has been modified by the influence of neo-Hindu movements and spiritual personalities, e.g. Sathya Sai Baba is accepted by devotees in the Vaishnava, Shaiva and Shakta forms. Generationally, the later generations have imbibed the spirit of unity in diversity and transcending barriers of caste, language and denominations, emerged as the modern South African Hindus. One can agree with Brinsley Samaroo (in Lal 2000: vii): 'Indeed, in the same way that these overseas Indians continue to be inspired by Bharat's spiritual development, they now have lessons for the ancestral place in religious tolerance and in dealing with a culturally different western world.'

The *girmitiyas* were a group of people whose only wealth was faith in the divine and the unquestioning obedience to moral and ethical norms. This paper has uncovered the incalculable strength of the *girmitiyas*, to endure their pains and ensure their own and their off-springs' well-being. They knew that the *yugas* return to seek redress or provide solace. The diaspora Hindus' faith and fortitude and a life of hard labour are acknowledged in the following: David Cameron, elected prime minister of the United Kingdom for a second term recently, was addressing the Hindu Community of London at the Swaminarayan Mandir at Neasden, London before the votes were cast. Words uttered there went a little deeper than mere electioneering, when he said that Britain should seek inspiration from Hinduism to become a better country. He further declared that the *Ramayana* should be studied because it is 'even more relevant in modern times' and the values of family, community and voluntary service that emerge from *Ramayana* and Hinduism are surely needed by Britain (*Post* 20-4 May 2015, p. 7). Such acknowledgement of the Hindus and Hinduism should lead to proper appreciation of the *girmitiya* Hindus.

The above is vindication of the Hindu *girmitiyas* of the diaspora, and their religion. The indentured labourers, including Hindus, 'paid with their life's blood so that their descendants might live in comfort and decency' (Nowbath in Henning 1993: 2). The various facets of lived experiences mentioned here are intended to create a new appreciation of girmit and *girmitiyas.*

REFERENCES

Bahadur, G., *Coolie Woman: The Odyssey of Indenture*, Johannesburg: Jacana Media Ltd, 2014.

Cameron, David., 'UK Temple gets Landmark Status', in *Post*, 20-4 May 2015, Durban.

Das, J.P., *A Time Elsewhere,* Delhi: Penguin Books, 2009.

Doniger, Wendy, *The Hindus: An Alternative History*, Oxford: Oxford University Press, 2010.

Gandhi, M.K., *Public Opinion on Repatriation,* Ahmedabad: Hindi Navjivan, 1931.

——, *Satya ke Prayog Athava Atmakatha,* New Delhi: Sasta Sahitya Mandal, 1970.

Henning, C.G., *The Indentured Indians in Natal 1860-1917,* New Delhi: Promilla & Co. Publishers, 1993.

Hiralal, Kalpana, 'The Gujarati Hindu Community in KwaZulu-Natal', in A. Singh (ed.), *Indian Diaspora 21st Century Challenges*, Delhi: Kamala-Raj Enterprises, 2009.

Jain, Ravindra K., 'Reflexivity and the Diaspora: Indian Women in Post-Indenture Caribbean, Fiji, South Africa and Mauritius', in A. Singh, (ed.), *Indian Diaspora 21st Century Challenges*, Delhi: Kamala-Raj Enterprises, 2009.

Kelly, J.D., *A Politics of Virtue*, Chicago & London: University of Chicago Press, 1993.

——, 'Fiji's Fifth Veda: Exile, Sanatan Dharma and Counter-colonial Initiatives in Diaspora', in Paula Richman (ed.), *Questioning Ramayanas: A South*

Asian Tradition, Berkeley & Los Angeles: University of California Press, 2001.

Kumar, P., *Hindus in South Africa,* Durban: University of Durban-Westville, 2000.

Lal, Brij V., *Chalo Jahaji,* Suva: Fiji Museum, and Canberra: Australian National University, 2000.

Meer, Y.S. et al., *Documents of Indentured Labour in Natal 1851-1917,* Durban: Institute of Black Research, 1980.

Misra, Maria, *Vishnu's Crowded Temple: India since the Great Rebellion,* New Haven & London: Yale University Press, 2008.

Nowbath, Chotai and Lalla, *The Hindu Heritage in South Africa,* Durban: South African Hindu Maha Sabha, 1960.

Nowbath, R.S., 'The Emigrant Coolie', in Henning (ed.), *The Indentured Indians in Natal 1860-1917,* New Delhi: Promilla & Co., 1993.

Parvatiya, Liladhar Sharma, *Bharatiya Sanskriti Kosh,* Delhi: Rajpal & Sons, 1996.

Prasad, Shiv, *Girmit ki Yaad, in* Verma (ed.), *Fiji ka Srijanatmak Hindi Sahitya,* Delhi: Sahitya Akademi, 2012.

Rhodes, C.J., quoted in 'Myth that Race doesn't Matter' by Xolela Mancu, *Sunday Times,* 22 March 2015, Johannesburg.

Richman, Paula, 'Ways of Celebrating Ram's Birth, Ramayana Week in Greater Durban', in *Religions of South Asia,* London: Equinox Publishing, 2008.

——, 'The Arya Samaj and the aftermath of Indenture in Natal & Trinidad', in *Nidan,* vol. 21, Durban: University of KwaZulu-Natal, 2009.

Samaroo, B., 'Girmit Connections—Beginnings and Ending', in B. Lal (ed.), *Chalo Jahaji,* Suva: Fiji Museum, and Canberra: Australia National University, 2000.

Sannyasi, Bhawani Dayal, *Pravasi ki Atmakatha,* Delhi: Rajhans Prakashan, 1947.

Saran, P., 'Asian Indian Experience in the United States: Then and Now', in A. Singh (ed.), *Indian Diaspora: 21st Century Challenges,* Delhi: Kamla-Raj Enterprises, 2009.

Shapiro, J. (Zapiro), Cartoon—'Ganesha and Board of Control for Cricket in India', Johannesburg, *Sunday Times,* 27 October 2013.

Shukla, U.D., *Ramacaritamanasa in South Africa,* Delhi: Motilal Banarsidass, 2002.

——, 'Issues in the Rama Story: Genesis, Impact and Resolution', *Nidan,* vol. 21, Durban: University of KwaZulu-Natal, 2009.

——, *Ramcharitmanas in the Diaspora: Trinidad, Mauritius and South Africa,* Delhi: Star Publications, 2011.

Singh, Anand (ed.), *Indian Diaspora: 21st Century Challenges,* Delhi: Kamala-Raj Enterprises, 2009.
Sitaram, R., 'The Ramayana and World Order: Past, Present and Future', in *Nidan,* Durban: University of KwaZulu-Natal, 2004.
Tennyson, Alfred Lord, 'Ulysses', in Robin Malan, *Inscapes,* Cape Town: Oxford University Press, 1991.
Tulasidas, Goswami, *Ramacharitmanas,* Gorakhpur: Gita Press, 1999.
Valmiki, *Srimad Valmiki Ramayan,* Gorakhpur: Gita Press, 2001.
Verma, Vimlesh Kanti, *Fiji ka Srijanatmak Hindi Sahitya,* Delhi: Sahitya Akademi, 2012.

CHAPTER 3

The Phenomenon of Ramleela/ Ramlila Theatre in Trinidad

KUMAR MAHABIR
SUSAN CHAND

INTRODUCTION

Between 1838 and 1917, more than half a million Indians were transported to the Caribbean as indentured labourers[1] after the abolition of formal slavery in 1834 by the British Empire (Vertovec 2000: 43). India was a suitable source of cheap labour for the colonial planters because of the large population with the majority of its inhabitants accustomed to agricultural labour and similar climatic conditions as those of the Caribbean. Moreover, negotiations for immigration to the Caribbean were easy as these were facilitated by the British who were in control of both colonies (Munasinghe 2001: 67-8).

Indian immigration was governed by the system of indenture contracts where recruitment was carried out by the indigenous agents [*arkathis*]. Recruiters were given a fee for tricking, forcing and even kidnapping Indians into indentureship (Roopnarine 2003; Mohanty 2014; Mahabir 2015). However, some individuals migrated voluntarily because the wage offer of 25 cents per day (in Trinidad) was way above a wage of five cents a day for an average labourer in India (de Verteuil 1989). Drought and famine also pushed tenant farmers and agricultural labourers to migrate for a better future (Mohanty 2014: 59).

In 1838, the first batch of Indian labourers (244 adults) to the Caribbean arrived in British Guiana (now Guyana) from the port of Calcutta. In seventy-nine years of indentureship, Guyana (238,909) and Trinidad (147,592) received the majority of the indentured labourers from India (Vertovec 2000: 44; Ally 2002).[2,3]

EMERGENCE OF HINDUISM IN THE CARIBBEAN

In describing the cultural character of the Caribbean region, Gordon Lewis (1983: 3-4) stated:

> . . . every person of the Caribbean cast of *dramatis personae* has been a newcomer, the colonizer, the African slave, the sugar planter, the merchant, the overseer, the Asiatic estate worker, the colonial official, they came to be members of overseas communities that were culturally naked, devoid of inherited traditions and accumulated custom. . . .

In this historically created 'culturally naked' landscape, the development of culture in the Caribbean found its genesis. However, the cultural landscape in the Caribbean world did not arise out of nothing. In the words of Kenneth Parmasad, a Trinidadian author and poet (1999: 67-8): 'We have refashioned the landscape with our labour, . . . we have erected our sacred shrines and planted our flags in every corner, we have transformed the vegetation with new plants; the air vibrates with our rhythms.'

The Indian migrants were not devoid of 'inherited traditions and accumulated custom'. They brought their rich cultural heritage with them both in tangible (religious texts) and intangible forms (cultural beliefs, values).

The majority of the migrants to the Caribbean came from regions in north India such as Bihar (14 per cent), Oudh (part of present-day Uttar Pradesh and Uttarakhand, 24-8 per cent) and North-west Provinces (currently part of Uttar Pradesh, 48-52 per cent). Other migrants were from East Bengal (now Bangladesh), central India, south India and Punjab (Vertovec 2000: 45-6; Mohanty 2014: 61). There were individuals from the tribal areas of Bihar and Bengal known as *jangalis* or 'hill coolies'.[4]

The religious composition of the migrants was varied. Approximately 85 per cent of the indentured labourers, particularly to Guyana and Trinidad, were Hindus, 15 per cent were Muslims and 0.1 per cent were Christians (Jain 1993: 23). Among Hindus, there were various castes including Brahmanas, Kshatriyas, Bhumihars, Rajputs and Thakar, as well as farmers, Ahirs [cowherds], and artisans, fishermen and boatmen. Low-caste migrants like chamars and other Shudras came mainly from South India (Mohanty 2014: 86; Clarke, 2013: 20; Jayaram 2006; Naidu 2007).

During indentureship, working and living conditions on the plantations were harsh. Each family was crammed into a single unit in the barracks.[5] Labourers sometimes toiled for 12 hours a day, irrespective of the weather or their health. They were closely monitored by the plantation manager, the magistrate and the police. Severe penalties, punishments and deferred payment were imposed to extract hard labour from the workers. Prejudice based on the Indians' physical appearance, language, religion and culture was common (Wood 1968; Ally 2002; Mohanty 2014: 62). The British planters further degraded their social status by calling them *coolie* meaning cheap labour (Clarke 1993: 121).

Amidst the difficult working conditions, Indians sought comfort in their religious and cultural practices. Workers came together during the evenings and weekends at organized activities like wrestling matches, stick fighting, playing of traditional games (*kabaddi, gulidanda, luha/lohar, ekabuka*), singing of *bhajans* [devotional hymns], *alhas* [narratives] and reading from the *Ramayana* and *Mahabharata* (Mahabir 2007; Edmonds and Gonzalez 2010; Mohanty 2014: 72) which some migrants would have brought along. Plantation owners allowed Hindus to practice their religion on the sugar estates (Naidu 2007). Hinduism in the Caribbean paved the way for migrants in the New World to redefine and reconstruct Indian culture and religion.

HINDU FESTIVALS IN TRINIDAD & TOBAGO

Today, Trinidad & Tobago has a population of 240,100 Hindus (18.2 per cent of the total population of 1,245,773). They also include 51.25 per cent of the east Indian population (468,524).[6] Hinduism is the second largest religion after Roman Catholicism in this multi-ethnic society. Hindus in Trinidad have been celebrating religious festivals such as Divali, Navratri, Ramleela/Ramlila, Phagwa, Shivratri, Kartik, and Ganga Dashara since 1860s (Edmonds and Gonzalez 2010: 179, Mahabir 2007).

Divali is the largest Hindu festival in the Caribbean and second largest national festival after Carnival in Trinidad & Tobago. It is celebrated as the Festival of Lights (in October or November). Divali is based on the Hindu epic, *Ramayana*, which relates the story of Lord Rama's triumph over the demon king Ravana of Lanka and the rescue of his wife Sita from the clutches of Ravana. In Trinidad, both Hindus and non-Hindus join in lighting of thousands of *diyas* (clay lamps) and are colourfully attired in *sarees* and *shalwars* (for women and young girls) and *kurtas* (for men and young boys). After the *diya* lighting, everyone partakes in sumptuous east Indian cuisine.[7] Every year, the display of fireworks on the night of Divali is eagerly anticipated by young and old. Divalihas been a national holiday since 1966 (*Indo-Caribbean Cultural Council* 2006).

Phagwa or Holi is also known as the Festival of Colours. It is often celebrated in the middle of March. Just as their counterparts in India, Hindus in Trinidad celebrate Phagwa with gaiety, smearing coloured powder (*gulal*) on each other's faces and bodies and spray coloured crystals (*abeer*) using water pistols (*pichkarees*). A traditional folk song, *chowtal*[8] is sung during this festival. Also, like Trinidad's Carnival, it is a communal, joyous event in which participants release their inhibitions and mingle with all segments of people in the community (Mahabir 2007).[9]

Ramleela/Ramlila is celebrated about ten days before Divali during the months of September to October. It is a 5 to 10 day 'open-air' drama based on the *Ramayana* which depicts the life of Lord Rama and his conquest over the demon king, Ravana. The Ramlila play culminates with the torching of the effigies of Ravana as well as his brother and son. Ramlila is celebrated during Navratri, which is dedicated to the worship of Mother Durga (Riggio 2010: 107).

EMERGENCE OF RAMLILA/RAMLEELA[10] IN TRINIDAD & TOBAGO

Ramleela, Ramlela or Ramlila (Rāmlīlā) is a theatrical folk performance based on the Hindu epic, *Ramayana*. Rama's *lila* or play narrates the story of the life of Rama, the king of Ayodhya, a kingdom in northern India 7,000 years ago. Rama is believed to be the seventh *avatar* (incarnation) of Vishnu (one of the three supreme deities of Hinduism) and the most worshipped and adored gods of the Hindus. The *lila* or divine play depicts Rama's mystical birth, years of youth, marriage, exile and abduction of his wife Sita by the demon king of Lanka, Ravana. The play also includes the battle and release of Sita from Ravana, the slaughter of Ravana, and finally Rama's triumphant return to his kingdom in Ayodhya (*Encyclopaedia Britannica* 2015).

According to historical accounts, Ramlila was first composed by sage Valmiki between 700 and 500 BC in Sanskrit. There are approximately 300 versions of the *Ramayana* including oral and written forms. The popular Sanskrit versions are the *Adhyatma Ramayana,* the *Bhagvata Purana,* the *Mahanataka* and the *Prasanna Raghava* (Ramanujan 1991: 33; Balkaransingh 2010: 89). However, with the decline of the Sanskrit dramas during the fourteenth to nineteenth century, folk theatres shifted to performing in numerous regional languages (*Encyclopaedia Britannica* 2015).

In north India, Ramlilas were made popular through the Avadhi version of the *Ramayana,* called *Ramcharitramanas* (meaning 'The Lake of Rama's Deeds'), written by Goswami Tulsidas in sixteenth century (Balkaransingh 2010: 92). This devotional text in Avadhi, known as *Manas,* was accessible to all ranks of the society. As mentioned earlier, a large percentage of Indians who came to Trinidad were from the provinces of north India (today's states of Uttar Pradesh and Bihar) and spoke Bhojpuri, Avadhi, Magadhi and Maithili (Brereton 1981: 103, Jayaram 2004: 149, Richman 2010: 78). Thus, chanting portions of the *Manas* in Avadhi and Bhojpuri was a core feature of Ramlila in Trinidad (Richman 2010: 78).

Although, Indian Hindus carried only a few belongings to Trinidad, they are said to have brought the *Manas,* either in memory or book form. Most grew up hearing the text recited and watching it enacted (Richman 2010: 79). In the words of Kamalwattie Ramsubeik, President of the National Ramleela Council of Trinidad & Tobago (NRCTT), '. . . our ancestors, the indentured servants, came clutching *Ramayana* under their arms . . .' (*The Sunday Guardian* 2008).

Since their arrival to Trinidad, Hindu immigrants have adapted and maintained their religious traditions (Singh 2012: 55). Initially,

Ramlila was performed in the rural villages of Trinidad. According to Rampersad (2013: 16): 'The first Ram Lila performances would have been held in an open community space that was available and accessible, and that was central enough for people from neighbouring villages to make it their annual pilgrimage destination. Ramleela was seen as a pilgrimage site, as it still is even today.'

The earliest documented record of Ramlila in Trinidad can be traced back to 1880 in Dow Village, California, in Central Trinidad. 'Dow Village Ramlila' has an unbroken history of over 135 years of performance. In early days, it was an annual, open-air event held in a village recreation park or *maidan* which was a part of the Gordon Sugar Estate (Balkaransingh, 2010: 95) or in the area of silk cotton tree on the outskirts of Dow Village (Sookhai 2007 cited in Riggio 2010: 126). The second oldest Ramlila celebration documented is the 'Chaguanas Ramlila,' later known as the 'First Felicity Ramlila'. This name was given to differentiate it from other Ramlila events such as the 'Maha Sabha Ramlila' of Felicity and the 'Pierre Road Ramlila' in Charlieville (located north-east of the First Felicity Ramlila) (ibid.: 96). 'The First Felicity Ramlila and Cultural Group has been in operation for almost a century. Other popular sites for Ramlila plays included St. John's Trace (Avocat), Felicity, Pierre Road, Sangre Grande, St. Augustine, and Cedar Hill (Ramsubeik 2013: 12).

Hindu religious organizations such as the Sanatan Dharma Maha Sabha (SDMS), SWAHA (a non-profit Hindu organization) and independent community groups have been instrumental in promoting and propagating Ramlila in Trinidad. Additionally, the National Ramleela Council of Trinidad (NRCTT) has played a pivotal role in launching Ramlila forward nationally, regionally, and internationally since its formation in 2001.

THE EVOLUTION OF RAMLILA PHENOMENON IN TRINIDAD & TOBAGO

Ramlila is exclusive to Trinidad & Tobago, despite the fact that there are comparatively more Hindus living in neighbouring Guyana (28.4 per cent) and Suriname (27 per cent) than in Trinidad & Tobago (18.1 per cent). It is the only play performed annually at dozens of venues for over 100 consecutive years in the region, and the only outdoor folk theatre of its kind in the Western Hemisphere (*Divali Magazine* 2013: 2).

Time and Season

As an open-air theatre in Trinidad, Ramlila is believed to have emerged when the indentureship contracts ended and the Indians sought to reconstruct their community life in a new society but fashioned after their cultural traditions in rural India (Rampersad 2013: 22). Ramleela became a popular festival during the period of the establishment of Indian villages in Trinidad in the 1870s (Parmasad 1999: 68).

As indentured labourers settled in the communities, they recalled their evenings in their native villages in India. Having no access to a Hindu calendar, they observed the seasons and celebrated some of the major festivals like Phagwa and Divali. In Trinidad, the blossoming of the *poui* trees (*Tabebuia serratifolia*) herald the beginning of Phagwa, which corresponds to the spring season in India (March-April). Similarly, Divali is celebrated in the month of September or October or November. Ramlila is performed ten days before Divali (Interview 21 March 2015 Chase Village, Trinidad). According to Jagessar Ganesh (2007), Association President of the Dow Village Ramleela, 'going to the bamboo patch and doing prayers and such things before we cut' was an important memory from his childhood. Because the bamboo cannot be cut during *pitri paksh* (the memorial period of remembrance of the departed souls), which comes before Dussehra, and thus Ramleela, it has to be cut some three or four weeks before Ramleela (cited in Riggio 2010: 127). This indicates the time of the season when Ramleela was to be held in the years where no Hindu calendar was available.

Language

According to a *pundit* of Charlieville (central Trinidad), it is believed that the first performance of Ramlila in Trinidad was rendered in a variety of Hindi called Bhojpuri. As early as the 1880s, Bhojpuri was spoken by indentured Indians in Trinidad. Therefore, memorizing, understanding and chanting of the *Ramcharitmanas* in

Bhojpuri as well as watching and acting in Ramlila plays were not an impossible task. The *chaupais* (four line verses) from the *Ramcharitmanas* was read in Avadhi and explained in Bhojpuri. The text's verses were intelligible to nearly all, and many knew certain verses by heart. The Ramlila *natak* or play was written by Ramdeo Benarsi, Trinidadian, in Bhojpuri for the local audience. In the late 1950s, the translation of the *chaupais* was changed from Bhojpuri to Standard English because most of the children of the indentured labourers were being introduced to the English language through school systems. By the 1970s, English had nearly replaced Bhojpuri as the oral language of Hindus, except elderly monolingual kin (Interview 21 March 2015, Charlieville, Trinidad; Richman 2010: 78, 82; Ramsubeik 2013: 12).

According to Raviji (2013: 64), at least five languages, Avadhi, Bhojpuri, Hindi, Sanskrit, Creole English are used in a single Ramleela performance. Standard Hindi and Sanskrit are used in reading the sacred text, Creole English is used for explanation of the text, Bhojpuri in folk songs and devotional hymns (*bhajans*), and Hindi and English for narrating the 'open-air' Ramleela plays.

An Ancient Style Maintained

Trinidad has preserved the oldest style of Ramleela in the world which has been derived from the ancient villages in India. Three features characterize the ancient form of Ramleela. First, it has retained the open-air format. Second, the oral delivery is based on Tulsidas' version of the *Ramcharitmanas* which includes narrations, chants, music and song (Richman 2010: 79). Third, the performers display the *Lokadharma* performance by miming the dialogue. *Lokadharma* is a realistic and amateurish mode in traditional Indian performance which involves very natural expression and movement reflective of daily life which is passed down from generation to generation (Rampersad: 2013: 22).

Ramleela as a Site of Pilgrimage

The absence of temples (*mandirs*) in the early indentureship period in Trinidad made Ramleela a popular site of pilgrimage for the immigrants. This annual pilgrimage instilled a sense of physical, mental and spiritual discipline among the immigrant devotees. They identified themselves with the story of the *Ramayana* and sought *darshan*[11] from the divinity which was embodied in the personification of Rama (ibid.: 18). Watching Ramleela enabled spectators to receive *darshan* of Lord Rama; and playing Ramleela allowed actors to steep themselves in Rama's deeds. Thus, both viewers and actors gained knowledge and merit (Richman 2010: 80). Personally seeing the divinity at close-range motivated the devotees to attend Ramleela celebrations year after year. Other members of the community attended Ramleela to consolidate the community, as well as to be entertained and to relive and reconnect with mythical India.

Selection of Characters

In the early Ramleela performances, the role of divine characters (*svaroopas*) was specifically assigned to pre-puberty high caste Brahmin males. Males with fair-skin and soft feminine features were preferred to act instead of females (Rampersad 2013: 22). Additionally, minor roles were ascribed to actors (*patras*) who were both Brahmin and non-Brahmins.

In the 1930s, only Brahmins were selected to play the major divine characters. They believed that gods like Rama should be played by Brahmins because of the conviction that they were pure and spiritually superior and more adept at fasting and performing rituals than non-Brahmins (Singh 2012a: 75). They wanted to assert themselves as (potential) socio-religious leaders of the Hindu community. However, in the latter half of the twentieth century, Ramleela productions were not strictly bound to caste distinctions. Actors were drawn from every stratum of the local village where Ramleela was staged. Non-Brahmins comprised farmers, shopkeepers, small grocers and people who worked in the nearby Woodford Lodge sugar-estate (Balkaransingh: 2010: 108; Richman 2010: 99).

From the time Ramleela began in Trinidad & Tobago in the 1880s, there was always a shortage of Brahmins to play lead roles. Sometimes, non-Brahmins, including Kshatriyas, were invited to perform the role of a deity in the play. However, divine characters continued to be played mainly by Brahmins (Interview 21 March

2015, Charlieville, Trinidad). Today, the actors are recruited from every segment of the society.

Gender and Ramlila

Before the 1960s, Ramlila was only performed by male actors who went through various preparatory rituals, including fasting for three months which was intended to purify the body and mind. During performance days, the principal actors would abandon their homes and live in temples or small sheds (*kutiyas*) provided by the supportive villagers. The actors followed a strict vegetarian diet and lived on the compound where Ramlila took place (Maharaj 2012). Women were not allowed to act in religious plays due to the censorious attitude among Hindus towards female performers and the ritual impurity assigned to menstruation (Singh 2012a: 74). It was felt that women should be confined within the four walls of the house. However, in the 1960s, females—primarily of pre-puberty age—were assigned minor roles. Women performed in communal scenes like Rama and Sita's wedding, *Bharat-Milap* (Rama meeting his brother Bharat) and Rama's return to Ayodhya. By the 1970s, women were eventually selected to perform major roles in many of the productions. However, pre-pubertal girls were preferred over adult women due to the continued stigma of impurity associated with menstruation. By the 1990s, women had more socio-economic opportunities in the society. The increasing influence of Western and secular world views facilitated the inclusion of women as major performers in Ramlila (ibid.: 76; Ramsubeik 2013: 14; Interview 27 September 2015 Cunupia, Trinidad). For instance, there are Baal Ramlila's female chanters of Ragoonanan Road and Felicity (central Trinidad) and Lopinot's all-female cast. Almost all troupes now include female players.

RAMLILA AS A VILLAGE THEATRE TODAY

Today, Ramlila performances are held in over 35 venues across Trinidad. Approximately 22 groups continue to perform 'on the ground' in large spaces and using up to 100 players. The Ramlila plays run for 8 to 11 nights and are usually held from 6 p.m. to 8 p.m. nightly (Ramsubeik 2012; Dowrich-Phillips 2010: 17). In the mid-twentieth century, Ramlilas began in mid-afternoon and ended soon after dark. Villagers who lived near the *grong* (ground) heard the *tassawhich* signalled the opening time (Richman 2010: 82).

As an open-air form of theatre, Ramlila involves lengthy preparations of the space, props, costumes and musical instruments. The production of Ramlila varies from venue to venue across Trinidad. Each production reflects the character of its village, *mandir* (temple), and organizing committee (Riggio 2010: 126).

However, in this paper, the First Felicity Ramlila will be discussed mainly due to its grand scale production as well as its significance in being the host of the longest running play, only next to Dow Village Ramlila.

The Preparation: Performance Space

In communities heavily populated by Hindus in Trinidad, playgrounds and recreational parks are converted into open-air theatres for the staging of the ten nights of Ramlila. Ramlila is currently performed in *maidans* (village playground) as well as on *manch* (traditional stage). The *maidan* Ramlila runs for 10 to 11 days, whereas the *manch* Ramlila is staged for 3 to 6 days. *Maidan* Ramlila is most popular in Felicity and Dow villages. During the year, the *maidans* are used for village sports like football, cricket, and kite flying or for recreation. However, Ramlila totally transforms these recreational parks both in appearance as well as activity (Balkaransingh 2010: 96-7). The ground (colloquially, *grong*), is demarcated from ordinary space by a bamboo railing, and undergoes ritual consecration after which footwear must be removed before entering the *grong* (Richman 2010: 79-80). The performance space is usually rectangular or spherical.

The day before the first day of the *leela* or the play, the *pundit*, with members from the Ramleela Committee and cast will circumambulate the grounds. They would worship the Mother Earth by sprinkling rice and water. They would invoke 10 cardinal points: East, West, North, South, Northeast, Northwest, Southeast, South-west, Up, and Down. The consecrated inner playing circle marks the epic geography of the drama (Riggio 2010: 131).

In the village of Felicity, the Ramlila performance space measures about 150 ft long and 110 ft wide in the middle of the playground.[12] A 3-ft high oval-shaped fence of bamboo or metal is erected around the area to cordon off spectators from the performers. Tall bamboo posts are erected at regular intervals along the fence. On top of these bamboo posts flutter *jhandis* (triangular flags) in red, yellow, black and white. A 50-ft high bamboo flag pole is planted at the centre of the oval-shaped 'theatre'. Numerous multi-coloured buntings and streamers extend from the middle of the central flag pole to the *jhandis* on the periphery of the oval barrier. The profusion of *jhandis* is a unique feature of the Ramlila *maidan* in Trinidad (Balkaransingh 2010: 98-9).

Within the oval fence, two raised platforms are built in the directions of north and south representing the kingdoms of Ayodhya and Lanka respectively. This is in contrast to the Ramnagar Ramlila in India where the positions of the kingdoms of Ayodhya and Lanka are along the north-east and south west directions, respectively (Riggio 2010: 110). The kingdom of Ayodhya is royally painted in yellow and gold, and decorated with braids and sequins. Brightly coloured canopies shade the king on his throne. Behind the king, there is a painted backdrop depicting the palace. The kingdom of Lanka is decorated in shiny green, black and dark blue with red cloth and tinsel. The royal setting on the platform is same as the kingdom of Ayodhya. About 10 sq feet is demarcated for each kingdom on either side of the stage. As the story unfolds each day, the props change to reflect the physical environment of the scene being depicted (Interview 27 September 2015, Cunupia, Trinidad; Balkaransingh 2010: 99; Riggio 2010: 132).

At the north-east of the oval space is a third platform with a huge tent over it which houses the musicians, the *pundit* (priest who is the chief storyteller) and invited guests. The *pundit* who is the chanter is clearly visible, sitting in a raised, well-lit, roofed platform in the Ramlila ground. The chanter is symbolically and spatially pivotal to the content, shape, and pace of *Ramlilas* in Trinidad (Richman 2010: 79). The musicians sit and play on the carpeted floor. The sound system is located behind that third platform. In the south-eastern part of the performance space, another tent is erected which housesthe *tassa* (a form of kettledrum) drummers who perform during the 10-day period. The inclusion of *tassa* drummers is another unique feature of Ramlila in Trinidad (Balkaransingh 2010: 99).

The other areas demarcated within the performance space include the *ashrams* (hermitages) of sages in the story, the river Ganges and Ashok Vatika (the grove of Ashoka trees) where Sita was kept captive in Lanka. The audience pavilion is located on the western side of the oval space, and food stalls are located on the eastern side. The 'stage' is considered sacred during the entire 10-day performance of Ramlila (ibid.: 98, 100).

The Preparation of the Performers

In addition to the preparation of the physical space, the performers of *Ramlila*, also called *swaroopas* (players of divine characters) and *patras* (actors) undergo preparation for their respective roles. The performers are expected to be physically fit, especially if they are playing the roles of Hanuman (monkey god) as well as warriors. Rehearsals of their roles are also crucial. They pay close attention to the storyteller (the *pundit*) to mime the narrations or *chaupais* with corresponding gestures. The performers observe the rituals of purifying themselves because they believe that heavenly deities descend on the Ramlila *maidan* and interact with the ordinary humans during the performance. The actors refrain from consuming meat and alcoholic beverages (Mahase Maharaj 2007 cited in Richman 2010: 81; Singh 2012a: 76; Interview 21 March 2015, Charlieville, Trinidad).

The Performance

Most of the Ramlila performances run for two hours daily. Some begin in the mid-afternoon and end at sunset. Others like the Felicity Ramlila start from 7 p.m. and end at 9 p.m. Every performance begins with a *puja* (worship). All the performers arrive before time, fully attired to take part in the *puja*. They gather near the bamboo flag-pole in the middle of the performance space for the *puja* and the sanctification of the site (Richman 2010: 82; Balkaransingh 2010: 102; Interview 27 September 2015, Cunupia, Trinidad).

The village *pundit*, who is also the storyteller, conducts the *puja*. He narrates and sings *dohas*, *chaupais* and *sorthas* directly from the sacred text, the *Ramcharitamanas*, and plays the harmonium simultaneously accompanied by his musicians. The *pundit's* role is multifaceted: he is the chief storyteller, lead vocalist, musical director, stage manager and spiritual guide. He performs all his roles in the standing position (Balkaransingh 2010: 106). As chanter and director, the *pundit* provides English commentary during each scene.He not only recites an Avadhi verse to begin each scene, but also explains the religious logic that drives the scene, logic sometimes unfamiliar to today's youth (Richman 2010: 86).

First Felicity is one of the venues that begins its narrative with a *Jahajee Leela*, dramatizing the journey across the *Kalapani* (the oceans) carrying the *Ramayana*, the epic book (Riggio 2010: 132).

After the *puja*, the actors enter the performance space dressed regally, holding their weapons, e.g. bows (*dhanush*), arrows in quivers, swords (*talwar*), and clubs (*gadas* or *mukdar*). They wear colour-coded costumes, signifying their roles as sages (gold with long beards), deities (various colours), their allegiance to Ayodhya (gold), Hanuman's monkeys (red) or Lanka (black, dark blue, or sometimes green). They move around the field gracefully, keeping in rhythm with the *tassa* drumming. Their body movements are in line with the decorum befitting their roles. The actor shop and skip around the field. As the rhythm and tempo of the drummers change to a military mode, the performers shoot arrows and fight with *talwars* and *gadas* (Riggio 2010: 118; Balkaransingh 2010: 103-4; Interview 21 March 2015, Chase Village & Charlieville, Trinidad).

As the days progress, the props are rearranged to depict the respective geographical locations of the story. The scenes change from mount Kailash, the seat of Lord Shiva and his wife, Parvati, to the humble *ashram* (hermitage) of sage Vishwamitra. The action then moves to the Panchvati, represented by a grove of trees where Rama, his wife, Sita, and his brother, Laxman, spend their years of exile. The setting also includes Ashok Vatika, where Sita is held captive by the demon king, Ravana, of Lanka, before relocating to the battle scene between Rama and Ravana, and finally, there is the erection of the effigies of Ravana, his brother Kumbhkarna, and son, Meghnath (Interview 27 September 2015, Cunupia, Trinidad; Balkaransingh 2010: 107).

As the story accelerates to a climax, the battle intensifies with more vigour and aggression. Arrows fly into the air, sometimes close to the bodies of the players, and even the audience. The audience is excited as they witness the triumph of Rama over the destruction of Ravana and his army. The troops are often portrayed by children, who are allowed the freedom to chase, fight, die, then rise again, and carry on the battle in a gleeful playful fashion, while participating in a performance that has as one of its aims the education of its youth (Riggio 2010: 120).

In some villages, the performers march through the streets on the 10th day. They display the heads of the effigies of Ravana and his brother and son in the tray of a lorry. The heads are then affixed to the bodies of the effigies before they perish in the flames (Interview 21 March 2015, Charlieville, Trinidad).

On the 10th day (the last day of the play) in the village of Felicity, after the destruction of Ravana, the champions Rama and his entourage walk through the streets in full dress regalia, accompanied by the stately rhythms of *tassa* drums. This procession symbolizes the soldiers' triumphant return from Lanka to Ayodhya for the coronation of Rama. The villagers welcome the victorious Rama and his entourage. The stage extends to include the entire village (a radius of about 3 km) which becomes sacred ground. Hindus believe that any ground upon which Lord Rama walks becomes consecrated (Interview 21 March 2015, Chase Village & Charlieville, Trinidad; Balkaransingh 2010: 110).

PRESERVATION OF RAMLILA AS AN OPEN AIR THEATRE IN TRINIDAD

The preservation of Ramlila in Trinidad for over a century is attributed mainly to the 'faith' element among Hindus. Faith has been a major driving force behind the belief that goodwill overcome evil which is the central theme underlying this form of open-air theatre.

The devotion to Ramlila has been vividly captured in the works of two Nobel Laureates in Literature, Derek Walcott (1992) from St. Lucia and Sir Vidiadhar Surajprasad Naipaul (2001) from Trinidad & Tobago and other scholars (Brockington 1981; Singh 2012a).

In his Nobel Acceptance Speech, 'Fragments of an Epic Memory' in 1992, Derek Walcott gives a colourful description of the Felicity Ramlila *maidan*:

> . . . It was as if, on the edge of the Central plain, there was another plateau, a raft on which the Ramayana would be poorly performed in this ocean of cane, but that was my writer's view of things, and it was wrong. I was seeing the Ramleela at Felicity as theatre when it was faith. . . . They were not amateurs but believers. . . . They believed in what they were playing, in the sacredness of the text.[13]

As a non-Indian and non-Hindu as well as a St. Lucian native, he was moved by the spectacle of Ramlila and the faith of the actors. His observation resonated the emotional intensity and sacred devotion displayed by the actors. In essence, it was not the mechanics of the drama that drove the actors to excel in their performance but their inner faith and mystical experience of entering into an illusion of assuming 'divine proportions' (Singh 2012a: 76).

Naipaul grew up in Chaguanas where the Felicity Ramlila, which Walcott describes, was performed. For Naipaul, the dramatization of the Hindu epic, the *Ramayana* was a learning experience. In his collection of essays, 'Literary Occasions', Naipaul writes:

> . . . Everything in that Ramlila had been transported from India in the memories of people. And though as theatre it was crude, and there was much that I would have missed in the story, I believe I understood more and felt more . . . the Ramlila had given reality, and a lot of excitement, to what I had known of the Ramayana. (2001: 15)

The expression of faith has been also observed by the literary critic John Brockington (1981: 171): 'The whole thing is as much a religious ceremony as a dramatic performance, as well as having a significant role in the transmission of faith in Rama among the illiterate masses (cited in Singh: 2012a: 70).'

According to an informant attending Ramlila performances for a few decades, the content of the play has not changed and the faith of the Hindu believers continues on:

The *Ramayana* story through the enactment of *Ramlila* ignites a flame in the hearts of the audience that connects them to the Hindu '*dharma*' (faith) of their forefathers who came to Trinidad as indentured labourers. Many have adopted the western culture but have continued to adhere to Hindu religion. It is this *dharma* brought alive through Ramlila has preserved our Hindu culture'. (Interview 21 March 2015, Chase Village, Trinidad)

Faith as a driving force in the preservation of Ramlila year after year is also articulated in the words of a prominent member of SWAHA Gyaan Mandal, Deepak Kirtan Mandal of Trinidad & Tobago:

Even though there may be a profound emphasis on the external attractions of Ramleela, such as the elabourate costumes, the scintillating scenes by the versatile actors or the magnificence of the fire that consumes the effigy of Ravana, Ramleela can also deliver on intangible aspects which are not only felt once a year but can continually be felt as an inward positive momentum that builds the human spirit. (Boodram 2013: 36)

Coupled with faith element is the underlying belief by the performers and spectators that good will overcome evil. This is another contributor to the preservation of Ramlila for over a century in Trinidad. In his *Literary Occasions* (2001), Naipaul writes about the burning of the effigy of the evil-king Ravana:

. . . The pageant ended with the burning of the big black effigy of the demon king of Lanka. This burning was one of the things that people had come for; and the effigy, roughly made, with tar paper on a bamboo frame, had been standing in the open field all the time, as a promise of the conflagration. . . . (15)

Every Ramlila performance climaxes with the burning of the effigies of Ravana, as well as his brother Kumbhakaran, and his son Meghnath. People travel from far and wide to witness the closing scenes of the play which culminates with the torching of the effigies. The burning symbolizes the victory of good over the evil forces. Parents import moral lessons to their children. Also, Ravana's black effigy depiction of evil and wickedness, is not specific to any caste, class or race (Singh 2012a: 72; Riggio 2010: 119-20; Richman 2010: 86, 87).

Faith element is also observed in the manner in which the Hindu devotees as well as the non-devotees flock the Ramlila grounds night after night. Ramlila as a religious festival draws over 500,000 spectators to about 35 different venues across the country to see the religious folk drama staged by over 30 groups who participate in the ten-days of performances annually.[14]

Pundit Vishnu of Palmiste Park (South Trinidad) explains that Trinidad's distinctive role in preserving the Ramleela lies in the fact that: 'The Trinidad Ramleela survived when it died out in other places. . . . It survived here, so this was a patriotic thing' (Dutt 2006 cited in Riggio 2010: 115).

Cooperation and harmony are also contributors for the preservation of Ramlila in Trinidad. The spirit of cooperation was integral to the community life of Caribbean indentured Indians. The spirit of sharing, cooperation and mutual respect were inherent in the village life of India from where the Indians came. Rampersad (2013: 20) observes that: 'It was not uncommon to find Hindus, Muslims and Christians coming together to host and support each other's cultural expressions. Ram Lila was one such performance that brought them all together, even if some participants were not devotees.'

Ramlila has been preserved over the decades because it has been able to incorporate topics relevant to Trinidad into the *Ramayana* tradition. Topics such as white colonial oppression, the racial and caste issues, negative influence of Western culture, and more recently drugs, crime and violence are dramatized in the Ramlila plays (Singh 2012a: 71). Also, in the words of a *pundit* from South Trinidad, 'We don't change the *Ramcharitmanas* to suit us: we make it applicable to our lives' (Richman 2010: 99).

Finally, the preservation of Ramlila in Trinidad for more than a century demonstrates that it is both a historical metaphor as well as the attempt by Hindus to reconstruct their community in a new environment in the diaspora (Walcott 1993: 4). As a historical metaphor, Ramlila presented a number of themes that the indentured Indians were able to identify with. Its central theme of Rama's exile from his kingdom equated with their separation from their Motherland, India and crossing the cursed *kalapani* to a foreign land. According to Naipaul (2001: 16), 'Rama's unjust banishment to the dangerous forest was like something I had always known'.

Rama's triumphant return represented the end of indentureship and beginning of a life of freedom and prosperity. The character of Ravana became a metaphor for those who threatened or oppressed them and local issues whether those related to the colonial authorities, the estate bosses, or African-Trinidadian political leaders (Singh 2012a: 71-3).

CONTRIBUTION OF RAMLILA TO THE SOCIAL FABRIC OF THE EAST INDIAN COMMUNITY

Ramlila has provided a space for young boys to participate in the 'play' as well as to prevent them from engaging in deviant and criminal activities. Ramlila awareness motivates youths toward creating mind-awareness and intellect-equilibrium, and encourages spiritual practice, thus, resulting in a reduction of crime and wasted time (Bikramdass 2013: 42). According to a *pundit* of Charlieville, the boys are encouraged to participate in the play as well as to become part of the audience for ten days. Being specially chosen for specific roles in the play gives them a sense of self-pride and enthusiasm. Involvement in the production also serves as a religious recreation for the youths of the Hindu community (Interview, 21 March 2015, Charlieville, Trinidad). Additionally, teenagers and young adults players in Ramlila take pride in having renounced meat, salt, alcohol, or smoking during Ramlila scenes, subsequently some ended up giving up meat altogether (Richman 2010: 101).

Ramlila engages youths in meaningful activities that contributes to their well-rounded development and educates them about their religion (Boodram 2013: 36). Studies have shown that youths who participated in Ramlila secured academic success and entrance into prestigious universities worldwide (Maharaj & Persad 2013: 38).

Ramlila has promoted Hindu ideals like family life, moral values, social organization and politics, and has prompted Hindus to aspire towards high values and good behaviour. Furthermore, preparation and participation in Ramlila have fostered family-like bonds within the village. Ramlila has engendered a sense of community and self-esteem (Boodram 2013: 36).

Ramlila has established a bridge between people of two major religious groups in the Indian community, the Hindus and Muslims. Since the inception of Ramlila in Trinidad in the 1860s, Muslims have always been part of the audience. According to a local *pundit*, Muslims in the audience were so keenly tuned to the listening of the *choupais*, that when someone made a mistake in his or her recitation of any verse, Muslims were quick to point it out. The Muslim members of the audience are well-versed in the oral version of *Ramayana* rather than the written text. Today, Hindus and Muslims mingle freely in Trinidad (Interview, 21 March 2015, Charlieville, Trinidad).

Ramlila has shaped the politics of the country. Local ministers attend Ramlilas to gain favourable political support from the Hindu communities. However, state funds are very little and sometimes non-existent. A survey conducted by the Dow Village *Ramlila* Committee indicated that political support is instrumental in the recognition and promotion of the Hindu culture and impact positively on the success the Ramlila groups (Bikramdass 2012: 42).

Ramlila shaped the social and religious lives of the Hindus. Themes on life cycle and religious rituals provided models for familial and marital relations and values associated with them. A well-known local historian, Bridget Brereton (2012) noted that:

> As social realities changed for local Hindus, so different elements in the Ramcharitmanas were emphasised. As the traditional extended family, with the all-powerful father, the bullying mother-in-law and the down-trodden young brides, gave way to the nuclear family and more equal relations between men and women, those parts of the story which portrayed total obedience and deference to parents, and complete subordination of women, were down-played.[15]

On the other hand, new social realities are emerging. By 1980s and 1990s, Western influence has brought dramatic changes in the position of Hindu women in Trinidad. Consequently, an assertive, morally self-directed Sita is 'constructed' out of the text, to suit the new realities of Hindu life (Brereton 2012).

Today, there is technological advancement in the productions of Ramlila plays across the country. Some villages are now running the sound tracks from the popular television series *Ramayan* produced by Ramanand Sagar in 1986 in India. Traditional decorations of paper streamers and palm and mango leaves and lighting of *diyas* (earthen wick lamps) are being superseded with synthetic and commercial decoration and lighting equipment. Moreover, the advent of Indian films has brought texts and gods to life thereby deepening the aspirations for Hindu culture depicted in these films (Singh: 2012b: 62).

Ramlila has been able to develop without changing its content for over a century. Walcott (1992) aptly sums the above notion as: 'The performance was like a dialect, a branch of its original language, an abridgement of it, but not a distortion or even a reduction of its epic scale'.[16]

The epic story of Rama continues to be narrated and dramatized for 10 days shifting between Bhojpuri Hindi and English. It continues to evoke reverence from the audience and the performers. Hindus and Indians have added new dimension to Ramlila which has mirrored the changes in society.

CONCLUSION

As an open-air theatre in Trinidad, Ramlila has withstood the vagaries of time, space and globalization for over a century. The distinguishing feature characterizing this oldest form of folk drama is evident in its preservation over the years. Although, there have been some changes, the arena stage, and the scale of production have remained unchanged.

The epic story enacted in Ramlila continues to appeal to Hindus and non-Hindus alike due to its universal appeal to real-life situations. Ramlila has been instrumental in breaking down the age-old conventions of caste, male supremacy and power and racial and ethnic differences. It has promoted inclusiveness, harmony and cooperation. Ramlila has been one of the institutions by which Hindus have used to reconstruct their community in a new environment in the diaspora.

ACKNOWLEDGEMENTS

I wish to thank Rebecca Cave and Samantha Jagdeo for proof-reading this paper.

NOTES

1. Hugh Tinker (1993) in his book, *A New System of Slavery* makes a direct link between slavery and indentured labour, presenting 'a darker picture of [indenture] as a new system of slavery'. Indentured labour was based on *girmit* (contract) system between an emigrant and the employer for a fixed wage for five years. At the end of five years, the emigrant could reindenture or work elsewhere in the same colony. At the end of ten years he/she was entitled to a subsidized return passage.
2. See http://www.cariwave.com/East_Indian_Indentureship.htmfor details of the arrivals of the Indians during the Indentureship.
3. See *Government of Madras Annual Reports 1899-1916* for migrants to the Caribbean from the port of Madras.
4. See Report of the High Level Committee on Indian Diaspora (2000), p. 203.
5. The barracks (also known as 'coolie lines') were constructed of wood and were 100 ft long and divided into 10 ft long sections.
6. Trinidad & Tobago Census (2011). Today, the descendants of the indentured labourers in the Caribbean are called 'East Indians' or Indo-Caribbeans' and are distinguished as people of Indian origin (PIO).
7. Meals served on Divali nights are home-cooked and include at least three to seven different dishes of curry (*talkari*) eaten with *dalpuri* or 'buss-up-shut' (East Indian version of bread). Tons of sweetmeats are made and distributed free: *barfi*, *laddoos*, *gulab jamuns*, *kurma*, *jelebis* and sweet rice.
8. *Chowtal* songs are sung loudly and in high pitch accompanied by hand drums and cymbals.
9. http://www.discover-tt.net/arts_and_culture/ramleela_ramdilla_and_phagwa_holi_or_festival_colours.html
10. In this paper, the terms Ramleela and Ramlila will be used interchangeably. Both these terms are used in Trinidad while referring to the *Ramayana* plays. According to Riggio (2010) Ramleela is the phonetic spelling most commonly used in Trinidad, though the vernacular term Ramdilla is

sometimes used. However, Richman (2010) preferred to use Ramlila, the spelling employed by *Ramayana* scholars for such dramas in India and the Indian diaspora.

11. *Darshan* illustrates the concept of a devotee making eye-contact with the physical form of divinity. The devotee looks upon the deity with deep awe and reverence. He/she believes that the divinity returns his/her gaze to him/her, thereby empowering him/her spiritually. It is an 'auspicious sight' for the devotee, an instance of seeing or beholding, and being seen or beheld at the same time.
12. The playground is about 2 acres of land.
13. See Derek Walcott's book: *The Antilles: Fragments of Epic Memory: The Nobel Lecture*, 1993, p. 4.
14. See *Trinidad Express* news article: 'Drama as Ramleela Plans Announced' 16 October 2012.
15. See Prof. Brereton's article on 'The Ramayana: Mirror and Metaphor'. Retrieved on 11 June 2015: http://www.trinidadexpress.com/commentaries/The_Ramayana__mirror_and_metaphor-142723955.html
16. See Derek Walcott's book: *The Antilles: Fragments of Epic Memory: The Nobel Lecture*, 1993, p. 6.

REFERENCES

Ally, Brian, 'East Indian Indentureship', 2002, *Cariwave*. Online.

Balkaransingh, Satnarine, 'Ramleela and Divali', in 'Trinidad Space speaking through Indo-Trinidadian Rituals & Festivals: 1900-2009', Ph.D. thesis. University of Trinidad & Tobago, 2010, pp. 88-111.

Brereton, Bridget, 'The Ramayana: Mirror and Metaphor', in *Daily Express, Trinidad Express Newspapers*, 16 March 2012 (online).

Bickramdass, Pricilla, 'Boundaries and Limitations of the Ramleela', in *Ramleela: Free Open-air Folk Theatre in Trinidad and Tobago, Divali Magazine*, vol. 14, no. 2: 42, 2013.

Bickramdass, Pricilla, 'Boundaries and Limitations of the Ramleela (Abstract)', in *Ramleela: Free Open-air Folk Theatre in Trinidad and Tobago, Divali Magazine*. vol. 14, no. 2: 42, 2013.

Boodram, Shivani, 'Ramleela and Youths', in *Ramleela: Free Open-air Folk Theatre in Trinidad and Tobago, Divali Magazine*, vol. 14, no. 2: 36, 2013.

——, 'Ramleela and Youths (Abstract)', in *Ramleela: Free open-air Folk Theatre in Trinidad and Tobago, Divali Magazine*, vol. 14, no. 2: 36, 2013.

Clarke, Colin, *Religion and Ethnicity as Differentiating Factors in the Social Structure of the Caribbean*, MMG Working Paper. Max Planck Institute for the Study of Religious and Ethnic Diversity, Göttingen, 2013.

De Verteuil, Anthony, *East Indian Immigrants: Gokool, Soodeen, Sookoo, Capildeo, Beccani, Ruknaddeen, Valiama, Bunsee*, Port of Spain: Paria Publishing, 1989.

'Drama as Ramleela Plans Announced', in *Trinidad Express Newspaper*, 16 October 2012, Online.

Dowrich-Phillips, Laura, 'Ramleela: Trinidad's Epic Theatre', in *Caribbean Beat*, no. 105: 17, 2010.

Edmonds, Ennis B. and Michelle A. Gonzalez, *Caribbean Religious History: An Introduction*, New York: NYU Press, 2010.

Indo-Caribbean Cultural Council, 'The Splendour of Divali', in *Divali*, vol. 8, no. 2, 2006.

Jain, Ravindra K., *Indian Communities Abroad: Themes and Literature*, New Delhi: Manohar, 1993.

Jayaram, Narayana, 'The Dynamics of Language in Indian Diaspora: The Case of Bhojpuri/Hindi in Trinidad', in *The Indian Diaspora Dynamics of Migration*, ed. Narayana Jayaram, New Delhi: Sage, 2004, pp. 147-71.

——, 'The Metamorphosis of Caste among Trinidad Hindus', in *Contributions to Indian Sociology*, vol. 40, no. 2, 2006, pp. 143-73.

Lewis, Gordon K., *Main Currents in Caribbean Thought: The Historical Evolution of Caribbean Society in its Ideological Aspects, 1492-1900*, USA: The John Hopkins University Press, 1983.

Mahabir, Kumar, 'Indian Contribution to the West Indies/Caribbean', in *Contributions of PIO to their Countries of Adoption*, ed. Ajay Dubey (in press).

——, 'Editorial', in *Ramleela: Free Open-air Folk Theatre in Trinidad and Tobago, Divali Magazine*, vol. 14, no. 2: 2, 2013.

Maharaj, Mitra and Amral Persad, 'The Impact of Ramleela on Holistic Development (Abstract)', in *Ramleela: Free Open-air Folk Theatre in Trinidad and Tobago, in Divali*, vol. 14, no. 2, 2013, pp. 38-40.

McEachrane, Desiree, 'Ramsubeik takes Ramleela Tale to Carifesta' in *The Sunday Guardian*, 10 August, 2008.

Mohanty, Siba Sankar, 'Indian Diaspora in the West Indies: An Overview and an Insight', in *Indian West Indian through the Writings of V.S. Naipaul: Socio-cultural and Political Dimensions of Indian Diaspora* by Siba Sankar Mohanty, New Delhi: Jawaharlal Nehru University, 2014, pp. 55-102.

Munasinghe, Viranjini, 'Shifting Ethnicity: East Indians against Nation', in *Callaloo or Tossed Salad?: East Indians and the Cultural Politics of Identity in Trinidad* by Viranjini Munasinghe, Ithaca, New York: Cornell University, 2001, pp. 67-79.

Naidu, Janet, 'Retention and Transcultural of Hinduism in the Caribbean', (online), in *Guyana Journal*, 2007.

Naipaul, V.S., *Literary Occasions: Essays.* Vintage eBooks, 2001.

Parmasad, Kenneth V., 'Ramleela and Hosay: Contestation on the Periphery: Towards 2000—Models for Multi-Cultural Arts Education', in *Caribbean Quarterly*, vol. 45, nos. 2-3, 1999, pp. 67-70

Ramanujan, Attipate K., 'Three Hundred Ramayanas: Five Examples and Three Thoughts on Translations', in *Many Ramayanas: The Diversity of a Narrative Tradition in South Asia*, ed. Paula Richman, Berkeley: University of California Press. UC eBooks Collections, 1991, pp. 22-48.

Ramanujan, R.K. 'Dance and Theatre: South Asian Arts', in *Encyclopaedia Britannica*, 2015.

Rampersad, Indrani, 'The Trinidad Ramleela/Ramlila', in *Ramleela: Free Open-air Folk Theatre in Trinidad and Tobago*, in *Divali*, vol. 14, no. 2, 2013, pp. 16-22.

Ramsubeik, Kamalwattie, 'History of Ramleela in Trinidad and Tobago', in *Ramleela: Free Open-air Folk Theatre in Trinidad and Tobago*, in *Divali*, vol. 14, no. 2, 2013, pp. 412-14.

——, 'Overview of Ramlila in T&T', in *National Ramlila Council of Trinidad and Tobago (NRCTT)*, 2015.

Raviji, 'Ramleela is Receiving Renewed Interest at Home and Abroad', in *Ramleela: Free Open-air Folk Theatre in Trinidad and Tobago*, in Divali, vol. 14, no. 2, 2013, pp. 64-6.

Richman, Paula, 'We Don't Change It, We Make It Applicable: Ramleela in Trindad', in *TDR: The Drama Review*, vol. 54, no.1, 2010, pp. 77-105.

Riggio, Milla C., 'Performing in the Lap and at the Feet of God: Ramleela in Trinidad, 2006-2008', in *TDR: The Drama Review*, vol. 54, no. 1, 2010, pp. 106-49.

Roopnarine, Lomarsh, 'East Indian Indentured Emigration to the Caribbean: Beyond the Push and Pull Model', in *The Journal of Caribbean Studies*, vol. 31, no. 2, 2003, pp. 97-134.

Singh, Sherry-Ann, *The Ramayana Tradition and Socio-Religious Change in Trinidad 1917-1990*, Kingston, Jamaica: Ian Randell Publishers, 2012a.

——, 'Trinidad Hinduism 1917-1945: Religious Transformation and Identity

Construction', in *Indian Diaspora in the Caribbean: History, Culture and Identity*, ed. Rattan Lal Hangloo, New Delhi: Primus Books, 2012b, pp. 55-69.

'The Caribbean', in *Report of the High Level Committee on Indian Diaspora* by Ministry of External Affairs, New Delhi, 2000, pp. 191-8.

Tinker, Hugh, *A New System of Slavery: The Export of Indian Labour Overseas, 1830-1920.* London: Hansib Publishing, 1993.

'Trinidad and Tobago', in *Report of the High Level Committee on Indian Diaspora* by Ministry of External Affairs, New Delhi, 2000, pp. 199-208.

Trinidad and Tobago 2011 Population and Housing Census: Demographic Report, Ministry of Planning and Sustainable Development. Central Statistical Office, The Republic of Trinidad and Tobago, 2011.

Vertovec, Stephen, '"Official" and "Popular" Hinduism', in *The Hindu Diaspora: Comparative Patterns* by Stephen Vertovec, New York: Routledge, 2000, pp. 39-62.

Walcott, Derek, *The Antilles: Fragments of Epic Memory: The Nobel Lecture*, USA: Farrar Straus Giroux Publishers, 1993.

Wood, Donald, *Trinidad in Transition: The Years after Slavery*, London: Oxford University Press, 1968.

Websites

Retrieved on 22 February 2015 from http://shodhganga.inflibnet.ac.in/handle/10603/18354

Retrieved on 23 February 2015 from: http://www.pewforum.org/files/2012/12/globalReligion-tables.pdf

Retrieved on 23 February 2015 from: http://indiandiaspora.nic.in/diasporapdf/chapter16.pdf

Retrieved on 25 February 2015 from: http://www.guyanajournal.com/hinduism_caribbean.html

Retrieved on 3 March 2015 from: https://guardian.co.tt/sites/default/files/story/2011_DemographicReport.pdf

Retrieved on 3 March 2015 from: http://www.cariwave.com/East_Indian_Indentureship.htm

Retrieved on 10 March 2015 from: http://www.nrctt.org/overview-of-ramleela-in-t-t/

Retrieved on 6 April 2015 http://ark.cdlib.org/ark:/13030/ft3j49n8h7/

Retrieved on 11 April 2015 from: http://www.trinidadexpress.com/featured-news/Drama_as_Ramleela_plans_announced-174506501.html

Retrieved on 4 June 2014 from: http://www.trinidadexpress.com/commentaries/The_Ramayana__mirror_and_metaphor-142723955.html

Retrieved on 27 September 2015 from:http://legacy.guardian.co.tt/archives/2008-08-14/Womanwise/wwise4.html

Retrieved on 29 September 2015 from: http://www.discover-tt.net/arts_and_culture/ramleela_ramdilla_and_phagwa_ holi_or_ festival_colours.html

CHAPTER 4

Church and State, Religion and Politics: The Hindu Stance on Education in Mid-twentieth Century Trinidad

VASHTI SINGH

HISTORICAL BACKGROUND

Trinidad & Tobago was first colonized and brought under Spanish rule, French influence and later British rule in 1802. Following the emancipation of black slaves in 1834, Britain perceived that control over the education system would give added impetus to anglicization as a core principle of English colonization.[1] Provision for universal education in cooperation with religious bodies who were already providers of education was unavoidable. However, the search for initiatives that would further Anglicization in schools took precedence. According to Seesaran (1974: 29), 'The prestige of the English was obviously increased for the Anglican Church was officially recognised as the co-partner of the State in the field of education.' On the other hand, the Roman Catholic Church constituted a bulwark against Anglicization. By the 1840s, the British government recognized that the influence of French and Spanish Roman Catholic priests in denominational schools would serve only to propagate and intensify resistance to English culture, values and beliefs. Government, therefore, felt an urgent need for secular schools on account of the diversity of races, religions and languages; in the belief that this type of schools would open accessibility to all (Ramesar 1980).

Governor Lord Harris introduced universal public education through the Ward School System in 1851.[2] Lord Harris stipulated:

'That the instruction to be given at the training and primary schools be secular and without direct religious or doctrinal training' (Anthony cited in *The Sunday Express*, 17 June 1984: 11). The stated principle of secularism was only meant to divert attention from the real problems of a complex diverse society. The Ward schools were intentionally designed to integrate and assimilate a rigidly divided multi-religious and multi-ethnic society on the basis of Anglicization. Universal secular education was also intended to reach the East Indian immigrant population who first arrived in 1845 as indentured labourers to work on sugar plantations. The vast majority of immigrants were Hindus (80 per cent) with a smaller group of Muslims (14 per cent). A minority of Sikhs, Buddhists and Christians also came (6 per cent). Both Hindus and Muslims adhered to their respective religious practices, cultural heritage and language as strong determinants of identity.[3] A survey which had been conducted in 1868 recorded only 3 Hindu children among 1,221 pupils enrolled in the Ward Schools (Brereton, 2005). This enrolment stands as a strong testimony to the fact that Hindus as well as Muslims rejected secular education.

In 1869, Sir Patrick Keenan, an Irish educationist, was invited by the Secretary of State for the colonies to address the shortcomings of the education system in Trinidad which gave credence to the plight of Hindus and Muslims. Keenan (1969: 38) documented: 'I cannot recall to mind any other case of a people who having voluntarily come to a strange land which they have enriched by their labour, were—morally and intellectually so completely neglected as the Coolies have been during the past twenty-four years.'[4] In addition to government's neglect of suitable provision for East Indian education, inefficient administration and inadequate supervision of the Ward schools coupled with Anglicizing and secular motives engendered strong opposition from a well entrenched Roman Catholic Church (Hamel-Smith 1983). Keenan who was himself a devout Catholic understood the concerns of his fellow Catholics and other religious bodies. Based on his recommendation, Governor Arthur Gordon introduced a partnership between the church and state in education in 1870.[5] Keenan's earnest desire was for east Indians to have an equal opportunity to participate in and to derive benefit from the advantages of this new national system of education.

While Keenan endorsed the establishment of separate schools for east Indian children under the management of the Canadian Presbyterian missionaries who first arrived in Trinidad in 1868, he also warned against the dangers of proselytism. To the contrary, Fergus (1986: 38) underlined: 'The school system under the management of the Canadian Presbyterian Church took on the role of Anglicising the East Indian.' The Canadian Mission (CM) was the main provider for east Indian education into the twentieth century; however conversion, the passport to academic success, was too great a price for most Hindus and Muslims to pay (Samaroo 1982).[6] Around 1928 to 1930, Hindu and Muslim leaders understandably stood up against proselytism in CM schools with a strong demand for their admission into the denominational system on equal terms with the Christian churches. The Marriot Mayhew Commission (1931) advised that east Indians to organize themselves on a model similar as the Boards of Management of Christian Churches as government was only prepared to grant aid to schools under a Head of Denomination (Government of Trinidad & Tobago, Ministry of Education, 1983).[7] The pertinent question was: Did either the Hindus or Muslims have a 'Head of Denomination' on the island?

According to Campbell (1985: 129) government's intention was 'to use genuine divisions in the Indian community as an excuse for inaction on both the questions of a share of the ecclesiastical grant and a share of government's subsidies for education'. The east Indian diaspora was faced with the formidable challenge to establish its own schools. The first non-Christian school to be recognized was the El Socorro Muslim School in 1949. This achievement served as an incentive for Hindus. In the general elections of 1950, Bhadase Sagan Maraj emerged as a strong Hindu political leader when he won the Tunapuna seat as an Independent. His prime objective was to unite Hindus and build Hindu schools.[8] His political opponent, Dr Eric Williams, chief minister of Trinidad & Tobago who would later become the first prime minister (1950: 56) indicated: 'In the last analysis, however, the question of the provision of State or denominational schools is a political one and must be determined by the British west Indian people themselves. The author merely indicates his preference for a fully State controlled system—that is, a democratic self-governing state.' Hindus objected to a fully state controlled education system, especially one which unavoidably would be operationalized on the continuation of a tradition of secularization and Christian-European nationalist education.

A key area of focus in this paper is an interrogation of the relationship between the church and the state, and religion and politics to conceptualize the interconnected and overlapping realms which strengthened the Hindu stance on education in mid-twentieth-century Trinidad.

CONCEPTUAL FRAMEWORK: CHURCH AND STATE, RELIGION AND POLITICS

One of the main characteristics of democratic regimes in the Western world is the separation of the church and the state. The discussion of separation is often associated with a pronounced distinction between the concepts of theocracy and secularism. Theocracy is a form of government that supports privileged members of the ruling religion to the detriment of others (Croft 2013). Secularism can be defined as a modern political and constitutional principle that embraces two basic propositions. The first is that people belonging to different faiths and sections of society have equality before the law, the Constitution and government policy; the second proposition identifies that there can be no mixing up of religion and politics (Jayaram 1997). The two propositions imply conformity to a more general principle—the realm of validity of religion in the political public domain and the larger society is necessarily limited.

The separation of the church and the state and the secularization it is intended to safeguard are widely accepted core principles of American liberal democracy.[9] The state has no role or authority in defining beliefs relating to God and worship. The free exercise of religion is guaranteed and meant to protect the people's right to express their views without fear of government's intervention (Peach 1986). The state is neutral between religions and permits citizens to believe or not believe in God, to engage or not engage in religious practices or to join religious organizations according to the freedom of their own conscience. While in contemporary American society the wall of separation between the church and the state remains standing, the main source of classical or early Islamic theology is unity between the church and the state. For Muslims as well as Hindus and other religious believers across the globe, there cannot be any unsanctified aspect of life that lies outside the scope of religious laws and persons who uphold them (Kilcullen 2012).[10] Hence, today the question arises, 'What possible basis is there for a separation of Church and State, or religion from politics?'

An article entitled 'Separation of Church and State' in the Boisi Center Papers on Religion in the United States (2007: 20-1) underscored: 'Church-State separation is at once simple in concept and irredeemably complex in practice. It is both a pragmatic strategy for maintaining religious vitality and a principled expression of the belief that theological and political legitimacy are distinct.'[11] Current thinking on church-state issues in America reflect that in future the contours of religious and political liberty will continue to shift as compromises are made and cultures are integrated. In this instance, Hegel's culturalist approach is significant because it sidesteps the rigidity attendant on more judicial determinants to church-state separation (Buchwalter 2006).[12] For Hegel, what counts as a society's understanding of the separation of church and state, including the criteria for making that separation, is determined and validated in a process of public discourse. This process is characterized by overlapping consensus and an understanding of differences as a product of a functioning culture that embraces everyday religious and political orientations.

The contentious issue for secular democratic governments is whether a democracy is ideally underpinned by a society in which religion within the private realm has little influence on politics in the public sphere. One argument is that this type of government cannot regulate or prohibit private religious belief and worship or prevent citizens from organizing politically and pursuing policy objectives which are aligned with their religious values, as long as they do not violate the Constitution (Stepan 2001). Secular democracies must avoid establishing or showing favouritism to churches with no toleration of other religious beliefs; or swinging the balance so much in favour of separation of church and state that religious convictions are ignored, disrespected or persecuted.[13] According to Driesen (2010: 4), 'heavy-handed ruling against religion in democracies runs the risk of provoking counterproductive, anti-democratic forces which lie within religious fundamentalism and furthermore obscures the full breath of options open for healthy relationships between church and state'. This autocratic approach weakens the potential religious and political processes that can help to legitimize and strengthen new democratic regimes.

In order for secular democratic regimes to earn legitimacy, it would seem logical to root and ground essential democratic and political rights in the most sacred values of the predominant culture, even if it is religious. Although he does not explicitly use the term 'public good', Gill (2008) emphasized that common belief systems, including religious ones, can be useful for society both in the interests of politicians seeking legitimacy as well as religious leaders seeking relevance and survival. Secularism is not about curbing religious freedom; it is about ensuring that freedom of thought and conscience applies equally to all religious believers and non-believers alike. Therefore the conceptual framework presented on church and state, and religion and politics leads to a central point: some separation of the church and the state is a fundamental requirement for a secular democracy, but the total removal of religion from politics and vice versa, is neither required nor always ideal. Any radical separation of the latter is undesirable since a genuine vibrant democracy depends on the degree to which both domains complement and mutually enrich one another to be recognized as reciprocal guarantees of strength.

HINDU INITIATIVE IN EDUCATION AND POLITICS

The year 1952 recorded the unification of Hindus as a powerful collectivity deemed necessary for educational advancement provided in their own schools. The first act of Bhadase Sagan Maraj as a

Member of Parliament was bringing together the two warring factions of the Sanatan Dharma Association (SDA) and Sanatan Dharma Board of Control (SDBC) to form a stronger pressure group and Hindu religious organization, which is known today as the Sanatan Dharma Maha Sabha(SDMS). The SDMS was incorporated by Ordinance No. 41 on 26 June 1952 (*The Trinidad Royal Gazette*, vol. 121, no. 52, 26 June 1952: 463). Bhadase was elected as the first President General of the SDMS. By virtue of his position, he also became Head of Denomination for Hindus. The SDMS was accorded recognition as a school building authority on 25 July 1952 (Narayansingh cited in *The Trinidad Express*, 26 February 1995: 9) From its inception, the SDMS reflected a desire of the Hindu community at large to have meaningful participation in both political and educational opportunities that were taking shape in Trinidad in the mid-twentieth century. Political gain created a pathway for Hindus to build their own Hindu denominational schools and avoid their incorporation into the proposed state secular system of education.[14] Hindus were now a more united force conscious of the impact of politics on Hindu initiative in education.

Following adult franchise in 1946, a brief period of alliance politics between some White and Coloured politicians resulted in political bargaining to bridge urban-rural differences. The bargaining process favoured education to disadvantaged rural East Indians as Bhadase Sagan Maraj intended to transform the rural Hindu community from one of illiterate cane cutters to one with equal opportunities for access to schooling. The illiteracy rate in the Debe area was estimated to be over 80 per cent in mid-twentieth century Trinidad. According to Seetahal-Maraj (1991: 39), the Head of the Hindu Denomination, Bhadase Sagan Maraj had communicated to the Minister of Education and Social Services his intention as follows: 'Hindus would not have to travel long distances to receive an education and instead education would be taken to them, even if it meant building a school in every trace of the Debe Penal area.' The minister was 'a real friend of the Indians' and felt much sympathy for the Hindus in their struggle to access education.[15] Wherever Hindu schools were erected by the Hindu community, the minister visited the sites and took the issue to Cabinet for approval. Within a relatively short four-year period (1952-6), the SDMS had built 41 primary schools. The noteworthy evidence was that only 11 of them were granted financial assistance from the government due to poor building construction.[16] Evidently, the founding of Hindu schools was facilitated through alliance politics over the decade 1946-56.

SDMS schools inevitably had become enmeshed in politics within the complex framework of Bhadase's religious and political leadership. In 1953, Bhadase Sagan Maraj launched the People's Democratic Party (PDP) and subsequently won five of the twenty-four seats in 1956 elections, then renamed as the Democratic Labour Party (DLP). This meant that the President General of the SDMS, a Hindu Head of Denomination also became the official leader of the Opposition. Bhadase Sagan Maraj chose to consolidate his religious and political leadership by becoming the President of the major sugar union, the ATSEFWTU (All Trinidad Sugar Estates and Factory Workers Trade Union). The PDP as a predominantly Indo-Trinidadian political organization readily drew support from the Hindu rural masses. Meanwhile, Dr Eric Williams led the nationalist struggle into the decisive formation of the People's National Movement (PNM) in 1956: a party which had immense support from Afro-Trinidadians in urban areas (James 1962).[17] The merger between Hindu religion and politics was accentuated by the racial divide and presented a unique and highly contentious issue for the newly founded Hindu schools.

The erection of Hindu schools featured prominently in the 1956 election campaign. Dr Eric Williams described the SDMS schools in the rural East Indian areas as 'political cells of the PDP' (Campbell 1992). With reference to the the term 'denominational politics' he emphasized: 'Another group builds schools for the specific purpose of fostering political activity and demands as a condition of service the votes of the staff. In effect, the teacher is not voting for a party, but a member of a religious order' (Williams cited in *PNM Weekly*, vol. 1, no. 6, 23 July 1956: 6). In its new role as a denominational body in education, the SDMS chose to respond. Simbhoonath Capildeo, in his capacity as an executive member of the SDMS as well as a Member of the DLP Opposition believed that Dr Eric Williams' quest for power had led him to take the extreme step of insulting the second largest religious group in the colony.[18] Capildeo seized the opportunity to reinforce that the SDMS of Trinidad & Tobago as a religious organisation of Sanatanist Hindus of the Colony, incorporated by private bills passed by the Legislative Council after due scrutiny; and furthermore 'the participation of individuals in politics was the common freedom enjoyed by all persons in the colony' (Capildeo cited in *The Trinidad Guardian*, 5 August 1956: 8).

Simboonath Capildeo aptly underscored:

> For the 105 years of their existence and suffering, Sanatanists of this colony have had to sit by and watch their numbers decimated by proselytising activities of non-Sanatanists. They have suffered in silence during these long years and to use the words of the 1946 census, their importance have been dwindling from year to year. When in 1952 they were granted recognition, we believed that this discrimination against us will end. (ibid.)

Hindus felt that the Hindu community suffered discrimination in education to the extent that in the year 1956 'out of every 100 Indians more than 51 could neither read nor write' (Government of Trinidad & Tobago, Education Department, 1957). This argument not only supported the need for Hindus to have their own schools but sanctioned Hindu participation in frontline politics.

The PDP was said to have functioned on purely religious lines. Ryan cited in Vertovec (1992: 84-5) affirmed that the SDMS was in fact a pillar of strength for Bhadase Sagan Maraj: 'The PDP in fact had never really functioned as an autonomous political party with a constitution. . . . It felt no need to organise since the branches of the Maha Sabha and the priesthood were easily converted into political instrumentalities.'[19] To his political advantage, Dr. Eric Williams highlighted that he had no objection whatsoever to the participation of denominational bodies in politics, however 'if the denominations enter the political arena they must develop and put forward political programmes' (Williams cited in Special Supplement to the *PNM Weekly*, vol. 1, no. 8, 9 August 1956: 1). Thus, while Dr Eric Williams identified with the Hindu educational endeavour, his point of powerful attack was that the President General of the Hindu SDMS was also the Political Leader of the PDP.[20] As a Hindu denominational body, the SDMS felt that their initiative taken to build schools and eradicate illiteracy should have been readily endorsed and supported by the state.

The state acknowledged the right of Hindus to own schools but only on condition that the physical structures set up met the requirements of the law. According to Dr Eric Williams: 'The PNM emphatically states that Hindu schools . . . are entitled to the same rights, privileges, duties and obligations as the schools and colleges of all other religious denominations, subject only to respect for and conformity with the Education Ordinance and law of the land' (Williams cited in Special Supplement to the *PNM Weekly*, vol. 1, no. 10, 23 August 1956: 6). While insistence on conformity to the law is understood, the political divide strongly impeded educational advancement of east Indians. The SDMS school building programme was severely hindered following the PNM victory at the polls in 1956.[21] Dr Eric Williams was critical of the Hindu schools which he commonly referred to as 'cowsheds'. In response, Bhadase Sagan Maraj stated: 'It is better to be educated in a cowshed than not to be educated at all' (Narayansingh cited in *The Trinidad Express*, 26 February 1995: 9).

The period of alliance politics (1946-56), contrasted sharply with the slow rate of rural development that characterized the subsequent period of 'nationalist' politics when the urban based, predominantly African People's National Movement would be pitted against the rural-based, predominantly Indian People's Democratic Party in the 1960s and 1970s (Singh 1994: 226).The success of alliance politics which facilitated the founding of SDMS schools essentially evolved from a merger of politics and Hindu religion.

According to Jain (2005: 468): 'To understand this alliance of politics and religion we must look to the major activity of Bhadase Sagan Maraj, his dynamism in creating East Indian educational institutions, something inevitable in the special configuration of denominational education in Trinidad.' Bhadase's dual role as religious leader and politician did well for Hindu schools to feature in denominational education at a time when the nationalist movement recognized government schools as an integrating force for nationalism and de-emphasized differences based on religion within the education system.

HINDU RESISTANCE TO A PROPOSED STATE SYSTEM OF EDUCATION

Having entered the denominational system of education, the SDMS carefully aligned with the position taken up by a well entrenched Roman Catholic Church against the introduction of a fully state controlled secular system of education. The state and the church in Trinidad were on opposing sides of the Aristotelian theory of the Ideal State as illustrated in the proposed 'Great Debate of 1955' between Dr Eric Williams and Dr Dom Basil Mathews.[22] In conformity with Aristotle's perspective that the state is the Supreme Being, Dr Eric Williams argued in favour of the introduction of state schools as follows: 'I see in the denominational school the breeding ground for disunity; I see in the State school the opportunity for cultivating a spirit of nationalism among the West Indian people and eradicating the suspicions and antagonisms growing in our midst. I place the community above the sect or race' (*The Trinidad Guardian*, 15 September 1991: 1). Dr Dom Basil Mathews stated his intention to engage in discussions with partial reference to Aristotle's philosophy which embraced certain aspects of the relationship between religion and the state. Dr Eric Williams cleverly indicated that in order to fully understand the debate, Aristotle's philosophy should be discussed in its entirety. The Catholic Church agreed to Dr Dom Basil's expedient withdrawal from the debate.

In sum, Dr Eric Williams desired an opportunity to expound upon Aristotle's argument that 'the goal of the state' was to educate with a view towards 'the ends of the state' and preservation of its institutions (Davidson 1900). The achievement of this goal required consensus among all groups based on virtues to promote 'the good life for the whole community' (Barnes 1995). The Catholics, the SDMS and other denominational bodies recognized that they were expected to accept a secular education system designed to serve the state without due consideration for values derived from their religious beliefs.

Thirty-six years, later in 1991, Dr Dom Basil Mathews presented a critique on the proposed 'Great Debate of 1955'. While Aristotle's ancient Greek philosophy focused on the belief that the state was the Supreme Being and a true citizen is loyal to the state; the Greeks were non-believers who were opposed to Christian values. Dr Dom Basil Mathews emphasized: 'The state could not dictate to the church what their policies should be. The church was determined to retain the moral and spiritual values, and that could not be translated through the secular state' (*The Trinidad Guardian*, September 1991: 1).[23] The stance taken by the Catholic church in 1955 strengthened SDMS's endeavour to defend the preservation of the Hindu religion against secularism and emerging nationalists attacks during the establishment phase of Hindu schools (1952-6), The SDMS in an orthodox sense was now considered a church.

In the mid-1950s, the teaching of religion in government schools including Hinduism proved to be a controversial topic of debate. Dr Eric Williams conveniently interpreted as the truth Mahatma Gandhi's perspectives on India's secular education system and the question of religious instruction. The former pointed out that the Indian educational system was a secular one and Mahatma Gandhi, Hinduism incarnate, repudiated not only state-aided denominational schools but also religious instruction in state schools.[24] Dr Eric Williams cited Mahatma Gandhi in his newspaper *Harijan* dated 16 July 1938 as follows: 'Religious instruction in the sense of denominational religion has been deliberately omitted. Unless there is a state religion it is very difficult if not impossible to provide religious instruction as it would mean providing for every denomination. Such instruction is best given at home.' (Williams cited in Special Supplement to the *PNM Weekly*, vol. 1, no. 8, 9 August 1956: 2). Dr Eric Williams pointed out that nine years later in April 1947, Mahatma Gandhi had made his disapproval of religious instruction in state schools even more precise in the following statement: 'I do not agree that government should provide religious education. . . . The government can only teach others based on the main principles common to all religions and agreed to by all parties. In fact, ours is a secular state' (ibid.). Contrary to Dr Williams' interpretation, Mahatma Gandhi's disapproval of religious instruction in secular state schools based on the principles of equality and consensus require further interrogation.

It is noteworthy to consider Mahatma Gandhi's question focused on secular India: 'Should religious instruction form part of the school curriculum as approved by the State?' (Kumar 2007: no pagination). Gandhi outlined:

> The state interference would probably always be unwelcome. . . . A curriculum of religious instruction should include a study of the tenets of faith other than one's own. For this purpose the students should be trained to cultivate the habit of understanding and appreciating the doctrines of various great religions of the world in a spirit of reverence and broad-minded tolerance. This if properly done, would help to give them a spiritual assurance and a better appreciation of their own religion'. (ibid.)

Gandhi's major concern was whether the state can effectively deliver a curriculum to embrace all religions and promote desirable virtues. Hence, Gandhi essentially did not disapprove of religious instruction in secular state schools; he welcomed teaching the doctrines of all great religions of the world in India's schools if this could have been implemented.[25] In the Trinidad context, the SDMS concurred with other denominational bodies that religious instruction should be offered in government schools. However, Hindus strongly desired their own schools cognizant of the fact that both government schools and even Church schools were already aligned between the motivations and existing outcomes of Anglicization under the Christian-European model of education.

Given the inextricable link between religion and language in shaping a society, Dr Eric Williams was firm in his conviction that the teaching of the Hindi language in Hindu schools would accentuate racial and ethnic differences to the detriment of building a national identity.[26] In his address entitled 'Education for Democratic Citizenship in the Caribbean' (1955), Dr Williams denounced the teaching of Hindi in schools thus: 'It is not that this recognition is wrong, as I have said before, non-Christian denominational schools can't be wrong, and Christian denominational schools right . . . but it will be suicidal to aggravate this religious diversity and religious difference by a linguistic differentia-tion.' (*The Trinidad Guardian*, 20 May 1955: 6). A rhetorical question emerged from this argument: 'How can any responsible person argue that in 1955, the second, third generation offspring of people brought here one hundred or even forty years ago, who do not speak Hindi in their homes , have a right to demand Mother tongue in the schools?' (Ryan 1972).[27] Unavoidably, this linguistic controversy elicited widespread public reaction.

East Indians organized themselves and raised a formidable issue based on the principle of fairness: 'If Latin, Spanish and French are expected to be learnt by children in the schools and the expenditure for teaching them is met from the general revenue, then why should not the Indian who forms thirty-seven per cent of the colony's population be given the facilities to learn Hindi?' (*The Trinidad Guardian*, 20 May 1955: 6). Dr. Eric Williams and some members of the Creole community were hostile to what they described as an upsurge of 'non-Christian religion' associated with a vigorous and claimant insistence on 'indigenous culture'.[28] Interestingly, a Christian Indian, who was a member of the PNM, responded that many Indians consider Hindi 'the mother tongue'. He cited Milton Kerwitz as follows: 'language as the carrier and preserver of a people's culture may be of primary importance in sustaining living ties between the alien and the country from which they emigrated' (*The Trinidad Guardian*, 7 June 1955: 8).[29] From the very inception of indentureship in 1845, Hindus and Muslims had recognized the need for language preservation to maintain ties with Trinidad and India.

Hindus feared cultural absorption and loss of their Hindi language and religious identity within an 'integrated secular state school system' under the Afro-based PNM party. Dr Eric Williams thus drew upon a distinction between the words Hindu and 'Indian culture' as stated by Jawaharlal Nehru, India's first prime minister, in his book entitled *The Discovery of India*: 'It is incorrect and undesirable to use 'Hindu' or 'Hinduism' for Indian culture. . . . A Christian or Muslim could, and often did, adapt himself to the Indian way of life and culture, and yet remained in faith an orthodox Christian or Muslim. He had 'indianized' himself to become an

Indian without changing his religion.' (Special Supplement to the *PNM Weekly*, vol. 1, no. 8, 9 August 1956: 1).[30] Dr Williams aspired to place national integration above any denomination or race. While this might be seen as admirable, the fundamental question that arose for Sanatanist Hindus was—'integration on the basis of what?' (*The Trinidad Guardian*: 16 January 1955: 3b). Bhadase and others warned that the *Ramayana* and Hindu dharma were in danger if non-Hindus held political office (Vertovec, 1992). The onus was on the present generation of Hindus to mobilize political support and take a stance on denominational Hindu edu-cation towards creating a pathway for positive social change.

THE HINDU STANCE ON EDUCATION

The Hindu religion emerged as a battleground with intense focus on a two-dimensional struggle which solidified the stance on education taken by Hindus to provide denominational primary schools. First, Hindus sought the establishment of their own schools and intensification of Hinduism in resistance to government's proposed integrated secular system of education premised on the Christian-European tradition. Simultaneously, the Hindu religion became a driving force for the mobilization of political participation to ensure the realization of Hindu schools and academic achievement among generations of Hindus for economic and social advancement towards a better quality of life.

In view of the incursion of nationalism and the controversies surrounding cultural absorption, the SDMS felt that the imperative of academic achievement in Western education for Hindus must complement a cultural awakening towards the consolidation of a collective Hindu identity (Singh 2002). First the wide range of geographical origins of Hindu-indentured immigrants from different parts of northern India to Trinidad thwarted genuine attempts to arrive at a consensus on socio-cultural variations. The continuous arrival of new immigrants complicated deliberate initiatives towards social and cultural amalgamation among Indians on the sugar estates. The situation placed a serious responsibility on Hindu schools to institutionalize Hinduism and create a more homogeneous culture which would stand above religious divisions.[31]

The SDMS intention was to bring about religious change through education aimed at continuous social and ideological reconfiguration of Indian communities.

The SDMS Parishad (Council of Pundits) accepted the mantle of leadership and worked towards coordination of activities between temples and schools through standardization of a publication for Hindu pupils called *My Prayer Book*, a collection of Sanskrit *mantras* (with English translations) and tenets of Hinduism.[32] Given that the academic component of the curriculum of Hindu schools was modeled on the Christian-European educational pattern operative in the society, Bhadase Sagan Maraj was firm in his conviction that teachers in Hindu schools should be teachers of religion as well (Seetahal Maraj 1991). SDMS pundits and teachers taught Hindi classes and religious instruction to enable pupils to know their sacred texts, namely the *Ramayana*, *Bhagavad Gita* and *Mahabharata*. There was also curriculum inclusion of Indian civilization, India's cultural heritage and art forms such as music, dance and drama. Western education was complemented by opportunities for retention of traditional eastern culture.

Hence, SDMS schools offered Hindu children an education within a community of religious and cultural experiences conducive to the development of Hinduism and an awareness of a collective Hindu identity which government schools could not give.[33] Activities in SDMS schools and affiliated temples led to the founding of branches which required locally-composed boards to coordinate religious activities. The boards and their practices were overseen nationally by the SDMS which convened Trinidad-wide assemblies of local representatives. These operations provided for Hindu education and religious organizational activities which meshed with Hindu participation in frontline politics throughout the 1950s and 1960s.

CONCLUSION

The year 1952 marked a turning point in the history of Indian diaspora in Trinidad on account of Hindus' access to education in their own schools. A critical part of this history involved the interplay between the church and the state, and religion and politics. First, the SDMS attained significant control of orthodox Hinduism which afforded an opportunity for Hindus to constitute a 'church' in the technical sense within the denominational education system. In the battleground for education against the state, the Hindu religion was not only 'standardized' but it also became 'politicized'. Although Bhadase's role as a religious leader came into conflict with his political agenda, he understood the socio-political forces at work and seized the opportunity to unite Hindus into a very powerful group than they had previously been. The experience did well for Hindu schools to feature in denominational education at a time when the nationalist government recognized schools as an integrating force of nationalism and de-emphasized religious and cultural differences within the educational system.

The concept of the Aristotlean Ideal State was clearly premised on citizens' obedience to secularism over religion. It was an entirely different approach to embrace the Hindu denomination in the thrust towards a state system of education, especially one which would unavoidably be operationalized on favouritism for the continuation of a tradition of Christian-European nationalistic education. In stark contrast to church and state separation in the Western tradition, the emerging reality was that Hindus' everyday religious beliefs and practices potentially supported politics in a movement forward for Hindu denominational education. Further, while church and state concerns the relationship between institutions that are structurally independent of each other, religion and politics deal with two spheres of activities in the life of the same person. As members of a religious group as well as citizens of the secular society, Hindus felt that their ethical convictions for social equality rooted in the Hindu religion gave them a legitimate right to engage in political activities and take a stance on education.

The researcher concludes that working out relations between the church and the state, and religion and politics in secular democratic states, presents many complexities and overlapping realms within which practical solutions can be found to strengthen religious and political processes. Hindu religion and politics merged to seek redress for Hindu exclusion from the total ensemble of historical principles and practices that governed church and state in education. Of profound significance, Hindus understood that the merger of Hinduism as a religion and politics could open the way for the establishment of Hindu schools to deliver education to generations of young Hindus. The founding of Hindu schools inspired not only academic achievement but religious institutionalization, cultural homogeneity and a distinctive Hindu identity. Today, in the twenty-first century, the curriculum of Hindu schools in Trinidad affords Hindu children an opportunity to maintain religious and cultural attachments to their motherland, India; and to develop a deeper understanding of how to preserve the shared heritage memory of their ancestors' struggles and achievements.

NOTES

1. Anglicization can be appropriately defined as 'the process through which non-English people become assimilated or bound into an English-dominated cultural and ideological system' (Williams cited in Coupland 1990: 19).
2. Lord Harris was a Liberal politician and colonial administrator who served as the Governor of Trinidad from 1846 to 1856. The Liberal Party was one of two major parties in the United Kingdom in the nineteenth and early twentieth century. It endorsed a political philosophy or world-view based on the ideas of liberty and equality. The Ward Schools Lord Harris introduced for all races were the forerunner of today's government schools in Trinidad & Tobago (Anthony cited in *The Sunday Express*, 17 June 1984: 11).
3. Immigration from a country as vast as India with varying geographical conditions meant grappling with a complex and rather different facets of an ancient culture and its transplantation in a strange land. Between 1845 and 1917 approximately 143,000 indentured labourers came to Trinidad from the subcontinent of India channelled through two main ports, Calcutta in the North and Madras in the South (Jha 2005).
4. Immigration from India was also referred to as 'coolie immigration'. The term 'Kuli' was also applied to other Asiatic peoples as well as to natives of India. In the Hindi language it meant 'porter' or 'labourer'. It was also the official designation for the very lowest class of East Indian labourers (Grant 1923).

5. Sir Authur Gordon was regarded as one of the most successful and hardworking Governors of Trinidad (1866-70).Though himself an Anglican he intended to reduce the long-standing alienation felt by the Trinidad Catholics as well as the dispossessed East Indian immigrants (Singh 2002). The dual system of education between church and state still exists in Trinidad today.
6. In 1891, 27 per cent of Christian Indians in Trinidad were Presbyterians (Ramesar, 1994). However, there were some who only accepted conversion to gain employment as teachers in CM schools and upward social mobility (Seesaran 2002).
7. The Marriot Mayhew Commission (1931) was appointed by the Secretary of State to consider educational problems on West Indian islands, including Trinidad. A major problem for Hindu leadership in education was the existence of two rival Hindu organizations: the Sanatan Dharma Association (SDA) and the Sanatan Dharma Board of Control (SDBC) apart from a third, the Arya Samaj. The SDA and SDBC organizations originated from controversy between the Presbyterians and Catholics who respectively approved and disapproved of divorce legislation. To compound the situation, the President of the SDA, Saran Teelucksingh was an Anglican and his counterpart of the SDBC, C.B. Mathura was a Catholic (Jain 2005).
8. The realization of Hindu schools was an imperative to eradicate illiteracy. The Census of 1946 recorded the illiteracy rate among East Indians as 50.6 per cent which was far greater than any other racial group (Colony of Trinidad & Tobago 1948).
9. At its core, American liberal democracy is based on the premise that democratic governance requires that those powers are moderated by the constitution. The First Amendment of the United States Constitution reads 'Congress shall make no law respecting an establishment of religion, or prohibiting the free exercise thereof' (Church 2004).
10. East-West comparative perspectives have shown that historically the relationship between church and state has taken a variety of forms from the religion dominating the state to the state dominating religion, one often trespasses in the realm of the other over power, authority, law and unavoidably education (Bereday and Lauwerys 1966).
11. The Boisi Centre for Religion and American Public life is a research institute at Boston College committed to fostering scholarly discussion about the role of religion and how it functions in the United States.
12. George Wilhem Friedrich (1770-1831) was a German philosopher who recognized the need for some separation of church and state while

he appealed for a more integrated relationship between religion and politics.

13. The latter perspective indicates that further separation of church and state is not necessarily associated with higher levels of democratic rights and freedom.
14. Bhadase Sagan Maraj knew that if East Indians and Hindus specifically were to occupy their rightful place in the ladder of economic and social advancement, they required not only Western education, but education in an environment conducive to promoting and retaining the tenets of their faith (Mohammed 1995).
15. Considering the political divide between the two major races, Africans and East Indians, it is meaningful to consider that the minister was of Syrian origin and his wife was an East Indian (Singh 2011).
16. For construction of many schools financial costs were absorbed by Bhadase Sagan Maraj himself who had acquired considerable wealth through war surplus trading. His political affiliations also propelled the SDMS school building programme (Seetahal Maraj 1991).The first six schools were established through additions and refurbishing of pre-existing structures built by the community on private land. Necessary renovations were completed at the expense of the community (Narayan-singh cited in *The Trinidad Express*, 26 February 1995: 9).
17. A similar configuration of divisions based on religion, race and geographical location is still apparent in national elections in Trinidad at present.
18. To heighten the accusation, Dr Eric Williams stated there was a link between the SDMS of Trinidad (a purely religious organization representing Hindus) and the intolerant fanatic Hindu Maha Sabha in India which he charged was responsible for the assassination of Mahatma Gandhi (Malik 1971). Capildeo responded: 'there never has been, nor is there any connection of any kind whatsoever between the Hindu MS of India and the SDMS Inc. of Trinidad and Tobago. . . . The Trinidad MS was incorporated in May 1952; Gandhi was assassinated in January 1948. There could be no possible connection between the two events' (*The Sunday Guardian*, 5 August 1956: 8).
19. The SDMS lack of organization and apparent conversion of religious affiliations into political forces stands as testimony that for Hindus there can be no clear-cut distinction between religion and politics or church and state.
20. On the contrary, it was a deliberate attempt on the part of Bhadase Sagan Maraj to consolidate his religious and political leadership with a central focus on provision of education for Hindus.

21. As many as ten Hindu schools already constructed were condemned and consequently never opened their doors. Yet Hindu children in rural districts remained without access to education (Singh 2002).
22. Dr Dom Basil Mathews pursued studies for the Catholic priesthood at Mount St. Benedict in Trinidad and was ordained priest in the Order of St. Benedict in 1935. Count Finbar Ryan, D.D. (Doctor of Divinity) had endorsed Mathews as Williams' opponent to discuss the concept of Aristotle's Ideal State and debate secular vs. denominational education in contemporary Trinidad.
23. The statement rejects heavy-handed ruling by a secular state over churches. It was this approach that deterred Dom Basil Mathews from participating in the Great Debate of 1955; it negated religious and political discourse against the advancement of democracy.
24. Dr Eric Williams drew upon a comparative perspective between Trinidad and India not only as secular states but in recognition that Hindu immigrants in Trinidad revered the religious teachings of Mahatma Gandhi. The comparison was meant to be politically expedient.
25. Mahatma Gandhi's argument is consistent with the view that a secular state should not curb religious freedom or expression; instead a secular democratic government ensures freedom of thought and conscience must apply equally to all religious believers as well as non-believers.
26. The core argument was that a new nation necessitates the cultivation of a new national identity and language played an important role in nation building and identity formation in a muti-religious, multi-racial and ethnically diverse Trinidad.
27. Notably, the linguistic diversity of the first Indian immigrants was a characteristic feature of the immigrant community. However, Indians in Trinidad, similar to those in other sugar colonies, gradually came to create a common tongue, sometimes referred to as 'Plantation Hindustani' (Tinker 1974). They intended to develop and retain this shared language among themselves.
28. Throughout the colonial period, 'Creole' was an identity that distinguished someone born in the Caribbean rather than in Europe or Africa. It therefore meant evolving cultural, racial and social forms (Khan 2004). It also meant non-alignment with the need for preservation of Indian indigenous languages.
29. The statement signifies that language is not just a means of communication, it is an expression of culture and who people are as individuals, communities and nations with due regard for cross-cultural exchanges.

30. While Jawaharlal Nehru's comment is accurate, religion has proven to be inseparable from culture and its social and historical settings.
31. It should be noted that caste divisions (with the priestly Brahmins at the top and leather working Chamar caste of the lowest untouchable groups at the bottom) among post-indenture Indian communities were generally only a reflection of a person's social status than a governing influence on it, status was derived from factors such as wealth, occupation, political power and education (Mayer 1967).
32. The Prayer book is still used in both primary and newly-established secondary SDMS schools in Trinidad.
33. The state was left with no alternative but to recognize the invaluable incorporation of Hindus into the dual system of education given their collective and communal solidarity in organized religious and political endeavours.

REFERENCES

Barnes, J. (ed.), *The Cambridge Companion to Aristotle*, Cambridge: Cambridge University Press, 1995.

Bereday, G.Z.F. and J.A. Lauwerys, *Church and State in Education*. London: Evan Brothers Limited, 1966.

Boisi Centre for Religion and American Public Life, 2007, *Separation of Church and State*, vol. 1 of the Boisi Centre Papers on Religion in the United States. Retrieved on 15 May 2015 from http://www.bc.edu/centers/boisi/publications/boisi_center_papers.htm

Brereton, B., 'The Experience of Indentureship: 1845-1917', in John Gaffar La Guerre and Ann Marie Bissessar (eds.), *Calcutta to Caroni and the Indian Diaspora* (3rd revd. edn.), The University of the West Indies, St. Augustine, Trinidad: School of Continuing Studies, 2005, pp. 29-45.

Buchwalter, A., 'The Relationship of Religion and Politics under Conditions of Modernity and Globality: An Hegelian Account', *An International Journal in Philosophy, Religion, Politics and the Arts*, vol. 1, nos. 1 & 2, 2006, pp. 64-73.

Campbell, C.C., 'The East Indian Revolt against Missionary Education 1982-39', in John Gaffar La Guerre (ed.), *Calcutta to Caroni: The East Indians of Trinidad.* (2nd revd. edn.), St. Augustine, Trinidad: Extra Mural Studies Unit, UWI, 1985, pp. 117-31.

Campbell, C.C., *Colony and Nation: A Short History of Education in Trinidad and Tobago 1834-1986*, Kingston: Ian Randle, 1992.

Church, F., *The Separation of Church and State: Writings on a Fundamental Freedom by America's Founders*, Boston: Beacon Press, 2004.

Colony of Trinidad and Tobago, *Census 1946*, Trinidad and Tobago Government Printing Office, 1948.

Croft, J., 2013, The Difference Between Secular Law and Secular Culture. Retrieved on 1 June 2015 from http://www.patheos.com/blogs/templeofthefuture/2013/07/the-difference-between-secular-law-and-secular-culture/

David, T., *Aristotle and the Ancient Education Ideals*, New York: Charles Scribner's, 1990.

Driessen, M.P.D., 'Religion, State and Democracy: Analysing Two Dimensions of Church-State Arrangements', *Politics and Religion*, vol. 3, no. 1, 2010, pp. 55-80.

Fergus, C.K., 'Education and the Movement for Self-Government in Trinidad and Tobago 1931-56, unpublished M.A. thesis, Department of History, The University of the West Indies, St. Augustine, Trinidad, 1986.

Freire, P., *The Politics of Education: Culture, Power and Liberation*, Massachusetts: Bergin and Garvey Publishers, Inc., 1985.

Gill, A., *The Political Origins of Religious Liberty*, New York: Cambridge University Press, 2008.

Government of Trinidad and Tobago, Education Department, *Statistician Report 1956*, Port-of-Spain: Government Printery, 1957.

——, Ministry of Education, *Education in the West Indies: Marriott Mayhew Commission 1931-2. Proposals Relating to Trinidad*, Port-of-Spain, Trinidad, 1983.

Grant, K. J., *My Missionary Memories*, Halifax: The Imperial Publishing Company Limited, 1923.

Hamel-Smith, A. L., 'The History of Education in Trinidad 1990-1938', unpublished M. Phil. thesis, Department of History, The University of the West Indies, St. Augustine, Trinidad, 1983.

Jain, R., 'Exclusion and Inclusion: Ethnicity and Race Relations in Trinidadian Indian Diaspora', in John Gaffar La Guerre (ed.), *Calcutta to Caroni and the Indian Diaspora*, op. cit., 2005, pp. 460-79.

James,C.L.R., *Party Politics in the West Indies*, San Juan: Trinidad Inprint Caribbean Ltd., 1962.

Jayaram,T., 1997, Secularism defined. Retrieved on 5 June 2015 from http// www. imsc.res.in/~jayaram/Articles/frontline/node1.html

Jha, J.C., 'The Indian Heritage in Trinidad', in John Gaffar La Guerre and

Ann Marie Bissessar, *Calcutta to Caroni and the Indian Diaspora*, Trinidad & Tobago School of Continuing Studies, The University of the West Indies, St. Augustine, 2005, pp.1-28.

Keenan, P., *Report Upon the State of Education in the Island of Trinidad*, Dublin: H.M.S.O, 1869.

Khan, A., *Callaloo Nation*, Durham and London: Duke University Press, 2004.

Kilcullen, J., *Separation of Church and State*, Sydney: Macquarie University, 2012.

Klass, M., *Singing with Sai Baba: The Politics of Revitalisation in Trinidad*, Virginia, Waveland Press, 1991.

Kumar, R., 2007, Remembering Gandhi on the 60th Anniversary of India's Independence. Retrieved on 1 March 2010 from http:www.globalpolitician.com/23579-gandhi.

Malik, Y.K., *East Indians in Trinidad: A Study in Minority Politics*, London: Oxford University Press, 1971.

Mayer, A., 'Patrons and Brokers: Rural Leadership in Four Overseas Indian Communities', in M. Freedman (ed.), *Social Organisations*, London: Frank Cass, 1967.

Mohammed, C., 'The Journey of a Footstep', *Naya Savera*, Barartaria, Trinidad: Cassims Concepts and Designs, 1995, pp. 27-8.

Peach, L., 'Supreme Court Docket: Does Religion belong in the Schools?' *Social Education*, vol. 50, no. 3, 1986, pp. 166-9.

Ramesar, M.D., 'The Development of Administration and Control in Trinidad and Tobago Education', *Journal of Association of Principals of Public Secondary Schools*, vol. 1, no. 1, 1980, pp. 11-15.

Ryan, S., *Race and Nationalism in Trinidad and Tobago: A Study of Decolonisation in a Multi-racial Society*, Toronto and Buffalo: University of Toronto Press, 1972.

Samaroo, B., 'Missionary Methods and Local Responses: The Canadian Presbyterians and the East Indians in the Caribbean', in B. Brereton and W. Dookeran (eds.), *East Indians in the Caribbean and Struggles for Identity*, London: Kraus International Publications, 1982, pp. 93-115.

Seesaran, R., 'Church and State in Education: Trinidad 1814-1870', unpublished M.A. thesis. Department of History, The University of the West Indies, St. Augustine, Trinidad, 1974.

Seetahal-Maraj, B, *Master and Servant: Bhadase Sagan Maraj*, St. Augustine, Trinidad: The Publications Committee of the SDMS of T&T Inc., 1991.

Singh, K., *Race and Class Struggles in a Colonial State: Trinidad 1917-1945*. Calgary: University of Calgary Press, 1994.

Singh, V., 'Denominational and State Conflict: The Experience of the Sanatan Dharma Board of Education 1952-96', unpublished MA thesis, School of Education, The University of the West Indies, St. Augustine, Trinidad, 2002.

Singh, V., 'East Indians and Educational Equity: The Ordinances of 1870, 1875, and 1890', *Yatra: The Journey*, vol. 3, issue 2, Trinidad & Tobago: High Commission of India, 2011, pp. 14-15.

Stepan, A. 'The World's Religious Systems of Democracy', in J. Linz. and A. Stephan (eds.), *Arguing Comparative Politics*, Oxford: Oxford University Press, 2001.

The Boisi Centre for Religion and American Public Life, *Separation of Church and State*, 2007.

Tinker, H., *A New System of Slavery*, London: Oxford University Press, 1974.

Vertovec, S. A., *Hindu Trinidad: Religion, Ethnicity and Socio-Economic Change*, London and Basingstoke: Macmillan Education Limited, 1992.

Williams, C.H., 'The Anglisation of Wales', in N. Coupland (ed.), *English in Wales: Diversity, Conflict and Change*, Cleveland Multilingual Matters, 1990, pp. 19-47.

Williams, E.E., *Education in the West Indies*, Port-of Spain: Guardian Commercial Printer, 1950.

NEWSPAPERS

Anthony, M., 'How Government Schools Came About', *The Sunday Express*, 17 June 1984, p. 11.

Capildeo, S., 'Voice of the People: Leader of the PNM Criticised for Distorting the Facts', *The Sunday Guardian*, 5 August 1956, p. 8.

'Denominationalism Threatens Trinidad's Future', *The Sunday Guardian*, 16 January 1955, p. 3b.

'Dr Williams Urges Emphasis on Britain, Africa and India', *The Trinidad Guardian*, 20 May 1955, p. 6.

'Lecturer Praised for Ability to Resist Majority Sentiment', *The Trinidad Guardian*, 7 June 1955, p. 8.

'Ordinances for 1952', *The Trinidad Royal Gazette*, vol. 121, 26 June 1952, p. 463.

'The Great Debate', *The Trinidad Guardian*, 15 September 1991, p. 1.

Narayansingh, V., 'Rise of Hindu Schools', *The Express*, 26 February 1995, p. 9.

Williams, E.E., 'A Public Lecture Delivered at the University of Woodford

Square on 14 August 1956', *Special Supplement to the PNM Weekly*, vol. 1, no. 10. 23 August 1956, p. 6.

Williams, E.E., 'Address to the First Annual Convention of the PNM on 28 July 1956', *Special Supplement to the PNM Weekly*, vol. 1, no. 8, 9 August 1956, pp. 1, 2.

Williams, E.E., 'Nationalism for PNM: Denominational Politics', *PNM Weekly*, vol. 1, no. 6, 23 July 1956, p. 6.

CHAPTER 5

Hinduism Transformed? A Case Study of Hindu Diaspora in Thailand*

RUCHI AGARWAL

INTRODUCTION

Defining Hinduism can be a daunting task. However, it is referred to as Sanatana Dharma meaning the eternal tradition. This refers to the belief that the origin lies beyond human history, and the truths were revealed and passed on through the ages and were recorded in the Vedas. A clear definition is difficult because there is no known founder, no central revelation, and no institutional structure that fits with the huge diversity of religious traditions, beliefs, and practices. In fact, the emergence of the term 'Hinduism', to refer to the religion of India, itself has been under debate among academics. Scholars such as Robert Frykenberg (1989), Christopher Fuller (1992), Brian Smith (1989), and Heinrich von Stietencron (1989), among others claim that Hinduism was a term coined by British writers in the nineteenth century. Scholars, however, find no clear evidence that the term 'Hindu' was being used as a religious identity prior to its imposition by the Europeans in the colonial period (Smith 1959; Stietencron 1997). Thapar (1990) makes similar claims that Persian writers used the word *al-hind* to refer to India and to the people living beyond the Indus River as 'Hindus'. The term was used as a geographical and ethnic term and only later it was used

*The research findings of this chapter were earlier published in *Nidan*, vol. 27, nos. 1 & 2, 2015, pp. 42-55.

to refer to those practising native religions of India who were neither Muslims nor Christians (pp. 6-10). On the other hand, scholars like Lawrence A. Babb (1986), Alf Hiltebeitel (1991), Peter van der Veer (1994), Cynthia Talbot (1996), and David N. Lorenzen (1999) have questioned the claims that Hinduism was invented or constructed by the colonizing Europeans in the nineteenth century. They claim the term existed and was in use way before the 1800s. Lorenzen (1999) for example, in his essay suggests that a Hindu religion theologically and devotionally existing in the *Bhagavad Gita,* the Puranas, and the philosophical commentaries on the six *darshanas* formed a stronger self-conscious identity because of the rivalry between Muslims and Hindus during the 1200s and 1500s, and thus was firmly established before the 1800s.

In this paper therefore I argue that the term 'Hinduism' is very vague and Hinduism as a religion is extremely broad. This leaves room for changes in religious beliefs and traditions as Hinduism encounters the local beliefs and traditions central to the host environment where it travels. To assess these changes or transformations, the Hindu diaspora in Thailand is presented as a case study. This article is a result of qualitative research based on observations and interviews conducted with the representatives of the Hindu communities in Bangkok.

HINDUISM IN SOUTHEAST ASIA

Southeast Asia has shared long historical relations with India for over 2000 years that has resulted in the spread of Hinduism[1] in this region along with the South Asian practitioners (Coedes 1968). The Indian settlement in Southeast Asia has been documented since the sixth century BCE and has contributed greatly to the development of the national culture of the Southeast Asian countries. Several factors contributed to the Indian settlements in Southeast Asia including the Kushan invasion of India around the first century AD and their rule, expanding to include much of north India, exerted pressure on the local population to emigrate overseas. Other factors included the opportunities that opened for high caste Indians to pursue their fortunes outside of India (ibid.: 21-2). Other scholars suggest that the Indian contact with Southeast Asia was more commercial and that migrants brought the traditional arts, religious beliefs, and customs along with them. This historical linkage prompted more Indians to move to Southeast Asia to continue the old traditions of trade relations thereby forming the Indian Diaspora in a foreign land. The historical presence of Hinduism in Southeast Asia, dating back to over 2000 years, was able to create an important religious sphere for itself in a predominantly Buddhist country like Thailand. Thailand has a population of over 90 per cent Buddhists, yet many Thais engage features of Hinduism in worship that comes from these historical, cultural and religious influences.

The motivation behind Indian migration[2] to Thailand ranged from frustration to attraction. The factors included social, economic, or political coercion prompting people to leave their homeland in search of better opportunities. The Tamils and Gujaratis migrated in the late 1800s and were mainly involved in the gem and textile trades. A larger scale migration took place in the 1890s from north-west India followed by a wave of Sikhs and Hindus from Punjab (Bangkok's . . . 2009). According to Mani (1993), in the twentieth century, the most important factor bringing migrants to Thailand was economic. This included poverty-ridden life in the villages due to droughts, crop failures, and unemployment. Additionally, political problems like the India-Pakistan Partition in 1947 contributed to increasing numbers of Indians, both Hindus and Punjabis, from the Pakistan side moving to neighbouring countries. The fact that Thailand was a peaceful country and that family links already existed with earlier settled immigrants made it easier for the politically displaced families to create a new home in Thailand. Religion was important to these migrants as it provided social and financial support from the already established religious organizations of the earlier migrants. Others relied on support from their previously settled family members. Religion then acted as a force binding the different groups (former and more recent) of Indian migrants together. It was of course easier for these groups to settle in Thailand because of the existing historical grounds of Hinduism. A general feeling among the Indian community in Thailand is that living here is like being in a home away from home.

It is important to study religions and diasporas because of the strong connection they share. Smart (1999) suggests three reasons for this. First, the study of diasporas and their methods of adjustment provide understandings of the general forms of religious transformation. Second, diasporas may themselves affect the development of religion in the homeland whereby the wealth, education and exposure to foreign features transferred from diasporas may have important effects on organization, practice and even belief. Last, with the greater number of diasporas in the modern world, 'multiethnicity is now a commonplace' (Smart 1999: 421 cited in Vertovec 2009). Smart is right and his ideas are visually evident in the case of the Indian diaspora in Thailand. This paper will attempt to make parallels to Smart's ideas with the Indian diaspora in Thailand. Religion is an important part of the Indian diaspora (Vertovec 2000; Parekh 1993). The strong roots of belonging come from Hinduism, an ethnic religion of India (Parekh 1993: 140). Over 85 per cent of overseas Indians worldwide are Hindus who refer to their homeland as 'Mother India' with deep spiritual and emotional longings that are fulfilled through routine visits and pilgrimages. However, not every overseas Indian is a Hindu. Several religious minorities exist within the Indian diaspora including the Muslims and the Sikhs. The heterogeneity and diversity are the factors that distinguish the Indian diaspora from their counterparts in the respective countries (Singh 2003: 4-5). What really binds the Indian diaspora together are the emotions, acquaintances, customs, feelings and attachments for their motherland that appeal to generations of emigrants. These create a sense of belongingness and a unity in diversity through a unified identity of the motherland. Indian media plays an important role in preserving this identity among the ethnically diverse Indian diaspora by promoting the Indian values, customs, and the links to the motherland.

METHODS OF ADJUSTMENT TO THE HOST ENVIRONMENT AND THE RESULTING TRANSFORMATIONS

The long presence of Indian diaspora in a foreign land forces them to experience great social, religious, economic, political, and cultural changes. The focus here is on the changes evident on the cultural and religious context. Living away from home may induce the diasporic community to abandon some traditional practices, adopting new ones and evolving a distinct way of life overtime. To further elaborate on this, the next section will be subdivided into first changes with adjustment to a new environment for the Hindu migrants and second the changes resulting from the Thais encountering Hinduism. Luchesi (2004) in his study on the Tamil community in Germany provides an insight into the importance of community formation through religious and cultural organizations. He shows how the places of worship for the Tamil community started to emerge firstly in rented places and later moved to more permanent facilities all over Germany. These places served as an inspiring force bringing people together, connecting them to the homeland, and helping to create an idealized image of the homeland for the later generations in a foreign land. Thus Luchesi shows how religious places help to maintain a collective memory of the homeland through shared practices. Similarly in Thailand, Sikhs have their own gurdwara known as the Sri Guru Singh Sabha located in Phahurat (Little India) which is known to be the largest Sikh temple in Southeast Asia. The most well-known south Indian Hindu temple is the Sri Mahamariamman Temple on Silom Road that is not only popular among the diasporic Hindus but also among the Thais and the Chinese. Popularly known as Wat Khaek, the Sri Mahamariamman Temple was built in late nineteenth century in what is now the financial district of Bangkok. According to a news article on the NBC News.com. the current priest at this temple is from the fourth generation of the Tamil immigrants ('Bangkok's Surprising touch of India' 2009). Traditionally people belonging to the various Indian communities gather every Sunday at their respective places of worship to perform religious duties and these gatherings are evidently important social gatherings for the respective communities. For example, the Sikhs gather in gurdwaras and Hindus gather in their temples on Sundays in Bangkok. It is important to note that a community gathering on a Sunday in Thailand is an adaptation from the modern Western society. In India, Sunday gatherings are not so common. Worshippers in India generally visit their respective places of worship either based on their convenience or on days that are dedicated to personal gods.

For example, devotees of Hanuman will pay their respects by visiting a Hanuman Temple on a Tuesday and devotees of Durga do so on a Friday.

Since most countries including Thailand follow the Western calendar, Sunday is the day off, and so after a busy week of work, it proves to be an ideal day of the week to organize gatherings where people can revitalize and reunite with their fellow community members. Special religious activities like sermons, rituals, festival celebrations, or community meals are organized to bring the community together. One example of a special religious activity is the Navratri (nine days festival dedicated to Goddess Durga) organized every year to worship Durga. Special offerings, nine days of daily recitation of Durga prayers, and *homa* on the first and last days of the festival are organized with the collective help of community members. Navratri is an important Hindu festival and is celebrated by Hindus living in and outside of India.

In addition, special events like once a year *gau-dan* (donating a cow) are also organized annually at the Hindu Samaj Temple (the Hindu temple in Bangkok). The members of the Hindu community, through donations, support the event where a cow, an animal of great importance to the Hindu religion, is donated to a Thai temple. Even during the ancient times, kings and others donated cows to Brahmins as *gau-dan* during one's lifetime bringing great merit to the individual. The Hindu Samaj Temple organizes *gau-dan* in order to provide the diasporic Hindu community in Thailand with merit accumulating opportunities thus making them feel at home away from home.

HOW THE DIASPORIC COMMUNITY CONTRIBUTED TO THE DEVELOPMENT OF HINDUISM IN THAILAND

The earlier section did provide some insights into the fact that Hindu religious traditions performed in Thailand by the diasporic community have actually changed when compared to similar traditions followed in India. As Vertovec says, religious and cultural reproduction generally takes place over generations. Issues related to maintenance, modification or discarding of religious practices are raised among the later generations that are born and brought up in a foreign land. The religious and cultural practices, cultivated by parents at home, religious education at school and participation at places of worship shape the identities and activities of the second and third generation of migrants. The identity and activity between the second and the third generations set them apart from their immigrant parents (2009: 139-40). In places outside of India, the basic Hindu ritual procedures have been curtailed, refashioned, or eclectically performed. In most places, Hindu rites are popularized in order to appeal to the young, diaspora-born Hindus compared to the more conservative elders. For example, in Malaysia Hindu leaders complain that the inclusion of music produced in India has created the 'disco-ization' of Hindu rituals (Willford 1998 cited in Vertovec 2009: 142).

Sinha's (2005) work on the making of a new Hindu deity and rituals in the urban temples as part of the popular Hinduism in Singapore is another example of the refashioning of Hinduism. She shows how a new god in the diaspora is created, along with the integration of Western practices like celebration of Father's Day and collective cake cutting in the temple as a new form of devotional expression. She shows how Muneeshwaran, a rural guardian deity in Tamil Nadu (brought to Malaya over one hundred and seventy years ago), has been reconfigured as a god of urban residents and is popular with the third and fourth generations of Singaporean Hindus. His worship encompasses free and liberal use of deities, symbols and ritual practices associated with other religious traditions as mentioned earlier.

Additionally in relation to the idea of sacred space in Hinduism, Jacobsen suggests that among diasporic Hindus, India is no longer exclusive in claiming Hindu sacred places. Many local places, and rivers are seen as sacred to them (Jacobsen 2004 cited Penumala 2010: 421). In Thailand, the Chao Phya River has long been seen as a sacred river for the Thais—as sacred as the Ganges. As Suarez recorded in 1690 Engelbert Kaempfer, a resident in Ayutthaya mentions the Siamese view of the source of the Chao Phraya River as rising just like the Ganges in Bengal from the Himalayas and its various arteries penetrate Cambodia, Pegu, and Siam and join with the Ganges (1999: 156). With this sacredness, some of the Hindu rituals in Thailand that are to be performed at the Ganges are conducted at the Chao Phraya River instead. A Brahmin[3] in Bangkok does not see any problem in doing so as 'all rivers are sacred and you can't afford to visit India every time a ritual needs to be conducted at the Ganges'. Upon death, in Hindu tradition, the ashes of the deceased collected after cremation have to be immersed in the Ganges so that the deceased attains *moksha.* However, with the limitation of time and financial resources, many families scatter the ashes of the deceased in the Chao Phraya River where a Brahmin may be invited to conduct the ceremony.

Another example of a reshaping of Hinduism in Thailand is related to the sacred bath in the Ganges. On special events devotees (especially of the priestly class) take a bath in the Ganges to wash away their sins. These events include Ganga Dussehra and Kumbh Mela among others. Ganga Dussehra celebrates the birthday of Ganges and Kumbh Mela is a festival that celebrates the Ganges in all her fertility and power. It is the re-enactment of a cosmogonic event when, at a certain astrological event, the waters of the Ganges became nectar (King 2005: 171-2). As Acharya[4] mentions, for diasporic Hindus in Thailand, due to time and financial constraints, it is not always possible to travel to India to participate in these events. To fulfil the religious needs and also to maintain the Hindu traditions, Hindu Samaj[5] Temple in Bangkok organizes a bathing ritual for the devotees at the sea in Chonburi[6] instead. As a committee member[7] explained, the temple makes necessary arrangements, ranging from transportation to religious goods and Brahmins accompanying the devotees to help perform the bathing ritual which is open to anyone willing to attend. According to the same committee member, this is done so that the younger generation will become aware of the traditions and continue to practice them in the future. However, also evident is that an increasing number of Thai devotees have been joining the event over the years. When asked, Acharya explained that for Thai devotees ritual bathing is a new religious experience evoking the sense of sacredness within them.

MULTI-ETHNICITY A COMMONPLACE

The Thai population has been exposed to Hinduism from the early times as Hinduism was incorporated into the Thai society by the elites historically[8] and has been an important part of the Royal rituals. This historical integration of Hinduism in Thailand and in other parts of Southeast Asia has been widely studied by scholars like Coedes (1968), Hall (1981), Sandhu, Kernial & Mani (1993) among others and therefore my focus here will only be on more recent developments.

One of the very popular deities of worship in Thailand is Brahma, a Hindu god. It is interesting to note that Brahma is not a deity of worship in India any more but is very popular among the Thai devotees. The most significant and popularly known shrine devoted to Brahma is the Erawan Shrine in Bangkok built in 1956 to ward off the difficulties faced in the construction of the Erawan Hotel. In the Hindu tradition Brahma is one of the Trimurti (trinity) with Shiva and Vishnu being the other two gods. In the Thai context, however, Brahma is seen as a powerful deity. The Erawan shrine has given rise to several smaller shrines which business and homeowners build and use to make daily offerings to please the deity believed to be the owner of the land. Households maintain smaller shrines dedicated to the spirit of the place while businesses maintain shrines dedicated to Indian deities that have been incorporated into the Thai Buddhist tradition. The daily offerings at these shrines are believed to bring success to the businesses. It is interesting to note that these Hindu elements have become so integrated into the Thai society that they have been localized. Brahma, for example, has only a handful of temples dedicated to him in India where counting the total number of temples itself is a daunting task. However Brahma in Thailand has gained importance with the Erawan Shrine and is commonly seen by the Thai devotees as a Thai deity.

With this popularity, the Hindu Samaj Temple in Bangkok enshrined a Brahma statue. The purpose was to accommodate the demands of the host society. Because of Brahma's popularity among the Thai devotees, the Hindu Samaj Temple decided to import a

Brahma statue from Jaipur (India). A ceremony was conducted where the statue was taken in a procession from the Hindu Samaj Temple to the Erawan Shrine and brought back and enshrined. The event was attended with great enthusiasm by both the Thai and Hindu devotees. However, according to Acharya, since Brahma is not a deity of worship, there have been no festivities or rituals performed to venerate him in the Hindu Samaj Temple since his installation a decade ago. More recently a goddess, Gayatri, has been enshrined next to the Brahma image upon the request of one of the Hindu devotees. According to the legend in the *Varaha Purana*, Sarasvati (wife of Brahma) is addressed as Gayatri, the goddess of learning who is worshipped regularly once a year (Wilkins 2003: 111). She is considered the mother of the Vedas and the embodiment of the Gayatri Mantra. Acharya explains that Gayatri in India is better known from the Gayatri Mantra and it is uncommon to find her statues in Hindu temples. However, a Hindu devotee who worshipped Gayatri as his personal god brought in a Gayatri statue from Jaipur. According to temple sources, it took two years to get the committee members of the temple to give their consent to install the Gayatri statue which finally took place in February 2014. When asked for the reason for such a long wait both Acharya and Panditji provided the same explanation, a priest who must act as the host as well can be the only one to enshrine a Gayatri statue. In addition only those belonging to the three upper castes namely priests, warriors, and merchants can perform rituals related to Gayatri. Therefore it is not common to find Gayatri statues enshrined in temples in India.

When asked how religious the Hindus living in Thailand are, Panditji said he sees a diminishing importance of religious belief among the Hindu community. He rather sees the local Thais more involved in Hindu rituals and practices than the diasporic Hindus. According to him this is because the younger generation, born and brought up in Thailand, are influenced by the surrounding Buddhist environment and do not carry the Hindu beliefs as their forefathers did. Many visit Buddhist temples and perform Buddhist ceremonies as a way of assimilating into the host society, which they see as home. Panditji and his fellow Brahmin friends are invited more by the Thai devotees to perform Hindu rituals and ceremonies. He sees the popularity of Brahma and more recently Ganesa as the reason behind the increasing involvement of Thais in Hinduism. This has lead to the creation of a popular Thai Hinduism in a predominantly Buddhist country.

Brahma's popularity has already been discussed. The more recently evident popularity is that of Ganesha, an important Hindu deity. Ganesha has been widely accepted throughout India as a god for warding off obstacles. He is more popular in the western state of India, Maharashtra where a festival dedicated to him, Ganesha Chaturthi, is celebrated with great enthusiasm. The festival has historical and political importance. The tradition of community celebration was started by Chhatrapati Shivaji (a warrior king of the Maratha Empire in the seventeenth century) as a public event to promote traditions and nationalism. The festival was the highlight of all the seasonal festivities until the Marathas were defeated in the 3rd Anglo-Maratha war in 1818. Bal Gangadhar Tilak revitalized it in the late nineteenth century with a message freedom to revive the patriotic spirit. All classes of the society regardless of the caste differences were brought together against the British. Thus Ganesha Chaturthi was a festival for all castes or classes. Cultural events including dance, dramas, musical nights and religious gatherings were organized during this ten-day festival. Since then the festival has become of great significance to people in Maharashtra especially Mumbai where the city virtually shuts down as millions of people celebrate the festival. The festival has gained further popularity through television broadcasts and movies with Mumbai being the centre of Bollywood. This popularity has spread to places to where Indians have migrated, with Thailand more recently becoming one of them. In the past the celebration was limited to Indians in Thailand coming from Maharashtra, but over the years with the influence of the media, and Bollywood in particular, the festival is gaining popularity among the Thai devotees as well.

As the president of Vishwa Hindu Parishad (VHP) in Thailand, Susheel Saraff, said in an interview with the *Times of India:* 'Thailand is the only place in the world where there are more non-Hindu followers of an Indian God. The Shiva temple (in Ramindra),

Utthayan Ganesha Temple (in Nakhon Nayok) and VHP celebrate Ganesha Utsav with enthusiasm. Participation by locals gets bigger every year'. (8 September 2013)

The VHP Thailand started celebrating Ganesha Chaturthi in Bangkok seven years ago when they were granted permission from the Thai government to do so. The government, however, had a condition that the deities should be eco-friendly. Each year the number of participants increases and, to accommodate the increasing number of Thai devotees, the prayers are made available in both Thai and English. Idols of Ganesha are made and ceremonies are performed. At the end of a week of festivities, the idols are brought out in procession and taken for immersion in the Chao Phraya River. These processions have become increasingly attractive to the Thais and with the influence of the media more devotees join such events. With more Thai devotees becoming aware of the festival through the media, different Hindu temples and shrines conduct Ganesha Chaturthi to serve the religious needs of the believers. The celebrations are more Thai than Hindu with the incorporation of spirit mediums and Buddhist style offerings. The participation of Thai spirit mediums, business people providing financial support and in return using the event as a business marketing tool; and also the transvestites to the Hindu festivities is a new phenomenon. An increasing number of transvestites join Hindu rituals since they generally feel that it provides them a freedom to express their devotion. Because transvestites are marginalized in Buddhism, they are attracted to other religious beliefs that provides freedom of devotional expression. Their presence is very much evident in religious processions organized by Wat Khaek on festivals like Ganesha Chaturthi and Navratri. Additionally, businessmen joining these festivities have added the financial element that leads to commodification through the demand of services of the Brahmins, and trade in icons and other religious goods.

Although a number of changes have taken place in Hinduism among the diaspora, some changes remain unacceptable by the Hindu Brahmins. I have observed a number of times that the Brahmins at the Hindu temples in Bangkok do not allow spirit mediums to demonstrate their supernatural abilities on the temple premises. A number of times, spirit mediums exhibiting their supernatural abilities have been asked by the Brahmins to leave and sometimes even banned from entering the temple premises in the future. When asked, all of the five resident priests at the Hindu Samaj explained that the common Hindu belief is that the human body is not pure enough to enshrine spirits of any gods. Therefore spirit mediums promoting the idea that their bodies are enshrined with Hindu gods is not acceptable. In the Thai context, however, Hindu gods are very popular among the spirit mediums.[9] This provides evidence that spirit mediums have incorporated Hinduism into their spiritual lives in Thailand but this is still not accepted in Hinduism.

ACCULTURATION WITH THE HOST ENVIRONMENT

Baumann (2004) argues that the preservation of native religious traditions that are different from the dominant religious affiliation of the host country does not hinder the social integration of the group. Instead keeping the heritage of difference and merging with the host society's socio-economic patterns go well together (2004: 77). The different Indian communities in Thailand maintain their native religions and cultures in addition to taking part in the religious activities of the host country. In addition, securing jobs and their futures insert pressure on members of diasporic communities to acculturate into the new host environment. However, there is a two-way acculturation in the case of Thailand. The Thai Royal ceremonies are infused with Brahmanical rituals that were incorporated by the elites in the past. Representatives from the Indian community have been present at these royal ceremonies to observe and participate in the rituals. Additionally the Buddhist holidays are also observed at the Hindu temples and special ceremonies are organized where an active participation of the members of the Hindu community is evident. With effective acculturation, the newly and earlier settled Indians have acquired Thai language proficiency and have a picture or a poster of HRM the king in their homes to show their respect and their inclination to be part of the Thai society.

On the king's birthday, the Hindu temples have special observances, which sometimes include processions organized by the temple authorities.

TRADITIONS PRESERVED OR MODIFIED?

The Indian traditions are a mix of a range of diverse traditions that differ from one ethnic group to another and from one place to another. However, there are some traditions commonly found all over India. The tradition of welcoming guests has always been an important part of Hindu tradition. Guests are seen as gods visiting ones home and a common saying known to every Indian is *atithi devo bhawa* meaning guests are like gods. Visiting guests are given ut-most respect and special foods are prepared. The tradition continues wherever Indians go and are known for their hospitality to guests. Other important traditions are the rites of passage including birth, maturity, marriage, and death. In a Hindu family, a newborn baby is welcomed with a ceremony by tasting honey as the first thing upon birth. This is followed by a naming ceremony done ten to twelve days after birth and later with the ear piercing and first haircut ceremony, which are considered highly significant. The other rite of passage is observed by a sacred thread ceremony (*janeu* ceremony) which is held in some Hindu families which may traditionally be performed before the boy starts his studies. Upon reaching adulthood, a marriage is arranged which may vary from region to region. However, the common elements are the marriage vows made around the sacred fire and the elders and the priest blessing the couple. The last rite of passage is the death ritual that has a uniform pattern drawn from the Vedas. However, there might be variations between sects, regions, castes, and family traditions. A priest traditionally performs the death rites. The eldest son in the family according to the Hindu traditions cremates the body of the deceased. The traditions related to all the rites of passage are kept alive among the Indian diasporic communities. The form of performing the rites might change but the contents remain the same. For example, the naming ceremony is traditionally done at home in India but becomes a bigger event for Hindus in Thailand where the ceremony is held in hotels with parties thrown for relatives and friends to join in. The sacred thread ceremony is rarely held among Hindus in Thailand. Panditji mentioned that it is very rare for him to be invited to conduct the sacred thread ceremony. However, as confirmed by yet another head priest (who will be referred to as Ajan) of a popular Hindu temple in Bangkok, the marriages are conducted traditionally but have become more lavish at the same time. He explains how marriages in India last for several days but in Thailand the ceremonies are curtailed to just one- or two-day events depending on the convenience of the families. The rituals are curtailed and confined to only the most important rituals in a Hindu wedding. They also involve Western elements such as cake cutting at wedding receptions and the Thai element of seniors (boss or superiors) of the bride and the groom adorning the couple with flower garlands. It is to be noted that under the Hindu tradition, the bride and the groom themselves adorn flower garlands during weddings but under the Thai influence the tradition has changed to the seniors rather offering garland to the couple as a form of their blessing to the newlywed couple.

The question then arises as to how these and many other Hindu traditions are preserved among the diasporic communities. The parents play an important role in the preservation of traditions where children are taught and exposed to them by regular participation in these different rites of passages. In addition children are sent to International schools run by Indians so that they can learn the home language (Hindi or Punjabi) in a foreign land. Moreover, the food culture is maintained where Indian food is served during the weekdays while weekends are generally left for people to eat outside depending on their likings.

CONCLUSION

The purpose of this paper is to assess the transformation of Hinduism among the diasporas with an emphasis on the Hindu diasporic community in Thailand. Defining Hinduism is difficult as it is a mix of several traditions and belief systems. Scholars have been debating whether the term was introduced by the colonizing powers to refer to people believing in the religions of India or was already in use even before the European encroachment into South Asia. Hinduism is therefore vague and leaves a lot of room for changes that can be brought in by those believing in Hinduism. My focus in this paper was not to get into that debate but rather to concentrate on the existence of Hinduism and diasporic Hindu community in Thailand and the changes that have been brought about in the traditional Hindu practices by this diasporic community residing in Thailand. India and Southeast Asia share a long history of trade relations. These relations gave rise to an integration of Hinduism into this region and particularly into Thai society. The historical trade links, earlier settled Indian migrants, and the presence of Hindu gods in Thailand allowed the new Indian migrants to feel at home away from their home. However several changes in the Hinduism of Thailand have been evident and in this paper are assessed according to Smart's analysis of the three reasons why religion and diaspora share a strong connection. Several categories of changes are evident including those resulting from an adjustment of the Hindu diasporic community to the host environment and those resulting from the Thais encounter of Hinduism. Several of these changes were assessed in this paper with a conclusion that even though many changes have taken place, some elements, like customs, traditions and beliefs important to Hinduism remain unchanged. The Hindu diasporic community has been able to maintain and preserve its Hindu identity in addition to acculturating with the demands of the host society.

NOTES

1. Coedes uses the term 'Hinduism' to refer to the belief system practised in ancient India. As mentioned previously this term is a relatively modern invention.
2. I use the term 'Indian migration' for people belonging to different Indian communities who migrated to Thailand. These include the Hindus, Muslims, Parsis, Sikhs, and also includes those belonging to different ethnic groups, for example Gujratis, Tamils, etc.

3. Interviewed on 13 February 2014 in Bangkok. The Brahmin prefers not to be named and so I will refer to him in this paper as Panditji.
4. Interviewed on 22 August 2015 at Hindu Samaj, Bangkok. He is a Brahmin at Hindu Samaj but prefers not to be named and will be referred to as Acharya.
5. Established as Hindu Sabha in 1925 by Pandit Raghunath Sharma in order to serve the religious need of the diasporic Hindu community. The current Hindu Samaj (also known as Dev Mandir) was inaugurated in 1969 by Their Majesties the King and Queen of Thailand.
6. A province on the Bay of Bangkok at the northern end of the Gulf of Thailand.
7. He is a diasporic Hindu who has been a member of the Hindu Samaj working committee for almost a decade. The interview with him took place on 20 August 2015 at the Hindu Samaj Temple in Bangkok. He prefers not to be named.
8. For more information see Coedes 1968 and Kam-Aek 2007.
9. *See* Pattana Kitiarsa (2005), 'Beyond Syncretism: Hybridization of Popular Religion in Contemporary Thailand', *Journal of Southeast Asian Studies*, The National University of Singapore, vol. 36, no. 3, pp. 461-87.

REFERENCES

Baumann, Martin, 'Becoming a Color of the Rainbow: The Social Integration of Indian Hindus in Trinidad, Analysed along a Phase Model Diaspora', in Knut A. Jacobsen and Kumar P. Pratap (eds.), *South Asians in the Diaspora: Histories and Religious Traditions*, Boston: Brill, 2004, pp. 77-96.

'Bangkok's Surprising Touch of India', Asia Travel on *NBC News* 2009. Retrieved on 20 February 2014 from http://www.nbcnews.com/id/32541316/#.Uwdvsnkhnkk

Coedès, Georges, *The Indianized States of Southeast Asia*, Honolulu, Kuala Lumpur, Singapore, etc.: University of Malaya Press (French Orig.: Histoire ancienne desétats hindouisés d'Extrême-Orient. Hanoi, 1944), 1968.

'Ganapati Goes Famous in Bangkok', *The Times of India*, 8 September 2013. Retrieved on 20 February 2014 from http://timesofindia.indiatimes. com/city/surat/Ganapati-goes-famous-in-Bangkok/articleshow/22421328.cms?referral=PM

Hall, D.G.E., *A History of Southeast Asia*, 4th edn., London: Macmillan Press, 1981, pp. 12-46.

Heinrich von Stietencron, 'Hinduism: On the Proper Use of a Deceptive Term', in Gunther-Deitz Sontheimer and Hermann Kulke, (eds.) *Hinduism Reconsidered*, 2nd edn., Delhi: Manohar, 1997, 1989, p. 36.

Jacobsen, Knut, A., 'Establishing Ritual Space in the Hindu Diaspora in Norway', in K.A. Jacobsen and P. Kumar (eds.), *South Asians in the Diaspora: Histories and Religious Traditions*, Leiden: Brill, 2004, pp. 134-48.

Kam-Aek, Bamrung, *Influence of Hinduism and Brahmanism in the Early Rattanakosin Era*, Silpakorn University Research and Development Institute, Bangkok, 2007.

Keyes, Charles, 'The Destruction of a Shrine to Brahma in Bangkok and the Fall of Thaksin Shinawatra: The Occult and the Thai Coup in Thailand of September 2006', Asia Research Institute Working Paper No. 80: NUS, 2006.

King, Anna S., 'Waters of Devotion', in A.S. King and J. Brockington (eds.), *The Intimate Other: Love Divine in Indic Religions*, New Delhi: Orient Longman, 2005.

Kurien, P., *Kaleidoscopic Ethnicity: International Migration and the Reconstruction of Community Identities in India*, New Brunswick, NJ: Rutgers University Press, 2002.

——, 'Being Young, Brown, and Hindu: The Identity Struggles of Second-generation Indian Americans', *Journal of Contemporary Ethnography*, Sage publications, vol. 34, no. 4 August 2005, pp. 434-69.

Lorenzen, D.N., 'Who Invented Hinduism?', *Comparative Studies in Society and History*', vol. 41, no. 4, New York & England: Cambridge University Press, 1999, pp. 630-59.

Luchesi, B., 'Tamil Hindu Places of Worship in Germany', in Knut A. Jacobson and Kumar P. Pratap (eds.), *South Asians in the Diaspora: Histories and Religious Traditions*, Boston: Brill, 2004, pp. 116-33.

Parekh, B., 'Some Reflections on the Indian Diaspora', *Journal of Contemporary Thought*, vol. 3, 1993, pp. 105-51.

Parekh, B., G. Singh, S. Vertovec, *Culture and Economy in the Indian Diaspora*, London: Routledge, 2003.

Penumala, P.K., 'Sociology of Hinduism', in B. Turner (ed.), *The New Blackwell Companion to the Sociology of Religion*, Oxford: Wiley-Blackwell, Ch. 18, 2010.

Portes, A. and R. Rumbaut, *Legacies: The Story of the Immigrant Second Generation*, Berkeley: University of California Press, 2001.

Sandhu, S. Kernial and A. Mani, *Indian Communities in Southeast Asia*, Institute of Southeast Asian Studies, Ch. 36, 1993.

Sinha, Vineeta, *Contextualizing Muneeswaran Worship in 'Singaporean Hinduism:*

A new God in the Diaspora? Muneeswaran Worship in Contemporary Singapore, Singapore: Singapore University Press, 2005.

Smart, Ninian, 'The Importance of Diasporas', in Steven Vertovec and Robin Cohen (eds.), *Migration, Diasporas and Transnationalism*, Aldershot: Edward Elgar, 1999, pp. 420-29.

Smith, C. Wilfred, 'Comparative Religion: Whither-and Why?' in Mircea Eliade and Joseph M. Kitagwa (eds.), *The History of Religions: Essays in Methodology*, Chicago, 1959, pp. 31-58.

Suarez, T., *Early Mapping of Southeast Asia*, Hong Kong: Periplus Editions, 1999, pp. 130-57.

Thapar, R., 'Communalism and the Historical Legacy: Some Facets', *Social Scientist*, vol. 18, nos. 6-7 (June-July) 1990, pp. 4-20.

Vertovec, S., *The Hindu Diaspora: Comparative Patterns*, London: Routledge, 2000.

——, 'Religion, Migration and Minority Status', in *Transnationalism*, London and New York: Routledge, 2009, pp. 137-40.

Wilkins, W.J., *Hindu Gods and Goddesses*, Mineola: Dover Publications, 2003.

CHAPTER 6

Global and Local Realities: The Case of NRIs Living in Durban

GERELENE JAGGANATH

In the South African province of KwaZulu-Natal, the city of Durban comprises the highest concentration of Indian population (www.indiainafrica.com). The coastal city of Durban and the surrounding metropolitan area is known for its vibrant beaches and abundant tourist attractions. A rich history of Hindu religion, temples and the promotion of Hindu languages and arts, exists in Durban with its People of Indian Origin (PIO) community. Among the cities of the world, Durban is also rated as having the highest concentration of overseas Indians (www.thetimesofindia.com). It is against this background that the study explores the presence and migration experiences of a group of thirty Non-Resident Indians (NRIs) living in Durban. The study focuses on the accompanying wives (often referred to as 'trailing wives' in migration discourse) of the skilled and highly skilled NRI immigrants and in doing so, attempts to provide a snapshot of the NRI community. The overall aim of the study is to highlight the challenges of a relatively unknown Indian community in Durban and to contribute to the larger body of literature on Indian women in the diaspora.

This paper comprises two parts: namely, the introduction and research methods; followed by the socio-cultural practices and, local and transnational networks of the sample. It considers two key issues: firstly, the women's socio-cultural practices and the diasporic space they occupy in Durban; and second, it provides a cursory view of the founding of spiritual movement (Vihangam Yoga) in relation to the role of the NRI as a diasporic figure.

INTRODUCTION

This paper attempts to capture the way in which migrant women in the Indian diaspora inscribe their presence symbolically on their new environment in order to recreate a home away from home. It is written in a similar tradition of scholarly works as Constable 2008, 2009; McKay 2005; McKay and Gibson 2005 that goes beyond the study of individual migrants to include cultural practices and relationships. By considering women's sociality and community building capacity in the diaspora; their religious associations, evolving ritual practices, new friendships and changing normativities, the newconvivial spaces and cultural practices carved out in the migration context are foregrounded. Too often seen as secondary to their economic status and marginal social position, this study explores the rich and varied relationships that migrants develop and the creative imagination that links new places to a sacred past or homeland, through ritual performance and material objects (Johnson & Werbner 2010). Directly relevant to this study, is the key role women play in reproducing religious practice, specifically domestic religious practice, which has been undermined in lieu of larger economic processes.

In the past decade it has been acknowledged (see Rayaprol 1997; Palriwala and Uberoi 2008) that Indian migrants creatively engage with the places and locales where they live and work within the diaspora, sharing sociability with migrants and non-migrants alike through ritual performance, pilgrimages, mobilization for rights and religious worship, often shifting or reshaping known moral and social boundaries prevalent in the homeland. In doing so, Indian women migrants in the diaspora, form novel associations and friendships, facilitate collective action and defy persistent stereo types previously generated in migration literature such as being sub missive, 'trailing wives', 'tied migrants' (Cooke 2001) and 'docile bodies' (Johnson and Werbner 2010: 21). Following migration, the position of women in families of immigrant communities in general, undergo considerable transformation (for their advancement as well as to their detriment), particularly when women migrate to work, or as in this study, when they migrate and are unable to work. In the Hindu diaspora, Vertovec (2002) brings to our attention how complexities and permutations often characterize processes of modifying or 'streamlining' religious practices. By way of illustration, he refers to studies where in some places outside India basic Hindu ritual procedures have become truncated (Malaysia), refashioned (in Britain), or eclectically performed (in East Africa); in others, much of the style or corpus of rites has been virtually 'invented' in conjunction with social changes in the community (evident in Trinidad), and in still other places, basic rites have been mutually 'negotiated' so as to provide a kind of socio-religious bridge between migrants from regionally distinct traditions (in England, in Scotland, and in the USA) (Vertovec 2004: 21). In most places, many rites have been popularized in order to appeal to young, diaspora-born Hindus even to the disdain of conservative elders. Informative to the sample of Hindu women NRIs in Durban, and complementing Vertovec's permutations, is the navigation between the practice of religious rites inherited from India (regional rituals and norms) and for instance, the growing acceptance of a relatively new spiritual movement called Vihangam Yoga in the local context.

RESEARCH METHODS

This ethnographic study involved qualitative data collection techniques such as participant observation combined with interviews as well as informal focus group discussions. Ethnographers typically gather participant observations, necessitating direct engagement and involvement with the world they are studying. During their observations, the routine use of informal or conversational interviews allows them to discuss and probe emerging issues. Because of the 'casual' nature of this type of interview technique it can be useful in eliciting highly candid accounts from individuals (Reeves et al. 2008: 513) particularly within the context of migration where trust and rapport among mobile individuals and families is not always easily established. The fieldwork for this study was conducted between December 2014 and May 2015 among a sample of 20 Hindu NRI women (wives) and approximately 10 NRI men (spouses of the women) who have been living and working in

Durban over differing periods of time. The women were designated as 'dependents' on their husbands' work visas, which meant that South African legislation forbid them seeking formal/gainful employment. Some of the married couples had been resident in South Africa for more than a decade whilst others had been in the country for five years and less (one respondent had arrived 2 months prior to the interviews). The men were well educated and were either professionals or highly skilled in status. The sample of 30 NRI's belonged to diverse regions of the Indian subcontinent (including Gujarat, Tamil Nadu, Andhra Pradesh, Kerala, Bihar, Rajasthan, Maharashtra and Bengal) and half of the sample had previously lived in other parts of the world (such as Kenya, Canada, United States, United Arab Emirates and Singapore) before moving to South Africa. The ages of the men and women participants ranged from 28 to 52 years. The study presented several challenges particularly with regard to accessing information, including lack of official NRI demographics and their migratory movement, as well as the lack of participation by men in the study. Reliance on anecdotal evidence (these included comments and conversations overheard at meetings and social gatherings; gossip; random interaction with expatriates at public sites; impromptu speeches addressing NRI concerns) for this study was inevitable. Engaging women participants proved less challenging due to the ease of accessing their social spaces, while the men were constrained by work commitments and mobility at the time of fieldwork. Social gatherings attended by the researcher included: organization meetings, hosting of overseas guests at the homes of the participants, women's 'coffee clubs', public functions showcasing Indian arts and culture, and religious/cultural ceremonies (such as the celebration of Holi). Part of the fieldwork included personal invitations to the homes of some women over the six-month period. These first-hand experiences were supported and complemented by secondary sources including electronic media reports, scholarly articles, website data and a perusal of several diaspora blogs on the subject of Indianness, women in the Indian diaspora and spiritual movements. Accessing information about Indian nationals as skilled and highly skilled workers in Durban was problematic. NRIs began entering South Africa as recently as 1994 when South Africa became a democracy, yet scholarly studies and statistics on their backgrounds, integration and contribution to the post-apartheid economy remain invisible. Not only do such immigrant communities make significant contributions to the regional economy (through their expertise, job creation and skills investment locally and globally, through their remittances to India), they also bring a rich and diverse cultural presence (see Ganesh 2010; Bhat and Narayan 2010) to the local landscape as well as the Indian diaspora in Africa.

Ad hoc information at meetings and interviews, on the numbers of NRI's in the province of KwaZulu-Natal, were estimated at 500 families (approximately 2,000 people), while in the province of Gauteng, the numbers are significantly larger, bordering on 2,000 families (approximately 8,000 people). Access to the participants was made through a referral system via several organizations including Global Organization for People of Indian Origin (GOPIO), Durban Chapter, Indian Nationals in South African Nation (INSAN), the Women's Coffee Club (wives of government officials such as the Indian consulate officers, Indian bankers as well as engineers and IT specialists) and Vihangam Yoga (South Africa). The use of brief narrative excerpts of the women and men interviewed and the case studies of 2 young mothers in this study is meant to provide 'moments' of their lived experience in the Indian diaspora. For the purposes of this paper, the words NRI and expatriate are used interchangeably to refer to migrant Indians living and working outside of India.

The second part of the paper comprises an overview of two key aspects, namely, the cultural practices of the women in local and global contexts, and the local and transnational networks of the sample. The sub-sections therein, highlight the varied negotiations of the women in adapting to a new environment as individuals, mothers and accompanying wives. Whether the women's socializing, religious practice, language, marriage of children, food preference and dress codes were perpetuated or re-configured cultural forms, their experiences embody the attainments and barriers in navigating cultural capital in the diaspora.

CULTURAL PRACTICE IN THE INDIAN DIASPORA: TRANSNATIONAL RESOURCE OR BARRIER?

By focussing on the primary socio-cultural spaces of this group of women in Durban and India, it was possible to discern the most obvious practices, cultural forms and networks of the women and their spouses. As 'dependents' of their husbands, the ways in which accompanying wives of highly skilled and professional Indian expatriates perceive and cope with relocation, has been a neglected area in international migration discourse. Recent studies contradict the generalization of accompanying spouses as 'trailing spouses' and passive partners (see Raghuram 2004b; Williams and Balaz 2008) in the geographically multidirectional careers of their husbands. Comments made during focus group discussions with the women, were contrary to the notion that non-working/unemployed women lacked agency:

'. . . we cannot do nothing (anything) while our husbands work. . .'
'. . . we have to make a contribution to the family. . .'
'. . . just because we cannot be employed does not mean we cannot do other things to keep ourselves busy and independent. . .'

The sub-sections to follow amplify the above excerpts and address the efforts, attainments and obstacles of the sample in relation to the household, sociality and religious practice.

THE HOUSEHOLD

Eleven of the twenty women interviewed, were engaged in household-based, informal income generating activities such as catering services, cooking and baking specific Indian cuisine such as *biryanis*, savouries and sweetmeats to order, operating beauty salons where artistic skills such as *henna* or *mehndi* art for brides, threading and Ayurvedic massage were included, and hosting cooking classes in authentic regional Indian cuisine for groups of mainly local Indian women. The other nine women described themselves as 'home executives' (or 'stay at home' wives), five of whom occasionally assisted their husbands with basic administrative tasks. De Prie's (2014) study of accompanying expatriate wives of Indian knowledge workers in the Netherlands, aptly states that calling these women 'tied migrants', prioritizes economic capital over other forms of capital building and downplays female agency in spheres outside the labour market. The entrepreneurial activities of the accompanying wives of Durban NRIs subverts the 'dependent' visa status of the women and elevates the notion of women's agency in the diaspora. All twenty women had some form of tertiary education, six were professionals (teachers, accountants, nurses and social workers), and four had previously been employed as administrators, managers and community health care workers. Ten women had not been employed since their marriage. The women showed complete acceptance of the prioritization of their spouse's career (albeit temporarily for some) until migration circumstances changed and it became conducive to resume a dual earning and dual career lifestyle.

'I miss working but we have to make sacrifices for children . . .'
'Family comes first . . . I don't mind giving up work . . .'
'It's better to stay at home in another country till they (children) finish school . . .'

Unlike India, the women in Durban did not have full-time/permanent domestic helpers to clean and cook. Five women in the sample employed local domestic helpers on a part-time basis, to assist with cleaning only. Professional Indian women in relatively affluent families in urban India, have domestic helpers who are either paid servants or dependent relatives, such as parents or in-laws, to assist with domestic activities and childcare (Stivens 1998). The extended family support for the caring of children in India could not be replicated in South Africa. Those women with school-going children in the sample did not negotiate their full-time attention to raising young children in a foreign land. Where child care was concerned, the women accepted that gendered roles in the household were not debatable. These were decisions made jointly with their spouses and in-laws. Nine women in the sample had older children who were attending universities in South Africa and abroad, as well as adult children who had returned to marry in India. While casual discussions with these parents revealed a general open-mindedness regarding the choice of partners outside of caste and religious norms, there was a subtle though undeniable preference for a continuation of values that prevailed in India. Four women had married children, all of whom had chosen spouses from India, with the same religious and regional backgrounds as themselves. While the shift away from arranged marriage and caste/village endogamy was evident in this instance, the choices of the married children indicated a retention of norms and cultural practices adhered to in the homeland. The adult children who had been educated and had worked as professionals in South Africa and abroad, had chosen professional spouses with whom they had returned to India.

Sociality and Religious Practice

It was the norm for this sample to visit family in India for a 6 to 8 week period in December and January every year. In this time, the women adopted their'Indian' woman persona as opposed to their South African identity. They distinguished between the 'two worlds' by alluding to language, dress and religious practice.

In South Africa, they believed that the challenge of not speaking fluent English, differentiated them from the local community. They attributed this reason to the formation of inclusive social networks where they could identify with the backgrounds and transnational experiences of other expatriates, communicating freely in the regional languages and dialects. Language was also a barrier experienced by their children in local South African schools and while the women endeavoured to speak their mother tongue in the home environment, most had to find a balance by speaking both English and the vernacular so as not to compromise loss of the mother tongue. It was a noticeable concern of the women that their cultural heritage not be lost to the younger generation. Those women with school-going children, rigorously pursued the religious and cultural education of the children as crucial elements in the development of their Indian identity. 'They must know who they are and where they came from before they move into the world'. Some of these women spent much of their time sourcing religious literature written in English to further assist with the retention of the children's moral education while supporting their transition in English medium schools. Others actively engaged with language problems by educating themselves in the English language. One of the mothers found that while her young son excelled at written work, his oral presentations were lacking. Through her own research on the internet, she discovered simple and effective methods of supporting his progress and verbal communication in the classroom. She said, '. . . it took me a while to find a method that worked well for him but now he can speak with more confidence in front of the class'. In her study of Indian ICT professionals, Roos (2013: 153) also confirms how language is perceived as a limiting factor to develop oneself abroad, both from a personal and professional point of view, which initiates feelings of restriction and isolation.

While the women socialized and entertained South African friends and colleagues of their husbands, their own social relationships varied between mostly neighbourly, to a few strong and mutually dependent friendships with local South African Indians. Their relationships with other racial groups in Durban were friendly and civil but distant, showing a tendency to retreat into socializing within their own expatriate grouping. The women (together with their husbands and sometimes their children) attended several cultural functions, celebrations and trade fairs hosted by the Indian Consulate of Durban as well as visiting artists and musicians from India, celebrating the Indian arts and cultural heritage which helped facilitate exposure and networking among locals and expatriates. Studies by Radhakrishnan (2003) and Dickinson (2014) on diasporic subjectivities through classical song and dance indicate a long history of community bonding and Indian vernacular identities between the performing arts of the Indian subcontinent and South African Indian audiences. The sample of women predominantly sought the comfort, familiarity and support system of other expatriates who could identify with their global and local experiences. The women's coffee clubs provided an informal forum to socialize, share experiences and increase their knowledge about issues that affected them directly. Those women who were residing for longer periods of time in Durban, adopted a 'sisterly' role towards wives who had recently arrived in the country, 'taking them under their wing' by providing a support system that eased their transition and integration in the new country. Each 'coffee morning' meeting was held at a different home where activities (such as cooking, yoga and board games) followed a particular theme (such as Valentine's Day; Independence Day; Mother's Day, etc.). It was through the women's groups and support networks that the men and children formed stronger bonds of friendship. The friendships forged among the women expatriates, as well as the friendships formed between them and local Indian women, embodies the making of fictive kin and a 'sisterhood' that exemplify the significance of social networks in the diaspora. The case study of Gauri illustrates the agency and challenges of a young mother and entrepreneur in Durban and India:

> Gauri, the young wife of an IT specialist, showed a preference for her South African friends and lifestyle, indicating no desire to return to India or relocating to other parts of the world in the future. She was also the youngest of the women, who was quick to express the tedious regimen she endured abroad, fielding religious instruction from her orthodox mother-in-law in Rajasthan and her conservative husband who made sure she complied. Gauri remarked. . . . 'He is a different person when he is in India . . . he is more relaxed in Durban.' She occasionally relied on her local Indian neighbours to fetch her child from preschool while managing her half-day beauty studio from her home. Gauri believed that living outside of India, allowed her less cultural restriction and her husband more financial opportunity. She enjoyed the annual pilgrimage to India to visit her parents but felt pressurized when her children were chastised for speaking 'too much' English, engaging in the time-consuming preparation of food for the strict dietary requirements of her in-laws and adorning the traditional dress code (sari, red dot and sindhoor) expected of her. In Durban, she 'live(d) in jeans and T-shirts'.

In South Africa, the women wore mainly Western clothes (jeans, blouses, short-pants and sleeveless dresses) unless attending a religious or cultural event, unlike in India, where most wore primarily 'Punjabis' (*salwaar kameez*) and saris. Conversations with two of the men in the sample, affirmed a preference for their wives to adhere to traditional attire in India because they felt it was more appropriate in respecting their elders and because of male perception regarding the Western dress code in Indian society where Western dress was generally associated with '. . . women of dubious moral character' (a remark made by a spouse).

The interview discussions concerning religious practice in the local context, revealed that 13 of the 20 women considered daily ritual, prayers, auspicious ceremonies on the Hindu almanac and festivities and activities to be reduced, compared to the demands and expectations of the extended family in India. Based on focus group discussions, these rituals included a combination of daily morning and evening prayers, a monthly visit to an affiliated temple and the observance of auspicious dates accompanied by fasting and prayers specific to the regional religious Indian norms. Prayer, fasting and diet took on different meanings for the women locally as they followed the requirements specific to their lineage, caste and geographical backgrounds. Two of the women did not adhere to any specific Hindu religious or spiritual practice but fulfilled all obligations and religious commitments in India so as not to offend their elders. Eight men and women adhered to a mainly vegetarian diet which was characterized by being vegetarian at home but non-vegetarian outside the household (the women attributed this change in diet to adaptation, their exposure to being migrants and having to cook according to the preferences of their spouses guests/colleagues from differing cultural backgrounds); five of the women and men were strictly vegetarian (including no eggs, garlic and onion); and two of the couples were not vegetarian. Interestingly, while half of the sample imposed the vegetarian dietary preference on their children, it seemed that the younger generation was moving away from this practice. Vegetarianism, however, was noted by the sample as the dominant dietary practice among families in India and is considered the cornerstone of religious and spiritual discipline. Five of the women followed a more spiritual than religious lifestyle where meditation was the dominant practice as opposed to ritual and cultural observances. This group practiced Vihangam Yoga, an ancient form of meditation which will be discussed later in this paper.

The section to follow explores the transnational networks of the sample. It sheds light on the local formations of an NRI advocacy group (INSAN) and a spiritual movement (Vihangam Yoga), and the NRI as diasporic actor.

Local and Transnational Networks

Expatriates all over the world face a multitude of challenges as migrants. In South Africa, skilled, highly skilled and professional migrants from India have had to develop their own forms of recourse in resolving issues concerning visas, permits and other legal rights. While the new Modi-led Indian government, has indicated (in the media), an interest in the diaspora particularly with regard to the huge contribution of migrant remittances to the homeland, diplomatic intervention in different countries with differing jurisdiction has not always proved significantly effective.

INSAN was originally formed as an organization to address the challenges of expatriates in Durban. It has grown in membership and supports the queries of Indian nationals living across South Africa. This common association interest group (also referred to as Hometown Associations, see Koser 2007) was formed in 2013 by a small group of like-minded expatriate professionals. By networking with the local and global diaspora, they prompted an action-group that would respond to any challenges or threats experienced by Indian nationals working in South Africa. The recent xenophobic attacks experienced across South Africa during March to April 2015 for instance, sent shock-waves throughout the international community and amplified the relevance for such associations (in this instance, for NRI security) in Durban. While Indian immigrants were not directly targeted nor victims of the violence of local black South Africans against predominantly African nationals, the immediate suspension of permit renewals has forced many Indian immigrants to return to India. Indian nationals who have been residing in the country for many years (some cited ten years while others, five years) have had no alternative but to return to India because of the short period of time within which the drastic measures of the South African government have been implemented. INSAN has taken heed of calls for assistance, support and activism where Indian nationals have been compromised. The sample of NRI's in this study comprised the founding members of INSAN, which through 'word of mouth' had formed networks with key government officials, significant authorities as well as global and local organizations such as GOPIO, Indian Expats in Johannesburg (www.expatforum.come), Indian expatriates in Durban (www.expat-blog.com)and the India Club (an international organization for Indian nationals) with whom they maintain strong relations.

Within the discourse on transnational networks, the premise that migrants adapt their modes of spiritual belonging and theologies of a 'migrant faith' to the cultural, political, social terrains and urban regimes of the places in which they settle (Wong and Levitt 2010) is further elaborated. The role of NRIs in founding and promoting Vihangam Yoga in Durban supports this perspective and affirms that expatriates perpetuate transnational networks of cultural forms, in this case, spiritual awareness and education. Csordas' (2009) book *Transnational Transcendence: Essays on Religion and Globalization* elaborates for instance, the 'spiritual marketing' of Kriya Yoga in the United States. Through varying twists and turns, this form of yoga and its complex transnational journey, indicates how such practices are modified to accommodate foreign audiences and may only bear a nuanced resemblance to the founding movement of the homeland. Werbner (2002) refers to chaordic transnationalism, the forging of local configurations of cultural institutions that traverse the diaspora, based on long separations that mobilize migrants in the place of settlement as well as across different social locales. Migration opens up new horizons and possibilities for migrants wherever they journey, and these come to be embodied materially, performatively and spiritually in the place of settlement. As migrants travel, so does their cultural, religious and political 'baggage' move with them and is transformed and re-shaped in each new location. In this way, numerous yoga gurus, techniques and practices from India have traversed international boundaries and subsequently been remodelled, repackaged and marketed for receiving markets in the Western world. Similarly, the introduction and promotion of Vihangam Yoga (VY) to Durban and South Africa, could be said to reflect a locally modified version of the original practice in India—a sort of malleability of cultural forms that take on shifting significances and workings in the diaspora. An in-depth interview with Anand, an international coordinator of VY and his wife Jaya in Durban, revealed how the movement had been resuscitated in India in 1924 before finding its way onto foreign shores through the promotion of NRIs in different parts of the world. Decisive functions of women also arise significantly in religious community associations and collective religious activities where they often take the lead in its management and organization. Anand had established VY centres of learning and education programmes in the Middle East and Dubai where he worked prior to moving to South Africa. Both husband and wife were certified *ashthanga yoga* practitioners and worked together in promoting VY among their social networks and others in Durban.

Jaya, was a young mother of 2 schooling children. She played an integral role in supporting and coordinating the meetings, programmes and sometimes even the catering of her husband's numerous organizational commitments. She stated that her engineer husband Anand '. . . took on too much responsibility . . . and I stay in the back[ground] to give support.' However, by spending time with her in at their home, at meetings and social gatherings, it became obvious that Jaya played far more of a leadership role in the management of her family's activities. She consistently engaged newcomers and members in the expatriate and spiritual groups through her friendliness, her vast knowledge and her passion for finding ways in which to encourage membership, particularly among women. Her application of spiritual principals, organizational skills and time-management were an indication of her agency as a woman, mother and wife. She played an integral role in facilitating yoga workshops for women in the marginalized rural areas of KwaZulu Natal. She maintained that '. . . women are very important in Vihangam Yoga because they encourage others in the family to meditate . . . the more involved the woman . . . the better the family . . . the healthier the society.'

Vihangam Yoga, also referred to as Brahma Vidya (see www.vihangamyoga.org) is found in 35 nations world wide and constitutes more than 5 million disciples/committed participants. Interestingly, Kenya houses the largest membership numbers of local African and Gujarati *yogis*, outside of India. The transnational movement boasts a female dominant membership internationally. In the United States the movement was well supported and promoted by NRIs while in Europe (Germany and France), European locals dominated the membership. In the United Kingdom and

South Africa, the numbers were slowly increasing mainly among locals. Conversations with locals attending VY celebrations such as National Woman's Day, indicated that in historically designated Indian townships such as Phoenix, local youth and their families were attracted to the well coordinated functions hosted by VY members. The positive public response to free meals and inspiring spiritual discourse on weekends, particularly for poor, marginalized communities made the efforts of the movement rewarding. The Durban membership included a few NRI families and an increasing number of Indian (South African PIO's) and African locals. Anand and Jaya were planning a grassroots programme, to train a cohort of local teachers the meditation technique (within the week of the interview), to distribute the spiritual knowledge and practice in 20 rural villages in KwaZulu-Natal. The teachers would be instructed in English but would convey the knowledge in the Zulu language. Anand and Jaya, in this instance, epitomize a national pride and determination to promote global Indianness through humanitarian efforts and cultural awareness. The integration and community outreach of NRIs into the wider South African society through spirituality is worthy of closer scrutiny. Contradictory to their inclusive socialization with mainly expatriates, the fulfilment of the spiritual movement's objectives, facilitated expansive social engagement of expatriate members across ethnic boundaries.Such projects mimic the VY blueprint in India for alleviating poverty and promoting education awareness and employment among the most vulnerable communities.

The NRI

It is argued that such individual efforts to encourage and establish spirituality outside of the homeland is part of the social and cultural responsibility of expatriates. This service to humanity or *seva* is considered part of the moral obligation of fulfilling their dharma and patriotic self-image as NRI's. Other arguments include that the perpetuation of religious and cultural norms of the homeland in other social spaces is a mechanism for preserving, recreating and grounding social institutions and practices that bring familiarity and comfort to the migrant in foreign contexts. Both arguments maintain that the movement of people and their ways of being and doing is not a new phenomenon nor is it likely to change in the future of migration processes, even more so with India's position as an emerging global leader. Shukla (2003: 10) aptly states that the Indian diaspora confronts simultaneous nationalism and internationalism:

> The non-resident Indian, popularly called an NRI, is a diasporic figure who illumines the surprising complementarity of those two spheres of operation. In occupying a category created by the Indian government in the 1970s to repatriate investment from abroad, this migrant is lexically bestowed with a relationship to India and receives benefits that would not normally be available to those living outside the nations-state, such as the right to own property within borders, as well as the affirmation of political loyalties to what is perceived as an ordinary place. He gains meaning from his state of being abroad and yet is interpellated as an Indian national. It is precisely the NRI's citizenship in and of the world and all the influences that inhere therein, that have made him both a powerful preoccupation of the Indian nation-state and a site of anxiety for those concerned with a purer relationship to homeland.

In the media as well as Bollywood, the NRI who was once unloved and portrayed as the height of moral corruption, has in the past decade become the embodiment of the national ethos and triumphant capitalism (Therwath 2010: 3). Similarly, Khadria (2014: 31) alludes to skilled professional emigrants from India who are now looked upon as 'angels' and offer a perfected image of transnational 'global Indian citizens . . .' seen as being capable not only of bringing investment and technology to India but also of returning themselves in a circulatory mode of migration. The promotion of the Hindu religion and spirituality outside of India has been strongly driven by NRIs who expound the beliefs and mysticism of the motherland in innovative and dedicated ways that is not given much attention in the Indian diaspora discourse. Within such caveats of Hinduism and spirituality, the role of women as front-runners and supportive 'partners' in perpetuating these practices is marginalized by male expatriate trajectories. Evident among those few families practising VY was the negotiation between their spiritual and religious practice. While the former instilled spiritual perspective based on meditation and service to humanity was the dominant lifestyle in Durban, the latter (ritual performance and devotional prayer) continued to be practised alongside their spiritual identity, based on cultural expectations of the larger extended family and respecting the wishes of the elderly (mostly ageing parents and grandparents) in India. The newly formed spiritual movement in Durban, lends itself to further scrutiny of the variation and dynamism within not only the Indian diaspora but also the Hindu diaspora.

CONCLUSION

Studies considering the integration of NRI immigrants in post-apartheid South Africa demand sociological scrutiny against the long migration history of South African Indians, referred to as PIOs. The exploratory nature of this study and the small sample size of professional NRI migrants and their wives in Durban, provides a snapshot of this group within the context of the Indian diaspora. Although insightful about transnational migrant configurations in the Indian diaspora, the study cannot make any general claims about NRI's in South Africa *per se*. The study aimed to foreground local and global spaces (Durban and India), relationships (such as the 'sisterhood' among expatriates and local Indian women)and networks (facilitated Coffee Club, INSAN, VY) created by the sample in adapting and integrating in the contemporary South African context. A focus on the 'accompanying' wives of the NRIs, who are unable to seek employment or practice as professionals locally due to work permit and visa restrictions, shifted the migration lens away from the male migrant trajectory and the economics of migration. In doing so, momentary episodes of an under-researched community provided a glimpse into the transnational lives of the women and their families in Durban, and the role of the NRI in the Indian diaspora. The case studies of Gauri and Jaya and the comments of the women in the sample, elucidate the perceptions, activities and overall agency of the women. Fieldwork among this group indicated a range of cultural, religious and spiritual practices and norms that were either reproduced or re-shaped in adaptation to the local context. Trans-national cultural barriers and diasporic religious presence in this instance, gave rise to novel re-configurations of creating 'a home away from home', a territorial and affective space where migrants settle (temporarily or permanently).

REFERENCES

Bhat, C. and L. Narayan, 'Indian Diaspora, Globalisation and Transnational Networks: The South African context', *Journal of Social Sciences*, vol. 25, nos. 1-3, 2010, pp. 13-30.

Cooke, T.J. et al., 'A Cross-national Comparison of the Impact of Family Migration on Women's Employment Status', *Demography*, vol. 38, no. 2, 2001, pp. 201-13.

Csordas, Thomas, *Transnational Transcendence: Essays on Religion and Globalization*, Berkeley: University of California Press, 2009.

De Prie, S., 'Personal Development in a Transnational Space: Identities and Daily Lives of Indian Expat Wives in the Netherlands', MA thesis, Amsterdam: VU University, 2014.

Dickinson, J. 'Making Space for India in Post-apartheid South Africa: Narrating Diasporic Subjectivities through Classical Song and Dance', *Emotion, Space and Society*, vol. 13, 2014, pp. 32-9.

Ganesh, K., 'Beyond Historical Origins: Negotiating Tamilness in South Africa', *Journal of Social Sciences*, vol. 25, nos. 1-3, 2010, pp. 25-37.

Johnson, Mark and Pnina Werbner, 'Diasporic Encounters, Sacred Journeys: Ritual, Normativity and the Religious Imagination among International Asian Migrant Women', in *Asia Pacific Journal of Anthropology*, vol. 11, nos. 3-4, 2010, p. 21.

Khadria, Binod, 'The Dichotomy of the Skilled and Unskilled among Non-resident Indians and Persons of Indian Origin: Bane or Boom for development in India?', in *Dynamics of Asian Development*, ed. G. Tejada et al., Delhi: Springer, 2014, pp. 29-45.

Palriwala, R. and P. Uberoi, *Marriage, migration and gender*, Delhi: Sage, 2008.

Radhakrishan, S., 'Time to Show our True Colours: The Gendered Politics of Indianness in post-Apartheid South Africa', *Gender and Society*, vol. 19, no. 2, 2005, pp. 262-81.

Raghuram, P., 'The Difference that Skills Make: Gender, Family Migration Strategies and Regulated Labour Markets', *Journal of Ethnic and Migration Studies*, vol. 30, no. 2, 2004b, pp. 303-21.

Rayaprol, A., *Negotiating Identities: Women in the Indian Diaspora*, Delhi: Oxford University Press, 1997.

Reeves, S., A. Kuper and B.D. Hodges, 'Qualitative Research Methodologies' *Ethnography Practice BMJ*, vol. 337, 2008, pp. 512-14.

Roos, Hannelore, 'In the Rhythm of the Global Market: Female Expatriates and Mobile Careers: A Case Study of Indian ICT Professionals on the Move', *Gender, Work and Organization*, vol. 20, no. 2, 2013, pp. 147-57.

Shukla, Sandhya, *India Abroad: Diasporic Cultures of Postwar America and England*, Princeton: Princeton University Press, 2003.

Stivens, M. and K. Sen, *Gender and Power in Affluent Asia*, London: Routledge, 1998.

Therwath, Ingrid, 'Shining Indians: Diaspora and Exemplarity in Bollywood', in *South Asia Multidisciplinary Academic Journal*, vol. 4, 2010, pp. 2-16.

Vertovec, Steven, 'Religion in Migration, Diasporas and Transnationalism', in *Research on Integration and Immigration in the Metropolis*, Working Paper Series, 2 July 2002, pp. 2-33.

Additional Readings

Constable, N., 'Distant Divides and Intimate Connections: Migrant Domestic Workers in Asia', part I, in *Critical Asian Studies*, vol. 36, no. 4, 2008, pp. 399-420.

——, 'Distant Divides and Intimate Connections: Migrant Domestic Workers in Asia', part 2, in *Critical Asian Studies*, vol. 41, no. 1, 2009, pp. 143-64.

Koser, Khalid, *International Migration: A Very Short Introduction*, Oxford: Oxford University Press, 2007.

McKay, D., 'Translocal Circulation: Place and Subjectivity in an Extended Filipino Community', *The Asia Pacific Journal of Anthropology*, vol. 7, no. 3, 2005, pp. 265-78.

Willis, Katie and Brenda Yeoh (eds.), *Gender and Migration*. Cheltenham: Edward Elgar, 2000.

Williams, A.M. and V. Balaz, *International Migration and Knowledge*, Routledge: London, 2008.

CHAPTER 7

The Hindu Response to Climate Change in South Africa

SAGIE NARSIAH

INTRODUCTION

Throughout the ages, humanity has faced many challenges. Some of these challenges have evolved into threats to the very existence of humankind. The risk of contagious, fatal, untreatable disease is a case-in point. The threat of a nuclear holocaust is another. Yet, these threats pale into insignificance when one considers the spectre of climate change. It is this spectre which hangs like the Sword of Damocles over the entire Earth. It is climate change which threatens the existence of the majority of the earth's populations—humans, fauna, flora, the denizens of the oceans and seas. No inhabitant of planet Earth is immune from the effects of climate change.

Climate change, in its present form is largely a consequence of human action on the Earth. Moreover, there has been no other comparable force which has had the impact that humans have had in changing the earths' landscape. The extensive scientific literature on human induced land-use and land cover change is unequivocal in this regard. According to Lambin et al. (2001: 1)

> Land-use and land-cover changes are so pervasive that, when aggregated globally, they significantly affect key aspects of Earth System functioning. They directly impact biotic diversity worldwide; contribute to local and regional climate change as well as to global climate warming; are the primary source of soil degradation; and, by altering eco-system services, affect the ability of biological systems to support human needs.

The impact of human beings on the Earth is the product of various socially produced processes. In many ways climate change is an outcome of what is viewed as the triumph of modernity, the progress of humanity—higher standards of living characterized, indeed informed, by unfettered industrialization and consumption at unprecedented levels. Climate change is the product of the world's 'disenchantment'. Following Weber, the process of 'disenchantment' was prefaced by the discovery of universal laws, particularly those which govern nature. Nature itself was disenchanted—myth, magic and superstition, the unknowable gave way to laws of nature, empirical verification and, certainty. That which was sacred is now mundane even profane. The Earth and its resources imbued with a supernatural consciousness in a word 'god' (enchanted) was supplanted by human beings as 'god'.

This (re)conceptualization of nature had huge ramifications for humanity's development. Moreover, the human-environment relationship was transformed. No longer were human beings at the mercy of nature, indeed being dominated by nature, rather it was human beings who could dominate nature, even tame her to determined ends. Scientific knowledge was applied to the production of technologies which facilitated the domination of nature. Nature was no longer a barrier to human development. In a phrase, nature was moulded according to the will of man.[1]

What this signified was nothing less than the recreation of nature, a re-enchantment of nature. Some, like Smith (2008) have conceptualized this as a second nature—the creation of a productivist landscape. In a sense, this movement, during what is referred to as the Enlightenment, has meant that nature was re-fitted to satisfy a humanity that had embraced consumption as an end in itself—consumption for consumption's sake. The consequences are all too obvious now. And, it has been obtained within a relatively short period of time. There are polarizations on a global scale—a small global elite who consume resources at an astonishing rate—20 per cent of the world's population consuming over 80 per cent of the earth's resources. Growing inequalities, with a diminishing group of very rich and ever increasing group of poor, continue apace. This situation is untenable. Should it be allowed to continue our already precarious situation is sure to end in a global cataclysm. What is needed, therefore, is nothing less than a disenchantment *redux*. Just as the system, mainly economic in nature, was infused with clearly identifiable mores and values, which served to legitimize the rapacity with which the global commons was captured for the benefit of the few, it is incumbent on the citizens of the world to demand a new set of values which must benefit everyone, rich and poor.

And, this cannot be reduced to empty rhetoric and rabble rousing. The approach has also been apparent throughout history and often degenerates into a small cottage industry, which can be easily dismissed or confined to peripheral (lunatic) fringe. This is where those sectors of global society, like organized religion can play a crucial role. Climate change is too important an issue to be left to scientists and politicians. Organized religion needs to invoke moral authority to ensure that humanity does not descend to the point of no return. It has to ensure that narrow partisan interests are quickly marginalized.

Lynn White, who worked as a Professor of History at the University of California in the United States of America, wrote a seminal paper published in the authoritative journal *Science*, asserted that religion was core to the ecological crisis identified in the 1960s. White was obviously in agreement with Weber's argument in the *Protestant Ethic and the Spirit of Capitalism*. White (1967: 1207) asserted that 'since the roots of our trouble are so largely religious, the remedy must also be essentially religious, whether we call it that or not. We must re-think and re-feel our nature and our destiny.'

For White (1967: 1205), 'human ecology is deeply conditioned by beliefs about our nature and destiny—that is, by religion'. Since the 1980s, 1988 to be more specific, with the formation of the Intergovernmental Panel on Climate Change (IPCC), there have been calls for social and anthropological interventions. Organized religion has answered this call. There have been several inter-faith gatherings where there has been some consensus around the need for concerted intervention by organized religious formations on climate change. For example the World Council of Churches has held a number of conferences addressing issues of ecology and climate change as far back as the early 1970s. It was during the 1990s that interfaith initiatives began to gather speed. The relevance of religion to climate change was highlighted in the historic meeting in August 2000 where more than one thousand religious leaders gathered at the [United Nations] for the Millennium World Peace Summit of Religious and Spiritual Leaders, to discuss, among other major topics, the environment (Tucker and Grim 2001). There has also been much work continuing in education, research and outreach (Tucker and Grim 2001). This work continues to highlight the need for an ecumenical approach to climate change.

Among the myriad of world religions, around 30 per cent are Christians; 20 per cent identify themselves with Islam and around 15 per cent or just over one billion people identify with the Hindu religion. Being a major world religion Hinduism has a significant role to play in re-imagining conventions which may supplement the mitigation and adaption strategies promoted by major bodies researching climate change like the IPCC.

In what follows, a brief overview of climate change will be undertaken. Thereafter, the link between nature and Hinduism and the potential role of the religion in combatting climate change will be examined. The concluding sections will examine the local response to climate change in South Africa.

CLIMATE CHANGE

Climate change refers to the variability in the earth's climate over a period of time. The IPCC (1995: 56) has defined climate change as 'any change in climate over time whether due to natural variability or as a result of human activity'.[2]

There are other definitions such as that adopted by the Framework Convention on Climate Change (FCCC), but these serve to politicize climate change even further (Pielke 2005). What this leads to is political inaction and paralysis inaction. The Kyoto Protocol is a case in point—there is general consensus that the Kyoto Protocol was a failure in that the proposed limitations on carbon emissions have not been supported or implemented by the major polluters namely, the United States of America and China. For the purposes of this paper, the definition that was adopted by the IPCC will be used.

The IPCC was established in 1988 as an authoritative global body on climate change.

> It was set up by the World Meteorological Organization (WMO) and the United Nations Environment Program (UNEP) to prepare, based on available scientific information, assessments on all aspects of climate change and its impacts, with a view of formulating realistic response strategies. The initial task for the IPCC as outlined in UN General Assembly Resolution 43/53 of 6 December 1988 was to prepare a comprehensive review and recommendations with respect to the state of knowledge of the science of climate change; the social and economic impact of climate change, and possible response strategies and elements for inclusion in a possible future international convention on climate. Today the IPCC's role is as defined in Principles Governing IPCC Work, . . . to assess on a comprehensive, objective, open and transparent basis the scientific, technical and socio-economic information relevant to understanding the scientific basis of risk of human-induced climate change, its potential impacts and options for adaptation and mitigation. IPCC reports should be neutral with respect to policy, although they may need to deal objectively with scientific, technical and socio-economic factors relevant to the application of particular policies. (https://www.ipcc.ch/organization/organization_history.shtml).

The IPCC has produced a number of reports on climate change. These reports are dense volumes where data on climate change is presented. A number of distinguished scientists are members of the IPCC. The IPCC reports present data which has been subjected to exacting standards of scientific rigour. For the IPCC there is no doubt that human beings have impacted on the global climate system. The greenhouse gas emissions are at an historical high. It is this singular factor which is the main contributor to the phenomenon known as global warming. In short what this means is that temperatures on a global scale have increased. Not only have temperatures over land increased, but so too have those temperatures over the oceans. As a consequence, polar ice caps have diminished and so has the amount of snow. Furthermore, there is a coincident rise in sea-levels. In a series of graphs presenting data on the globally averaged land and ocean surface temperature, sea level change and, greenhouse gas concentrations, the trend is unequivocally upward. What is alarming is that over the last sixty-five years, since 1950, there has been a marked increase in all the indicators referred to above.

It is important to note that seemingly small increases in temperature have enormous implications. An increase in temperature changes weather patterns resulting in increased incidences of drought and floods. Increased ocean temperatures influence precipitation over large parts of the globe. For example, temperature increases over the southern Pacific Ocean leads to the *El Nino* and *La Nina* phenomenon which affects precipitation over the southern African region. These systems in turn influence food security. Droughts lead to crop failures, that is, lower yields. This in turn leads to higher prices for staple foods. The implications for the economy are serious because this leads to higher food inflation. Also the agricultural sector is unable to employ labour, seasonal or otherwise. Unemployment levels increase. The higher prices and the loss or lack of employment mean hardship for the poorest sectors of the population in particular. There is a domino effect with the middle classes in society taking strain having to find ways to service debt in the form of mortgages or car repayments. It is almost a global norm that the first instrument that central bankers use to address increases in inflation rates is to increase interest rates. The ramifications of global temperature changes are thus far reaching. Yet, these changes form part of a cycle that is in many ways, socially constructed.

According to the IPPC (2014: 4):

> Anthropogenic greenhouse gas emissions have increased since the pre-industrial era, driven largely by economic and population growth, and are now higher than ever. This has led to atmospheric concentrations of carbon dioxide, methane and nitrous oxide that are unprecedented in at least the last 800,000 years. Their effects, together with those of other anthropogenic drivers, have been detected throughout the climate system and are extremely likely to have been the dominant cause of the observed warming since the mid-twentieth century.

The IPPC investigation into the sources of global warming is revealing. According to the IPCC, the main sources of global warming are carbon dioxide from fossil fuel combustion and industrial processes; carbon dioxide from forestry and other land use, methane, nitrous oxide and fluorinated gases. Most emissions sources have decreased since 1970, except carbon dioxide emanating from the combustion of fossil fuels. The burning of fossil fuels is by far the greatest contributor to green house gas emissions at around 78 per cent. The implications of this are dire. The oceans act as a sink for the absorption of carbon dioxide. However, because of the huge amounts which have been emitted into the atmosphere the ability of the oceans to absorb these gases has decreased as the saturation point is reached. As a consequence, the oceans have become more acidic, by 26 per cent (IPCC 2014). An increase in the acidity of the oceans threatens aquatic life. The oceans are a source of our food supply.

Global climate change is associated with environmental cataclysm. For example, there have been a growing number of films which have been put out by various movie houses that portray extreme events—floods, snowstorms and the like. Although these are fictional accounts, the threat to human life on planet earth and the implications for human existence under this changed environmental regime are all too real. In the present era, it appears that art in many ways mirrors reality. The extreme environmental event is becoming commonplace on a global scale. The IPPC (2014: 7) noted 'changes in many extreme weather and climate events have been observed since about 1950. Some of these changes have been linked to human influences, including a decrease in cold temperature extremes, an increase in warm temperature extremes, an increase in extreme high sea level and an increase in the number of heavy precipitation events in a number of regions.'

On a global scale, there has been a decrease in the number of colder days and nights. There has been an attendant increase in the number of warm days and nights. During the past few decades, even the past few summers, temperature records have been shattered. Accordingly, heat wave conditions during the summer months are now reaching a norm rather than exceptional events which people experienced during their lifetimes. The IPCC attributes this change to human intervention through the emission of greenhouse gases, carbon dioxide in particular. These extreme events are destructive—there is extensive damage to infrastructure and in many cases there is loss of life. The old and the very young being the most vulnerable in communities are especially endangered. There is hardly any doubt that human activity, as argued earlier, rooted in religious belief, is responsible for the general phenomenon called climate change and global warming in particular.

It follows that religious belief has, whether overtly or implicitly, sanctioned the human practises which have informed climate change. Although some religious groupings have questioned climate change—climate change denialists—they have not refuted the scientific evidence. If the influence of religion could be held responsible for a phenomenon that threatens the very existence of the planet as we know it, then surely it could be harnessed for its salvation.

What is required is a revolutionary change in our use of fossil fuels. On a global scale, greenhouse emissions from the flaring of fossil fuels, needs to drop dramatically. The consequences of this not happening have been subject to a number of simulation exercises by organizations such as, apart from the IPCC, National Aeronautics and Space Administration's (NASA) Goddard Space Flight Center in the United States of America.

According to the Goddard Center, the main contributor to global warming is the occurrence, particularly during the last decade of, greenhouse gases like carbon dioxide and aerosols. While concerted global action which largely banned the ozone gases found in various aerosols and refrigerators resulted in the relatively quick recovery of the ozone over a short period of time, the same cannot be held true for greenhouse gases. According to the IPCC (2014: 8)

> continued emission of greenhouse gases will cause further warming and long-lasting changes in all components of the climate system, increasing the likelihood of severe, pervasive and irreversible impacts for people and ecosystems. Limiting climate change would require substantial and sustained reductions in greenhouse gas emissions which, together with adaptation, can limit climate change risks [. . .]. Cumulative emissions of carbon dioxide, largely determine global mean surface warming by the late twenty-first century and

beyond. Projections of greenhouse gas emissions vary over a wide range, depending on both socio-economic development and climate policy.

These risks are higher for disadvantaged groups in all countries. For example, rising sea levels will impact coastal habitats, for example, mangroves, which are essential to the replenishment of fish and other aquatic species; low lying areas will disappear. There are some island nations which will disappear underwater altogether. The Not in My Backyard (NIMBY) approach will simply not work here—climate change is a global phenomenon which demands a global response. The nature of this response is broadly categorized as mitigation and adaptation. These are not mutually exclusive and should be viewed as inter-linked. The approach has to be holistic. The approach has to be one that is at once political but depoliticized. All countries need to be in agreement and selfish, national interests need to be bracketed or suspended in favour of the global common good.

> Adaptation and mitigation responses are underpinned by common enabling factors. These include effective institutions and governance, innovation and investments in environmentally sound technologies and infrastructure, sustainable livelihoods and behavioural and lifestyle choices [. . .] mitigation options are available in every major sector. Mitigation can be more cost effective if using an integrated approach that combines measures to reduce energy use and the greenhouse gas intensity of end-use sectors, decarbonize energy supply, reduce net emissions and enhance carbon sinks in land-based sectors. (IPCC 2014: 26)

Simply stated, mitigation refers to the reduction of greenhouse gas emissions. Mitigation has been a major point of contention between the developed and developing nations. Initiatives such as carbon-trading/cap and trade are very creative measures akin to re-arranging the deckchairs on a sinking Titanic Earth. This process has been highly politicized and led to the collapse of a number of global climate change initiatives aimed at producing global agreements. The 2009 Copenhagen Conference, was an abject failure due to the reluctance of developed countries, in the main, acting in their own interests. Another attempt at securing a global compact on climate change was made in December 2015, in Paris, France.

While mitigation is essential on the global scale and is indispensable to national policy on climate change, it is adaptation—eliciting a change in human behaviour—that directly impacts people's way of life. The IPCC identified the personal sphere as one area to manage the risks of climate change. For the IPCC (2014: 27-9) 'personal, individual and collective assumptions, beliefs, values and worldviews influencing climate-change responses [. . .] emissions can be substantially lowered through changes in consumption patterns, adoption of energy savings measures, dietary change and reduction in food wastes'. Here religion has the potential to provoke a sea change in the attitudes and beliefs of its adherents. Posas (2007: 2) articulates this view: 'The complementary and unique roles of religion in addressing climate change stem primarily from religion's functions in society, ethical teachings, reach and influence, and ability to inspire adherents to action.'

HINDUISM, NATURE AND CLIMATE CHANGE

Hinduism is one of the major world religions. There are over one billion people who follow the Hindu faith, 94 per cent of whom are found in India; Hindus are only behind Christians, who make up almost 33 per cent, and Muslims with 23 per cent of religious adherents (Haluza-Delay 2014). Like many other religions, Hinduism does not subscribe to a singular view—there are multiple streams that inform Hinduism. Unlike some of the other major religions where there is one single text and multiple interpretations, there is no one singular text to which all Hindus subscribe. Hindus draw inspiration from a number sources such as the *Bhagavad Gita*, *Ramayana*, Upanishads, Puranas, and Vedas. There are a myriad interpretations of these texts. This paper does not provide an in-depth exegesis of these texts. Rather, this paper will refer to some Hindu concepts which may be useful in promoting behavioural change. These proposed changes may inform adaptation to climate which in turn may mitigate what is perhaps one of the greatest challenges to human beings.

Although, there isn't a singular Hindu view on nature or cosmology which informs the religion, climate change offers the potential to draw all Hindus together in pursuit of a singular objective—the amelioration of climate change. It is encouraging that such initiatives have already been activated, driven by an ecumenical imperative. For example, in December 2009, for example a Hindu Declaration on Climate Change was presented to the Convocation of Hindu Spiritual Leaders at the Parliament of World Religions in Melbourne, Australia. It is instructive to consider key passages from the declaration.

> The Hindu tradition understands that man is not separate from nature, that we are linked by spiritual, psychological and physical bonds with the elements around us. Knowing that the Divine is present everywhere and in all things. Hindus strive to do no harm. We hold deep reverence for life and an awareness that the great forces of nature—the earth, water, the fire, the air and space—as well as all the various orders of life, including plants and trees, forests and animals, are bound to each other within life's cosmic web.
>
> Our beloved Earth, so touchingly looked upon as the Universal Mother, has nurtured mankind through millions of years of growth and evolution. Now centuries of rapacious exploitation of the planet have caught up with us, and a radical change in our relationship with nature is no longer an option. It is a matter of survival. We cannot continue to destroy nature without also destroying ourselves. The dire problems besetting our world—war, disease, poverty and hunger—will all be magnified many fold by the predicted impacts of climate change [. . .].
>
> Sanatana Dharma envisions the vastness of God's manifestation and the immense cycles of time in which it is perfectly created, preserved and destroyed, again and again, every dissolution being the preamble to the next creative impulse. Notwithstanding this spiritual reassurance, Hindus still know we must do all that is humanly possible to protect the Earth and her resources for the present as well as future generations. (Hindu Declaration on Climate Change 2009)

Hindus, as articulated in passage above, realize an intrinsic link with nature. Nature is integral to the cycle of birth, death, rebirth and so on. The destruction of nature thus threatens the very existence of the religion. In many ways worship, by implication, care of nature is worship of the supernatural. The Hindu scriptures are fairly unequivocal in this regard—the concept of *bhakti* is linked to the worship/devotion to a supreme being. As the passage above indicates, the Earth is viewed as the 'Universal Mother'. The Earth is thus god or to invoke the feminine, a goddess. The Earth as goddess is known by various names such as Bhu; Bumi; Prithvi; Vasudha; Vasundhara and Avni (Agoramoorthy and Hsu 2011). She is to be worshipped and not defiled. 'Impure objects such as urine, faeces, spit, or anything which has these elements, as well as blood or poison should not be cast into water' (cited in ibid.: 106; cf. Narayanan 2001). The concept of dharma is interpreted as righteousness and nonviolence is viewed as the highest form of righteousness (ibid.: 1997, 2001). Water is a key element in Hinduism. Rivers are viewed as sacred. The Ganges is viewed as the most sacred river in Hinduism—it is a key element in the cycle of birth and death. Rivers are revered through holy hymns in the *Rigveda*—here reference is made to the 'Sarasvati river, which is now extinct which flowed into the Rann of Kutch and created an intricate network of fertile streams extending from today's Punjab to West Bengal. The climate those days was characterised by abundant rain and monsoons—the manifestation of the god Indra' (Agoramoorthy and Hsu 2011: 106; Narayaran 2001). Apart from water, animals sacred to Hindus are elephants and water buffalo, among others. Climate change threatens the habitats of these animals. Urbanization, for example threatens animal habitats.[3] It is an act of violence against other creatures who have an equal right to the earth. It violates the Hindu concept of dharma.

One of the key challenges to climate change is the depletion of forests and by implication the loss of carbon sinks. Alternatively, there is a need for afforestation so as to increase the absorption of carbon dioxide. Religious practises to which Hindus subscribe have a direct bearing on this issue. Agromoorthy and Hsu (2011: 106) (see also Narayanan, 1997, 2001) state:

> The planting of trees in the villages of ancient India was celebrated as the 'festival of trees,' according to Matsya Purana [. . .] the 'Varaba Dharmottara' claims that one who plants [five] mango trees will not suffer after death. The scriptures also condemn those who cut and destroy forest and trees. Another important text, the 'Arthashstra' [. . .] concerns a wide range of social issues such as fines for destroying sacred groves, and forests [. . .] 'Matsya Puranam' narrates a wonderful example of caring for the Earth. The goddess Parvati was planting a sapling of Ashoka tree (*Saracaindica*), and a sage asked her why she

was growing trees instead of raising children. Parvati replied that one digs a well where there is little water lives in heaven for as many years as there are drops of water in it. One large reservoir of water, she continued, is worth ten wells. One son is like ten sons; the planting of trees was thus her way of saving the universe.

The act of deforestation is an act of violence against nature. The wanton destruction of trees violates dharma—it is viewed as a sinful act. This will therefore impact on the cycle of birth and life. This message, rooted in religious belief must be harnessed in the struggle against climate change. In India, there has been destruction of catchment areas of major rivers which has led to large scale flooding. For example, the catchment area of the Ganges, viewed by many believers as the hair (locks) of god Shiva were subject to large-scale deforestation (Shiva's locks were denuded). Invoking this story and together with the assistance of scientists reforestation projects have led to recovery of parts of the catchment area.

There is a need for religious teachings to draw the attention of adherents to the violation of key principles in the respective religious practises. Rivers have been despoiled through industrialization and the discharge of sewage. Textile companies discharge dyes, for example, directly into water courses, rendering these water courses toxic. It costs far less to dispose of such material into water courses than subjecting them to expensive treatment. Simply put, there ought to be no law against pollution of rivers because it is the moral obligation of every Hindu to ensure that water courses are not polluted.

Custom and religious practises can be traced back to particular texts. These texts which for many may be divorced from their material circumstances and thus reduced to ritual, can now be harnessed in the struggle against climate change. These texts allow for the re-enchantment of nature. To plant trees is to obey the commands of the gods and goddesses, it is an act of worshipping nature and saving the planet. In the passage above which alludes to the goddess Parvati, an argument is made for reforestation and against deforestation. Such parables need to become more commonplace in everyday teachings and discourses.

Opportunities can be initiated for religious practise to be recontextualized. For example, at the Venkateshwara Temple in Tirupati, south India, one of the most well-known Hindu temples in the world, has moved away from serving sweetmeats (the *laddu*) to giving away saplings to devotees. There are a number of such initiatives in India. For example, Louise Fowler-Smith writes about the phenomenon of tree veneration she encountered in Tamil Nadu, south India. In ancient cultures across the globe, trees were protected and nourished. In Hindu texts, trees are considered the most important living forms on earth and are the object of veneration, being decorated with garlands and other paraphernalia. Trees are often viewed as the abode of the sacred and thus protected (Fowler-Smith 2009). The Chipko movement where women physically intervene to prevent the destruction of trees practises this understanding. This contrasts with the Western view where trees are simply viewed as an economic resource. This enchantment of nature, and the conception that she is sacred and must be respected and protected is a view which needs to promoted. The examples referred to here represent a tiny minority of strategies which are environmentally friendly. These strategies may be applied globally. But, India herself needs to ensure that environmentally sensitive approaches, rooted in religious texts and belief, need to be widespread on the subcontinent. This is all the more urgent given that India is third highest emitter of greenhouse gases in the world.

What this section has demonstrated is that the despoliation of nature and by implication the destruction of the earth through practises which are responsible for climate change militates against some of the most basic tenets of Hinduism, for example that of dharma and bhakti. The opportunity thus exists for the Indian diaspora to play a more active role in promoting this as a global message to address the destruction that climate change continues to wreak. We will now turn to South Africa, which has a Hindu population approaching almost one million adherents.

HINDUS AND CLIMATE CHANGE IN SOUTH AFRICA[4]

South Africa has one of the major populations of Indians outside the subcontinent. The Hindu religion is practised by the majority of South Africans of Indian descent. Although a minority group in South Africa's population of around 55 million, Indians show high levels of literacy and are active participants in the country's economic, social and political life.

Indians first arrived in November 1860 in Durban, South Africa. Although the majority enlisted to work as indentured labourers in what was then British controlled Natal, there were those from the merchant classes who also formed part of the cohort. The labourers worked primarily on the white-owned sugar cane farms on the north and south coast of what is now known as KwaZulu-Natal. South Africans of Indian descent have a rich, highly textured history. Much of it has been documented, but there are myriad of histories which remain to be written. Among those histories which remain barely interrogated are the nuances of cultural traditions drawn from various parts of India which found their way into the spatial melting pot which still has the greatest density of Indians in South Africa, Durban. One should keep in mind the various Indian groupings which derive from locations around India, all who may be categorized as Hindu but following different Hindu practises, for example the Tamils, Telugus, and Gujaratis, view them-selves as Hindus but have a myriad of religious practises which differ from one another.

Those indentured Indians who landed on the shores of South Africa over 150 years ago came with very little education. In cultural and religious matters there was an obvious lack, and indeed an absence, of nuance and sophistication. Pedestrianism was to be expected because the immigrants came from a largely agrarian background. Their religious activities were largely based on memory. The development of shrines and temples occurred against this background. And, those who were more knowledgeable than others took the lead. As the flow of immigrants increased particularly during the early twentieth century, the number of educated individuals arriving increased. Among these were religious leaders from India. These practitioners imparted knowledge to the locals. It should be noted, however, that the knowledge transfer was largely informal. Heritage was largely transferred verbally. The practical and linguistic skills related to rituals and in-depth knowledge of the religion were obviously lacking. As a consequence, there evolved over a period of time religious practices that were highly contextual. The rituals practised in the South African context differed from those in India. The Hindu religion of the early period in South Africa was confined to ritualistic practise around temples and shrines. Organized institutions for the training of Hindu priests did not exist in early twentieth century South Africa.

The arrival of the Arya Samaj in South Africa signalled a movement towards a more vedic, textual based Hindu practise, that was communicated in Sanskrit and tended to be more esoteric. The Arya Samaj group tended to adopt the Brahminical, caste-based practise in its early years. Women were not allowed to become priests. Towards the end of the twentieth century this practise changed as the organization moved away from appointing only Brahmin priests. In 1989, the first priest from Sri Lanka arrived in South Africa. These priests were also from the Brahmin caste and later in 1994, after India restored diplomatic relations with South Africa, a number of north and south Indian priests began to arrive in the country. These priests came with a different set of ideas and practices from those already existing in South Africa.

The arrival of foreign priests in South Africa gave rise to questioning of rituals and procedures practised by the locals. For example, the foreign priests used Sanskrit chants. These chants were unfamiliar to the locals. This caused difficulties with other groups who were not familiar with it. And, this added to the debate around authenticity—who was right? The locals or the foreigners? A major debate is raging at the moment regarding the practise of the ritual of *kavady*, a religious festival that is dedicated to a Hindu deity. It has proven extremely difficult to change practises which have been ingrained for a very long period of time. And, this is largely because of the way Hinduism has evolved in the South African context. Many of the rituals which are performed draw on the agrarian roots which informed the practise of Hinduism in its formative years in South Africa.

Many South African Hindu rituals do have a connection to the land, environment, geographical conditions and so on. Many of these rituals actually began with a perceived responsibility for nature and the environment. In other instances rituals began as care for a place. Virtually all Hindu rituals revolve around natural phenomena—rivers, trees and, mountains. For example in South Africa, anthills (the *puthu*) are venerated. When the land is moist, the ants create anthills and this is symbolic of fertility. For Hindus the *puthu* is symbolic of the appearance of a deity—a god or goddess. The reaction of Hindus when they apprehend such a phenomenon is to worship rather than destroy it. Trees also are worshipped in a similar way.

Hinduism in South Africa is often tied into various ritual practices. The offering of fruit, milk and other foodstuff to deities is an integral part of the ritual. With large numbers of devotees making these offerings to their respective deities there is a huge amount of fruit and milk used. Much of this is simply wasted. There has not been a concerted effort to try and address this issue. The example of the world famous Tirupati Temple springs to mind here—the *prasad* has been substituted by the offering of saplings. Trees are planted promoting the message of care for the Earth. In South Africa there is an opportunity to engage in such initiatives, given that the country is water scarce and the environment, particularly, the former bantustan areas have been despoiled under the apartheid regime.

The South African Hindu response to climate change, mirrors what is happening on the Indian subcontinent. The action against climate change is at an incipient stage. There is no concerted effort or systematic programme to address climate change. Yet, Hinduism has a very strong ethical and moral basis to argue for a concerted effort to mitigate and promote adaptation to climate change. For example, the Hindu voice against the South African government's adoption of coal fired power stations rather than green technologies like solar and wind power has remained unheard. The South African government has expressed a strong interest in rolling out nuclear power on a grand scale, yet there is little or no dissent expressed by religious groups.

If religions in general want to claim the moral high ground, then they would have to transform from within. The practises mired in ritual needs to be revisited and urgently updated to engage with issues of local and global import such as climate change.

Sermons on these issues need to become the norm rather than the exception. And, it has to be informed at the practical level, the protection of the environment in general and various components in particular such as trees and water courses. After all, they are central to life—trees produce oxygen and water enables life. Hard choices will have to be made to modify or even discontinue those rituals that despoil the environment in favour of practise that are environmentally friendly and indeed sustainable. Personal behaviours, related to over consumption needs to be directly addressed. In South Africa, the gap between the rich and the poor has been growing. South Africa is among the most unequal societies in the world. What inequalities indicate is a society that is becoming increasingly polarized. That key informants for this paper indicated that they are not aware of any major project on climate change in the Hindu community in South Africa, is of great concern. While this may be viewed as something of a lack, the positive is that there is enormous potential to engage with this issue.

CONCLUSION

This paper examined the Hindu response to climate change in South Africa. An outline of the nature of climate change was outlined. Climate change is a global issue. The main contributor to climate change are humans. While greenhouse gases such as carbon dioxide and methane are essential to life, over-concentration of these gases tips the global atmospheric balance. However, instead of sustaining life, the over-concentration of these gases threatens life. Human activities, linked to excessive consumption, has been identified as a key contributor to climate change. The primary contributor to greenhouse gases is the burning of fossil fuels. The burning of fossil fuels contributes close to 80 per cent to greenhouse gases in the atmosphere. This paper argues that since religion has provided the rational basis for the exploitation of the earth it therefore has the potential to take the lead in providing an alternative rationale for the salvation of the Earth.

This paper on the role of nature in Hinduism was briefly examined. Some of the very basic tenets of Hinduism such as dharma and bhakti (righteous living, non-violence) and devotion to god, have direct links to nature. Furthermore, these concepts can be invoked in the struggle of humanity against climate change, specifically the emission of greenhouse gases and the fouling of the earth in general.

Last, the lack of a Hindu response to climate change in South Africa, is noted in this paper. Unfortunately, climate change is not being taken seriously in the South African context. Part of the reticence could be traced to the evolution of Hinduism in South Africa. Furthermore, ingrained traditions and rituals are hard to transform or to even jettison. Yet, with planet Earth rapidly reaching the point of no return, an effort needs to be made to change behaviours. Furthermore, Hindus need to be part of an ecumenical movement to address these issues. We cannot afford to be partisan on this issue, after all, Hindus subscribe to the conception of a single humanity.

NOTES

1. The term is used consciously to highlight the gendered production of human landscapes.
2. This section relies mainly on the 2014 IPCC report on climate change. The IPCC is a compilation of authoritative research on climate change.
3. Certainly, as more people move to cities, more fossil fuels will be consumed. However, urbanization and population increase are not causal factors when it comes to climate change. Over-consumption is. The neo-Malthusian argument is well worn. The masses of poor people contribute far less to climate change than the minority of over-consumers who need to shoulder their share of the blame for the situation we find ourselves in.
4. This section is sourced largely from an interview with Prof. P. Kumar, emeritus professor in the School of Religion at the University of KwaZulu-Natal.

REFERENCES

Agoramoorthy, G. and M.J. Hsu, 'Ancient Hindu Scriptures Show the Ways to Mitigate Global Warming through Responsible Action', in *Anthropos*, 106, 2001, pp. 211-16.

Fowler-Smith, L., 'Hindu Tree Veneration as of Mode of Environmental Encounter', in *Leonardo*, vol. 42, no. 1, 2009, pp. 43-5.

Haluza-DeLay, R., 2015, 'Religion and Climate Change: Varieties in Viewpoints and Practices', in *WIREs Climate Change* 2014. doi: 10.1002/wcc.268

'Hindu Declaration on Climate Change', Presented for Consideration to the Convocation of Hindu Spiritual Leaders. Parliament of the World's Religions, Melbourne, Australia, 8 December 2009.

IPCC, 'Climate Change', *Synthesis Report. Summary for Policymakers*, IPCC, 2014.

Lambin, E.F. et al., 'The Causes of Land-Use and Land-Cover Change-Moving Beyond the Myths', in *Global Environmental Change: Human and Policy Dimensions*, vol. 11, 2001, pp. 2-13.

Narayanan, V., '"One Tree is Equal to Ten Sons": Hindu Responses to the Problems of Ecology, Population, and Consumption', in *Journal of the American Academy of Religion*, vol. 65, no. 2, 1997, pp. 291-332.

——, 'Water, Wood, and Wisdom: Ecological Perspectives from the Hindu Traditions', in *Daedalus*, vol. 130, no. 4, 2001, pp. 179-206.

Pielke, R., *Environmental Science & Policy*, vol. 8, 2005, pp. 548-61.

Posas, P.J., 'Roles of Religion and Ethics in Addressing Climate Change', in *Ethics in Science and Environmental Politics*, vol. 19, 2007, pp. 31-49.

Smith, N., *Uneven Development: Nature, Capital, and the Production of Space*, Athens: University of Georgia Press, 2008.

Tucker, M.E and J.A. Grim, 'Religion and Ecology: Can the Climate Change'? *Daedalus*, vol. 130, no. 4, 2001, pp. 1-22.

White, L., 'The Historical Roots of Our Ecologic Crisis', *Science*, vol. 155, no. 3767, 1967, pp. 1203-7.

CHAPTER 8

The Traditional Hindu Perspective on Environment and M.K. Gandhi's Standpoint

NAMITA NIMBALKAR

Sarvamvrityatishthati (He resides in every where).

Bhagavad Gita 13.13

INTRODUCTION

The current worldwide ecological crisis has only emerged during the past four decades and its effects have been felt within southern Asia more recently. As the region copes with decreasing air quality in its cities and degraded water in various regions, religious thinkers, academicians and activists have begun to reflect on how the broader values of religious tradition might contribute to fostering greater care for the Earth.

The religions of the world have traditionally expressed concern for environment and its creatures. They have accorded some moral significance to other creatures, and proposed some ethical responsibilities on the part of humans, although these ethical dimensions are usually secondary, or inferior, relative to responsibilities to other humans.[1] The numerous dos and don'ts laid down by ancestors in day to day activities point to the belief system of the harmonious co-existence of nature and human beings. They also had better realization as to what the ill-effects of the disharmony will be, when it arises. However, for reasons yet to be best understood, religious concerns for the environment faded with the rise of modern society.

The beginning of environmental ethics as a new discipline of philosophy began in the early 1970s. It challenged the anthropocentric or human centred view which assumed moral superiority of human beings to members of other species on earth.[2] An intricate relationship is observed between environmental ethics and values closely related to the behaviour of man towards the conservation of nature. Values, as Bharucha notes, lead to a process of decision-making which leads to action. For value education in relation to the environment, this process is learned through an understanding and appreciation of nature's oneness and the importance of its conservation.[3] It is an intellectual code of behaviour that regulates man's relationship with nature. It cannot be imposed by law but has to be articulated, systematized, codified and brought to the doorsteps of each and every individual.

The religious hermeneutical lens seeks answers from the scriptures, texts, rituals and, myths. O.P. Dwivedi in his *Dharmic Ecology* paper looks at religion as a strategy that puts into practice the Hindu concept of 'eco-care'. The paper is divided into two parts, the first part examines how the traditional Hindu concept of nature contains words of wisdom to conserve and protect nature and the second part explores the dynamics of M.K. Gandhi's philosophy towards environment ethics.

THE RELATION BETWEEN HINDUISM AND ENVIRONMENT

The tradition of frugality in Indian everyday life has been well documented and there are many anecdotal accounts of it. The common man in India has through the ages utilized and conserved the resources through recycling, re-using and deriving value out of whatever he could. However, as the population of India increases and as the modern lifestyle continues to demand consumer goods, the balance of sustainability is being shattered. With a renewed appreciation of the five great elements (earth, water, fire, air and ether) a new interpretation of social duty (*dharma*) expanded to include the ecological community and a recollection of an abstemious ethic, the Hindu tradition can develop new modalities for caring for the earth.[4]

Environmental ethics forms the core lore of Hinduism. Hindus revere rivers, trees, animals and birds. Nature is worshipped in India and it has never been considered a hostile element to be conquered or dominated. However, its rich natural resources are under heavy pressure due to a growing economy and exploding population.[5] A need is felt to seek the role religions can play in fostering moral thinking and acting about environment. Several scholars have opened up discussions about the role religious communities can play in protecting the environment. Does worshipping nature inspire Hindus to act in an environmentally conscious way? Is there any relationship between their reverence for bio-divinity and their care for biodiversity?

The religious traditions of India are rich and varied, offering diverse theological and practical perspectives on the human condition. The *Isa Upanishad* tells us that 'all this is for habitation by the Lord',[6] which means, everything from a blade of glass to the whole cosmos is the home of God. God lives in every corner of existence. Therefore, all creation is sacred, nature, life, mountains, rivers and animals are to be revered. This sense of the sacred in creation is fundamental to Hindu's relationship with nature.[7]

The Vedas, Upanishads, *Mahabharata*, *Ramayana* and Puranas contain messages encouraging the protection of the environment and inspire a sense of respect for nature. Sacred texts emphasizes that nature is not to be conquered. Humans are to live in harmony with nature and recognize that the divinity resides in all living elements, including plants and animals.

The Vedas, believed to have been written around 3000 BCE and considered sacred in Hinduism, contain one thousand and twenty-eight hymns dedicated to 33 different gods. Most of the 33 gods are nature gods. The hymns contain several references about protecting the environment and thus indicate an intimacy with the seers and people of that time. The *Rigveda* venerates deities like Mitra, Varuna, Indra, Maruts and Aditya who are responsible for maintaining balance in nature, whether the mountains, lakes, heaven, earth, forests or the waters. Seers recognized that changes caused due to indiscreet human activities could result in imbalances in seasons, rainfall patterns, crops and atmosphere and thus degrade the quality of water, air and resources. One seer admonished:

'Do not cut trees, because they remove pollution'. (*Rigveda* 6.48.17)
'Do not disturb the sky and do not pollute the atmosphere'. (*Yajurveda* 5.43)
'We invoke all supporting Earth on which trees, lords of forests, stand ever firm'. (*Atharvaveda* 12.1.27)
'Whatever, I dig of you, O Earth, may that grow quickly upon you. O Pure One, may my thrust never pierce thy vital points thy heart'.[8]

The concept of *Rta* or Cosmic Order originates in the *Rigveda* (10.85; 4.23, 9-12; 10.190). In the Vedic vision, the universe is not conceived as a haphazard mass of elements and events, but as an ordered whole in which each part inheres the whole and the whole is balanced by its parts. *Rta* is, in essence, the ordering principle of nature, the inflexible law of universal order and harmony, the universal cosmic flow which gives to everything from the vast galaxies, down to the nucleus of an atom, their nature and course, is *Rta*. *Rta* is observable everywhere. The eternal bond between man and nature is nourished by *Rta*. In the Vedic vision, this law of cosmic order is conceived to be manifesting at three levels: on the cosmic plane *Rta* governs the law of nature; on the socio-ethical level, *Rta* imparts justice and on the religio-spiritual level, *Rta* mirrored the ritual performances of the sacrificial ritual (*yajna*). *Rta* contributes to the maintenance of balance between the micro and macro levels of existence.[9] It is also believed that the Prajapati (the 'Lord of Creatures' of the *Rigveda*) is the creator of the sky, earth, oceans and the species. Prajapati is also their protector and eventual destroyer.

The Hindu belief is that the Earth is mother, the Earth is goddess, the Earth is Kali, the Earth is Prithvi, the Earth is Sita and—and she is the home of God. The Prithvi Sukta in the *Atharvaveda* (verses 12.1.1-12.1.63) is a beautiful hymn composed in honour of Mother Earth. The *Atharvaveda* teaches practitioners how to respect air, fire, water, trees and rivers. In the Prithvi Sukta the Vedic seer solemnly declares the caring and reciprocal attitude to Mother Earth: *mata bhumih putroham prithivyah*: [Earth is my mother, I am her son].

For the Hindu, the Earth evolves, breathes, is conscious, creates, destroys and recreates. Mother Earth is celebrated for all her natural bounties and particularly for her gifts of herbs and vegetation. Her blessings are sought for prosperity in all endeavours and the fulfilment of all righteous aspirations. A covenant is made that humankind shall secure the Earth against all environmental trespasses and shall never let her (Earth) be oppressed. A soul-stirring prayer is sung in one of the hymns for the preservation and conservation of hills, snow-clad mountains and all brown, black and red earth, unhurt, unsmitten, unwounded, unbroken and well-defended by Indra. The following hymn in the Bhumi Sukta of the *Atharvaveda* is infused with ecological and environmental values:

Earth, in which lie the sea, the river and other waters,
in which food and cornfields have come to be,
in which lives all that breathes and that moves,
may she confer on us the finest of her yield.
Earth, in which the waters, common to all,
moving on all sides, flow unfailingly, day and night,
may she pour on us milk in many streams,
and endow us with luster,
May those born of thee, O Earth,
be of our welfare, free from sickness and waste,
wakeful through a long life,
we shall become bearers of tribute to thee.
Earth, my mother, set me securely with bliss in full accord with heaven,
O wise one, uphold me in grace and splendor.[10]

Trees were worshipped and protected for their contribution to the sustainability of species, genetic diversity and ecology. The *Varaha Purana* mentions that trees have five types of kindness which are their daily sacrifice. To families—trees provide fuel; to passers-by—trees provide shade and a resting place; to birds—trees provide shelter; with their leaves, roots and bark trees provide medicines.[11]

The scriptures such as the Upanishads, the Puranas and subsequent texts to it sing praise to nature. The *Panch Mahabhutas* (the Five Great Elements), that is, Prithvi, Ap, Tej, Vayu, Akash, (Earth, Water, Fire, Air, Space) is the sum total of the environment which is derived from *Prakriti*—the primal energy.[12] By including the five elements, the ancient people recognized the importance of biodiversity. Hindus believe that the spark of the divinity is present not only in the human soul but also in other living things such as the Earth. The Divine reality is manifested in the form of *prana/ shakti* and forms the very fabric of religion. They also believed that the Divine resides within the universe and is not an outside an creation. The *Mundaka Upanishad* describes the Divine as follows:

The sky is his head, his eyes are the moon and the sun;
the quarters his ears, his speech the Vedas disclosed,
The wind is his breath, his heart the entire universe,
from his feet came the earth, he is indeed the inner Self of all things.[13]

Hindus believe in the cycle of birth, death and rebirth which is governed by *karma*. Hindus believe that the soul passes through a cycle of successive lives and its next incarnation is always dependent on how the previous life was lived.[14] It means that a person to reap the fruits of his *karmas* will have to be reborn again and may come back as a bird or another animal. This faith has made the Hindus hold on to the firm belief that every aspect of creation should be respected and revered.

The *Srimad Bhagvata Mahapurana* states that 'ether, air, fire, water, earth, planets, all creatures, directions, trees and plants, rivers, and seas, they all are organs of God's body; remembering this, a devotee respects all species'. The ancient people were wise to realize the importance of forests and every animal in the ecosystem. The Virata Parva, the fourth book of the *Mahabharata*, very categorically states, 'Don't destroy forest with tigers and don't make the forest devoid of tigers. Forests can't be saved without tigers and tigers can't live without forests because forests protect tigers and tigers protect forests.'[15] For Hindus, human beings are considered as but one link in the symbiotic chain of life and consciousness. Vegetarianism is practised to avoid the negative karmic effect. The basic concept is: seeing the presence of God in all, [living beings] and treating the creation with respect without harming and exploiting other [living beings] (*vasudevah sarvamiti*).[16] The *Srimad Bhagavata Mahapurana* confirms this fundamental principle: A good devotee is the one who sees in all creation the presence of God (*sarvabhutesu yehpasyedbhagvadbhavamatmanah*[17]).

The *Mahabharata* states:

The purchaser of flesh performs *himsa* (violence) by his wealth; he who eats flesh does so by enjoying its taste; the killer does *himsa* by actually tying and killing the animal. Thus, there are three forms of killing: he who brings flesh or sends for it, he who cuts of the limbs of an animal, and he who purchases, sells, or cooks flesh and eats it. All of these are to be considered meat-eaters.[18]

The *Mahabharata* (18.113.8) states: 'One should never do that to another which one regards as injurious to one's own self. This, in brief, is the rule of dharma. Yielding to desire and acting differently, one becomes guilty of *adharma*.' In the Moksadharma Parva, Chapter 182, verse 20 of the *Mahabharata* it is said that all living beings have a soul, and God resides as their inner soul: *sarvabhutatmbhutastho*. Ideally it means that the rights of other species should not be encroached upon.

The *Manusmriti* prohibits wanton destruction of both wild and cultivated plants.[19] It further emphasizes that violence against domesticated animals to be *himsa*.[20] The *Dharmashastras* states, 'Without doing injury to living things, flesh cannot be had anywhere; and the killing of living beings is not conducive to heaven; hence eating of flesh should be avoided.'[21] The *Chandgoya Upanishad* bars violence against 'all creatures' (*sarva-bhuta*) and the practitioner of *ahimsa* is said to escape from the cycle of reincarnation.[22]

Based on this belief, there is a profound opposition in the Hindu religion to the institutionalized breeding and killing of animals, birds and fish for human consumption. From the perspective of Hindu religion, the abuse and exploitation of nature for selfish gain is considered unjust and sacrilegious.[23] Reference can be made to the *Manusmrti* (5.38) which states, 'A person who kills an animal for meat will die of a violent death as many times as there are hairs of that killed animal'. The *Yajnavalkyasmrti Acaradhyayah*, verse 180, warns of hell fire (*ghoranaraka*) those who kill domesticated and protected animals: 'The wicked person who kills animals which are protected has to live in hellfire for the days equal to the number of hairs on the body of that animal'.

Another interesting aspect in Hinduism is the reverence to animals. The animal kingdom is considered as sacred. Hindu deities move around in their own *vahana* (vehicles) that are usually animals.

These animals are considered as sacred as God. This divine status provides animals a privileged status. To give a few examples, Lord Ganesha—the Remover of Obstacles, has a mouse as his vehicle. Symbolically the mouse signifies Ganesha's ability to destroy all obstacles. Similarly, another Hindu God, Shiva—the Destroyer, has Nandi, the bull as his vehicle. Nandi the bull symbolizes sexual energy and fertility. The Lord of Death, Yama visits on a He-buffalo, Lakshmi has the owl as her vehicle, Saraswati has the swan or peacock. There is thus an all-pervasive ethos among Hindus that perceives the animal and the human world as one unbroken continuum.[24] Of all the animals, the cow occupies the central position. It is considered to represent the Divine. Lord Krishna states in *Srimad Bhagavad-Gita*: chapter 10, verse 28: 'Among cows, I am the wish fulfilling cow' (*dhenunamasmikamadhuk*).[25]

There is a rich treasure trove in Hinduism with regard to its concern for environment and it can be succinctly concluded from the first verse of the *Isha Upanishad:*

> The whole universe together with its creatures belongs to the Lord (Nature). No creature is superior to any other, and the human being should not have absolute power over Nature. Let no species encroach upon the rights and privileges of other species. However, one can enjoy the bounties of nature by giving up greed.

M.K. GANDHI'S APPROACH TO ENVIRONMENT

There were many people in the past who could foresee the future and visualize the price mankind will have to pay while competing in the mad race of industrialization and urbanization. One among them was M.K. Gandhi revered as the father of the nation in India. Gandhi was a deeply religious person and his advocacy of simple living through the principles of non-violence (*ahimsa*) and holding to truthfulness (*satyagraha*) could give some Hindus pause as they consider the lifestyle changes engendered by contemporary consumerism. Nobody in his or her senses can suggest today, 'to destroy all machinery and mills', not even Mahatma Gandhi, who, too, however reluctantly accepted the fact that 'machinery has its place, it has come to stay'.[26]

In the strict sense of the term, Gandhi does not come under the category of environmentalist. This is not because Gandhi was indifferent to the environmental problem, but it was not of such great magnitude in his times. His experience as a global citizen (studied law in London, practised law in South Africa, national leader of Indian Freedom movement) cultivated in him an insight to anticipate the problems which the world would experience as the fruits of industrialization, economic growth, distribution of goods and services along with pollution of air, water, land, desertification, deforestation toxic wastes, urbanization, etc. Gandhi is a passionate champion of a life pattern based on three cardinal principles: Simplicity, Slowness and Smallness.[27] His view that 'Earth provides enough to satisfy every man's need, but not every man's greed'[28] serves as a role model of practising an environmentalism based on limited possession. Arne Naess, the Norwegian philosopher with whose name Deep Ecology[29] is inextricably intertwined, has testified that from Gandhi he learnt that the power of non-violence could only be realized after the awareness of 'the essential oneness of all life'.[30] Chandi Prasad Bhatt, Vimla and Sunderlal Bahuguna who have been at the helm of the Chipko Movement protest (to save trees) and Baba Amte, Medha Patkar of Narmada Bachao Andolan (protest against dam building on river Narmada) acknowledge that their inspiration has come from Gandhi.[31] It can be safely argued that Gandhi inspired and even fathered the Indian environmental movement.[32]

The Gandhian concept of non-violence is its practice in thought, speech and action. The notion of non-violence is also extended to include the responsibility which man should undertake to protect the biotic and abiotic world. He envisaged for a peaceful, just society, where man could cohabit in harmony and have reverence for all things living and non-living.

The influences which shaped Gandhi's thought were the teachings of *Isa Upanishad, Patanjali Yogasutras* and the *Bhagavad Gita* as well as John Ruskin's book *Unto the Last.* These influences catalysed his desire to lead a life of frugality and develop ideas that foster 'sustainable development'.[33]

The influence of Patanjali the compiler of *Yogasutras* is evident on Gandhi. The Yoga's ethical guidelines of *yamas* (restraints) and *niyamas* (observances) were practised by Gandhi in all sincerity. The *yamas* are the ethical precepts, essentially a set of rules of don'ts. The five *yamas*: (i) non-violence (*ahimsa*) towards all animate and inanimate creation; (ii) truth (*satya*); (iii) avoiding the use of materials obtained by illegitimate means and avoiding destruction (*asteya*); (iv) celibacy (*brahmacharya*) to keep check on the growing population and demand for resources; and (v) not amassing wealth beyond requirement (*aparigraha*). Gandhi also practised the *niyamas*, or the set of rules of do's which relate to cleanliness of surroundings and of the self. The practice of *shaucha* (purification) removes impurities which adversely affect our state of mind, and prevent the attainment of real wisdom and spiritual liberation from both of our environment and body. *Santosha* (contentment) suppresses the craving for what an individual does not have as well as discourages him from coveting the possessions of others. *Santosha* is the realization that happiness gained through materialism is only temporary. An individual must also consciously work at surrounding himself with a pure environment (including food, drink, friends, entertainment, home furnishings and transportation) to not add any external impurities back into our bodies or minds. Other *niyamas* are austerity (*tapas*), contemplation of one's life (*svadhyaya*) and devotion to God (*ishvara pranidhana*). The austerity through the practice of *yamas* and *niyamas* by Gandhi confirms deep respect for the environment.

Gandhi established *ashrams* in South Africa and in India. His *ashrams* were based on local self-reliance, equality of gender, participatory management. One is filled with awe and wonder to see Gandhi in his early formative years of his philosophy in South Africa, to live a minimalist life in the Phoenix Ashram (1904) and Tolstoy Farm (1910). While at the *ashrams* in India, Gandhi formed a tertiary school that focused on manual labour, agriculture and literacy, in order to advance his efforts for the nation's self-sufficiency. His emphasis on local self-reliance is what the environmentalist of today are stressing upon, when they speak about reduction of carbon footprint. It took almost a century for the policy makers and thinkers at the global stage to realize the thought process of Gandhi in conservation of environment.

Gandhi formulated an economic order in the context of this design of an ideal social order: a non-violent, non-exploitative, humanistic and egalitarian society. His approach to economics was through the avenue of truth and non-violence. Its goal is not pure material benefit, but the advancement of humanity on its road to progress by strengthening the characters and the development of personalities. 'No one's gain should be anybody's loss—financial, physical, moral or spiritual. If there is to be a choice, the preference should fall on the internal constituents of man rather than on the material.'[34]

The Gandhian thought is built upon a form of non-exploitative 'moral economics' in which everyone works for the common good without seeking to accumulate any more than they need, from individual to nation (through family, village, region, etc.) Gandhi's emphasis on the voluntary limitations of wants which he also sometimes referred to as voluntary poverty has put him at loggerheads with almost all his followers who considered themselves progressive-minded and wanted to lead the people of India into affluence. Gandhi was criticized in strong terms for wanting to keep the people in perpetual poverty and demanding ascetic austerity from them. But Gandhi never demanded ascetic mortification of the flesh from the people and neither did he practice it himself. Gandhi believed that for any change to be meaningful it must begin at the bottom and reflect in the changes in the realm of health, education, culture and economic development for the lowliest of the lowly.

Gandhi suggested an alternative economy for India. His observation of the Western civilization had made him wise enough to realize that short-term economic gains will do little good for the Indian society. Further, India lives in its villages. There is a chasm between the rich and the poor, urban and rural, of India. And as always, it will be the poor who will firsthand pay the price of development as they will get delineated from the use of natural resources, such as land, water and forests. Gandhi was aware that the growing chasm would divide the society, giving rise to conflicts.

The gnawing question to which we have to find an answer is: Is it possible for us to avoid the situation in the present century? It will be wise to recall the Talisman which Gandhi gave, 'Recall the face of the poorest and weakest man you may have seen and ask yourself if the step you contemplate to take is going to be of any use to him. Will he gain anything by it?'[35]

Gandhian thinkers have suggested many remedies to prevent the deterioration of environment. About those remedies Shri Thakurdas Bung says, 'For saving environment we will have to impose restrictions on industrialization, greater urbanization, wanton pleasure and frame a policy under which requirements of all around be fulfilled. We will have to follow the policy of 'Simple living and high thinking with an emphasis on "recycling of goods" instead of "use and throw" policy'.[36]

CONCLUSION

India has had a distinct civilization and culture that was very much in consonance with natural habitat. Nature (*prakriti*) was revered with utmost devotion and the civilization was known for its cultural and spiritual heritage in protecting its environment. These factors constituted an important element in sustaining the natural wealth but have been constantly neglected by the mankind. The Western concept/perception that nature and environment exist for the service of humanity has slowly crept into Indian society, promoting the values of unsustainable consumption and acquisitive materialism. Dwivedi rightly observes that 'culture and religions of the world can provide a solid foundation for changing people's attitude on the preservation and conservation of the environment. World religions and cultures particularly Oriental belief systems, do not inherently subscribe to the abuse and exploitation of Nature for material and selfish gains.' Unfortunately, 'culture and no part of the world have remained immune from makind's irreverence towards nature, an irreverence that has brought in its wake the destruction of our own habitat, our progeny and ourselves'. He also identifies that ethical values emanating from the world religions and cultures are some of the basic determinants of our behaviour towards nature.[37]

Gandhi's ideas are of great relevance today. These are relevant to the path of development we wish to pursue. Gandhi was of the firm view of 'consume only what you can produce'[38] and also a strong proponent of the need for an alternative process of development. The task of mankind is to 'cooperate judiciously and caringly with the Nature's Economy of Permanence'.[39]

To plead for an awakened interest in the age-old traditions is not to advocate a return to the conditions of antiquity but understanding the ancient traditions and wisdom will help to put into practice the eco-care vision of Hinduism. The guiding principle of *vasudhaiva kutumbakam*[40] (the world is one family) should be promoted for *sarva-bhuta-hite-ratah* (welfare of all beings).[41]

James Speth identifies two factors that are central to the environmental ethics—'the protection of their (people's) own sake of the living community that evolved here with us and our trusteeship of the earth's natural wealth and beauty for generations to come'. (Speth, 2004: 192). He also contends that 'to realize such a future, societies will have to free themselves from a variety of pernicious habits of thought, including the enchantment of limitless material expansion and what John Kenneth Galbriath has said 'the highly contrived consumption of an infinite variety of goods and services'.

NOTES

1. http://www.scu.edu/ethics/practicing/focusareas/environmental_ethics/lesson10.html, retrieved on 25 September 2015.
2. http://plato.stanford.edu/entries/ethics-environmental/#IntChaEnvEth, retrieved on 25 September 2015.
3. Bharucha, Erach, *Environmental Studies*, Hyderabad: Universities Press, 2005, p. 230.
4. http://fore.yale.edu/religion/hinduism/, retrieved on 29 April 2015.
5. India with its population of 1.4 billion is second only to China.
6. file:///C:/Users/Acer/Downloads/17IshaUpanishad%20(2).pdf, retrieved on 12 April 2015.
7. Ranchor Prime, *Hinduism and Ecology: Seeds of Truth*, London: Cassell Publishers, 1992, p. 72.

8. R.T.H. Griffith, *The Hymns of Atharva Veda*, California: Evinity Publishing Inc, 1st edn., 2009, p. 35.
9. http://www.exoticindiaart.com/book/details/rta-cosmic-order-IDD686/, retrieved on 27 September 2015.
10. Karan Singh, *Essays on Hinduism*, Delhi: Ratna Sagar, 1987, pp. 117-18.
11. *Varaha Purana*, 162.41-2.
12. www.greenfaith.org/files/top-10-hindu-teachings-handout, retrieved on 18 April 2015.
13. https://en.wikipedia.org/wiki/Mundaka_Upanishad, retrieved on 29 May 2015.
14. http://www.bbc.co.uk/religion/religions/hinduism/ataglance/glance.shtml, retrieved on 10 May 2015.
15. *Virata Parva*, 5.45-6.
16. *Bhagavad Gita*, 7.19.
17. *Srimad Bhagavata Mahapurana*, 11.2.41.
18. *Mahabharata*, 115:40.
19. *Manusmriti*, 11.145.
20. *Manusmriti*, 5.27-44.
21. http://www.hindupedia.com/en/Ahimsa_in_Scriptures#cite_note-17, retrieved on 15 May 2015.
22. *Chandgoaya Upanishad*, 8.15.1.
23. O.P. Dwivedi, 'Dharmic Ecology', in *Hinduism and Ecology: The Intersection of Earth, Sky, and Water*, ed. Christopher Key Chapple and Mary Evelyn Tucker, Cambridge, Mass.: Harvard University Press, 2000, p. 6.
24. Sehdev Kumar and Aaloka Mehndritta, 'Environmental Ethics—Ancient Traditions and Contemporary Dilemmas: A Hindu Perspective', *Journal of Hindu-Christian Studies*, vol. 6, 1993, p. 44.
25. http://www.bhagavad-gita.org/Articles/holy-cow.html, retrieved on 28 April 2015.
26. *Young India*, 5 November 1925.
27. http://www.mkgandhi.org/environment/jha.htm, retrieved on 25 September, 2015.
28. Pyarelal, *Mahatma Gandhi*, vol. X: *The Last Phase*, part II, Ahmedabad: Navajivan, 1958, p. 552.
29. Deep Ecology is a contemporary ecological philosophy that recognizes an inherent worth of other beings, aide from their utility. It provides a foundation for the environmental, ecology and green movements and has fostered a new system of environmental ethics. . . . Similar views have been propounded by Bill Devall and George Sessions in their work on Deep Ecology (1985) Holding the view that everything is connected

to everything else, they observe the changing trends of emerging deep ecological consciousness that goes beyond anthropocentrism. http://en.wikipedia.org/wiki/Deep_ecology retrieved on 24 September 2015.

30. Vinay Lal, op. cit., pp. 183-212.
31. Vinay Lal, 'Too Deep for Deep Ecology: Gandhi and the Ecological Vision of Life', in *Hinduism and Ecology: The Intersection of Earth, Sky, and Water*, ed. Christopher Key Chapple and Mary Evelyn Tucker, Cambridge, Mass.: Harvard University Press, 2000, p. 185.
32. Ibid.
33. T.N. Khoshoo, *Mahatma Gandhi: An Apostle of Applied Human Ecology*, New Delhi: Tata Energy Research Institute, 1995, pp. 1-2.
34. Rashmi Sharma, *Gandhian Economics: A Human Approach*, New Delhi: Deep & Deep, 1997, p. 33.
35. *Mahatma Gandhi, Last Phase*, vol. II, 1958, p. 65.
36. Bang Thakurdas, *Bharat: Kal, Aaj Ani Udya*, Wardha: Paramdham Prakashan, 2005, p. 22.
37. O.P. Dwivedi, *Environmental Ethics*, New Delhi: Sanchar Publishing House, 1994.
38. Anand Sharma, *Gandhian Way: Peace, Non-violence and Empowerment*, Academic Foundation, 2007, p. 154.
39. Savita Singh, *Global Concern with Environmental Crisis and Gandhi's Vision*, New Delhi: A.P.H. Publishing Corporation, 1999, p. 63.
40. *Mahopanishad* VI.71.
41. *Bhagavad Gita*, 5.25.

CHAPTER 9

Review of Pedro Machado's *Oceans of Trade: South Asian Merchants, Africa and the Indian Ocean, c. 1750-1850*

GAIL M. PRESBEY

Pedro Machado's background makes him an excellent person for the kind of study he undertakes in his book. He's a research associate of the Indian Ocean World Centre. He knows many languages, and has worked on various World History projects on slavery and on leprosy. His focus is on ocean trade and in particular the products of cloth, ivory and slaves (as they are considered a trade commodity).

OVERVIEW OF MACHADO'S BOOK

The main argument of the book is that Hindu Vaniya merchants based in the Kathiawar peninsula of Gujarat, India had an extensive Indian Ocean trade from 1750 to 1850. They had a thriving shipbuilding industry in Daman (pp. 80-5), skilled crews and cartographers who mapped the ocean depths and studied ocean and weather conditions (p. 92), and an organized network of cloth manufacturers, so that they could go to (what we now call) Mozambique and trade cloth for ivory, and eventually, for slaves and silver. Their cloth was greatly in demand due to its high quality, and the merchants were paying a lot of attention to African consumer demand in cloth. They ensured they manufactured and sold the kind of cloth that Africans most wanted, so Machado plays up the constructive role that African consumer choices made in the development of the trade (showing how receptive producers were to consumer demand). African demand particularly had to do with demanding a high quality cloth, which was used in their culture on specific occasions to mark high status events. Machado tries to show that the cloth was being considered a kind of currency, even though there were sometimes complaints about its fluctuation in value (pp. 128-30). The merchants traded cloth for ivory which was mostly used in India itself for ivory bangles which culturally symbolized wedded bliss, and so they were highly in demand (especially since the bangles were broken at the death of a marriage partner and so were not recycled).

The merchants had an extensive banking and credit system, and were able to insure trading ventures, and they worked with the Portuguese rulers to take advantage of their status as imperial subjects to benefit from lowered import and export tariffs. Conditions in the 1820s and 1830s changed dramatically due to a drought in Africa, during which time the amount of slaves for sale rose higher (perhaps because some were attempted to flee the drought, see p. 205). After 1833 when the British banned the slave trade, Brazilians were engaged in buying slaves in Mozambique as a way of avoiding the West African coast where they would more easily be detected by British ships trying to interrupt the slave trade. Baniya merchants traded cloth for silver, which then allowed them to purchase slaves; they bought and shipped slaves to both India and Aden and other Middle Eastern ports. They brought silver back to active silver markets in Kathiawar and Gujarat. They also exchanged slaves for silver with the Brazilians, and brought the silver back to India.

Machado's overall point is that the Vaniya merchants' participation in the Indian Ocean trade was substantial and multi-faceted, and that their presence as Hindu traders, in contrast to Indian Muslim or British traders, changes the more dominant historical narrative that imagines that they dropped out of their prominent role after they reduced trade to the Persian Gulf and Red Sea ports like Aden and Mocha (where they had been trading since the fourth century BCE, see pp. 18-19) due to discrimination and violence against Hindus (for example, a massacre ordered by the Imam of

Mocha, see pp. 22-3), or narratives that overemphasize British control of Indian trade. The merchants did not just drop out, they adapted, and searched for new markets in Southeast Africa.

In this book we see that the Vaniya merchants worked with Portuguese colonial officials to take advantage of their trade rules (see p. 55) and their courts, when it suited the traders (but they ignored these courts and used customary *mahajan* guild organizations when they thought it would be to their benefit, see p. 10), but these merchants were independent business people who were mak-ing their own business decisions and financing their own projects. They were not dependent on colonial rule and they weren't just doing the bidding of the colonizers. In fact, the Portuguese were jealous of the Vaniya traders' success and power (pp. 63, 155). It is important to notice this because 'Dependency Theory' shows how colonizers created dependency when it wasn't there before, by destroying what had been thriving economic systems. This is a portrait of the thriving economic system that would eventually be taken over by the British when they ruled India as part of the British Empire. Also, within the context of Portuguese influence on trade in India, the emphasis had been on the role of Goa, and little emphasis has been on the thriving Kathiawar peninsula and Gujarat; Machado corrects that deficit by filling in the details of the story of this vibrant more northern India-based trade.

Machado also shows that the Vaniya merchants had extensive working relationships with African businesspeople/agents called *patamares* who were gathering the ivory, as well as African traders of the Zambesi Valley called *Vashambadzi* who assumed the risks of the dangerous ivory trade (and were not 'slaves' but of slave status, see pp. 39-40, 191-3). He also discusses the long-distance traders of ivory in Yao in northern Mozambique (p. 185). His book therefore departs from a genre of history writing that focuses on European demands for luxury goods and how European consumer demand impacts world trade. He will instead talk about African consumer demand for cloth, and Indian consumer demand for ivory, which is usually not mentioned.

The author shows us how culture played a role in several crucial ways, such as, Vaniya merchant culture focused a lot on the extended family as agents that one could trust. In a 'verbal culture' with limited literacy (pp. 34, and 44, fn. 76), trust and reputation were crucial to thriving businesses, while talk and rumour could destroy a business. Semi-formal and informal organizations developed to monitor trust and control dangerous rumors (see pp. 46-9). Vaniya cultural preferences made them reluctant to own property since they preferred mobility; but they did own property that they were given to cover debts owed to them (p. 65). Ships crews had an authoritarian structure. Also, while they designed ships that could carry cannons and arms, they preferred to emphasize speed and maneuverability rather than to slow down their travel time by transporting heavy armaments (pp. 74-5).

Other important roles for culture included choices that Africans made about the cloth they wanted to buy. Cloth carried cultural and symbolic meaning. Cloth was used as 'a means of bestowing moral and social qualities, of marking both high and low status' (p. 123). Giving a gift of cloth could commit others to obligations in the future. There were important investiture ceremonies that used certain cloths. Africans also insisted on high quality cloth (p. 132). Some cloths were especially used to exhibit mourning, or to be worn at sacrificial ceremonies for the ancestral spirits (p. 135). Vaniya merchants paid great attention to their consumer markets' desires for products.

THE BOOK'S RELATION TO THE LARGER FIELD OF WORLD HISTORY

One very important reason to engage in the study of World History is to unlearn the Eurocentric distortions we have been taught in school and that are reinforced in many aspects of mainstream American culture (see Manning 2003: 38, 76; Wolf 2010: xx). The actual, more fully informed version of World History is fascinating. Eric Wolf, an important founder of the field of World History, emphasizes showing the interactions between Europe and Africa, Latin America and Asia. Historians as well as the general public routinely under-estimate the level of interaction, and we ignore the way that southern continents, for example, have impacted

Europe (since most history books focus on how Europe impacted other areas). Wolf also debunks the 'billiards' metaphor in which cultures and nations are seen as bounded and bouncing off of each other; instead we see peoples and cultures as permeable and malleable, being changed by their encounters in a context where national boundaries are not the walls we presume they are (Wolf 2010: 4, 6; Manning 2003: 285). It's not only consumer goods but also social practices that can be mutually influential. For example, according to Sinha, Britain and India both influenced each other's gender perceptions (Manning 2003: 97-8).

A key way in which Machado's book departs from the Eurocentric norm is that he is most interested in describing producers, traders, and consumers who are not European. So he does not chronicle the trade of items going to or from Europe. He does not have to delve into describing what Europeans wanted, or what they did, since the main agents are Indian and African. Yes, there are some Portuguese rulers and businesspeople, but they are not dominant in the story line that Machado is telling. He writes a 'South-South' history. Another key theme in World History is exploring race, class and gender as it impacts history. The challenge is always to find sources adequate enough to give us a sense of the daily life, struggles, cares, and interactions of those who don't appear much in official records or who haven't written their autobiographies. It is then that historians turn to a variety of sources, whether they are court records, business records (and Machado's study of traders depends a lot on inventories of ships, or records of business loans, etc.), or the archaeological study of material culture, or the linguistic study of the development of a language, to get at what daily life had been like. To seek out the stories of those who are of a race or ethnicity with lower prestige, or the stories of women who for centuries (with some important exceptions) did not write history books or their life stories is necessary in order for us to have a more accurate and objective historical record.

It was Eric Wolf who emphasized the theme of political economy in world history. It was also he who used commodity chains as a focus for studying links and interactions between regions. Following Marx, he wanted to study the growth of the world market (Wolf

2010: xxi, 21). Various authors of ours have followed these chains, all the way from production to consumption (as does Sidney Mintz in his study of sugar). Machado's study also looks at the production of cloth, the gathering of ivory and slaves, and the sale of these three items (that is, their destination, and the significance that consumers have given this item in their local context). While he follows the silver from the time that traders receive it from Brazilians to the places where it is used, he does not follow the trail to the production of the silver in any detail (perhaps because silver mining happens in a region beyond the Indian Ocean). Likewise, although he asserts that Indian cloth made it to Brazil (Machado, p. 158), he was not able to find much of that record, and he does not do a study of Brazilian consumers of Indian cloth.

As Kopytof notes, despite the widespread commoditization of people through slavery throughout various times in history, it seems unacceptable, and even a category mistake, from our current perspective. 'This conceptual polarity of individualized persons and commoditized things is recent and, culturally speaking, exceptional' (Kopytof 1986: 64). Nevertheless it can be jarring to study the slave trade in a blasé way that lists slaves along with cloth, ivory, and other commodities without and special reference to the moral distinction involved. Machado definitely downplays any controversy and portrays his Hindu merchants as engaging in the slave trade in a business manner, and not out of any inherent cruelty but rather in conformity to the way business was done in the time period.

When we turn to Machado's account of the lesser-known Mozambiquan slave trade, we also saw an extensive description of African agency in the many parts of the trade. For example, Vaniya merchants worked with African agents called *patamares* who gathered ivory, and African traders from the Zambesi Valley known as *vashambadzi* who for the most part assumed great risks in engaging in the dangerous ivory trade. These *vashambadzi* were of slave status but not technically 'slaves' (see Machado, pp. 39-40, 191-3). Machado also covers the long distance Ivory traders in Yao of northern Mozambique (p. 185). Machado shows many Africans to be serious business people with many skills.

As important as slavery is as a topic, it is just one way of focusing upon the important theme dwelled upon by Eric Wolf, which involves the question of how societies socially deploy their labour. Who rules or influences who? What choices do agents have over their own lives, even if their roles and choices are circumscribed? How are these roles and relationships contested? Slavery has ended (for the most part), but it is very interesting to note how it ended, and what forms of labour took its place. Oftentimes some of the alternatives were a lot like slavery!

While I have presumed that Wolf's approach to world history is a direct influence on Machado, since his book focuses on political economy and international trade, nevertheless Machado never mentions Eric Wolf. Also, Machado has chosen a topic that is barely covered in Wolf's otherwise seemingly exhaustive coverage of world trade. Machado emphasized that he would cover the history of extensive Hindu trading on the Indian Ocean, and he insisted that most books covered Muslim trade (or later, trade to and from India controlled by the British) while ignoring trade by Hindu merchants and companies. A look at Wolf's index sees that he only mentions Hindus on two pages (although there are 14 pages that mention Hindus or Hinduism one searches the book using google books). In contrast there are large sections in the index on Islam (with 22 pages mentioned under 'Islamic sphere' and 7 pages under 'Muslims' and 'Muslim Spain'). While Wolf has extensive coverage of the ivory trade, he does not mention at all that Hindus were involved in the trade. As regards shipbuilding in India, Wolf covers the Arab ship designers and builders, but he does not mention the extensive ship building engaged in by Hindu ship builders in Daman (see Machado, pp. 80-5).

In a chapter called 'Trade and Conquest in the Orient', Wolf covers India by emphasizing the roles of the British and the Muslims, hardly mentioning any of the history of Hindu traders that Machado covers. Wolf says that the British arrived in India as traders with the East Indian Company, and were able to trade due to their relationships with the Mughals, the Muslim rulers of India. He mentions that the British bought textiles dyed with indigo in Surat. Wolf says, 'Shipping was in the hands of Muslims who traded with the ports on the Red Sea; brokerage, commerce and money lending were dominated by powerful lineages of Hindu merchants' (Wolf 2010: 240). This is some acknowledgement of the role of Hindus in trade at the time (as bankers), but it is a mere fraction of their actual involvement, since Hindus were not only financiers but shipbuilders and distance traders. Wolf goes on to talk more about the Mughals and the British, but does not develop the story line of the role of the Hindus. His book has a map of India, that shows both Surat and Diu, but there is no mention of what trade goes on in the port town of Diu. But from reading Machado's account we know that a lot of long-distance trade went on in Surat and Diu, and that such trade preceded British involvement. While the Portuguese are involved in trade in Diu and Goa and Southeast Africa, they don't have enough funds, ships, and know-how to run large scale trading businesses themselves. In fact, the Vaniya traders have a greater business ability than do the Portuguese (Machado, pp. 63, 155). The traders position themselves to benefit from Portuguese rule when it benefits them (such as gaining access to lower import and export tariffs, see Machado, p. 55), and to avoid or circumvent Portuguese control when it doesn't suit them (using customary guild organizations called *mahajan* when it seemed to be in their interest, see Machado, p. 10).

Wolf has a five page description of India's caste system as it was set up in the 1400s (Wolf 2010: 45-50). He briefly mentions that it was mostly the Brahmins that 'furnished links with wider networks of trade and markets' (ibid.: 49). But he doesn't go into any descriptions of other aspects of Indian culture. In contrast, Machado dwells, not upon the religious practices of the Hindus, but of their family relations, since their family relations serve as a basis and a model for their business relations. Extended family members are wedded together in relations of trust, which then help them in the business world (Machado, p. 33). Vaniya cultural preferences also valued mobility, and so the merchants were reluctant to make large land and building purchases in Africa, although they did own some buildings, mostly those they were given as collateral for debts (ibid., p. 65). This preference for swift mobility also influenced their ship design (pp. 74-5). While culture is important, Wolf would caution us about how we refer to a group's culture. The old, nationalistic way of describing culture insisted that each culture had an inner nature whose unique expression explained their achievements in some sense. So we shouldn't be looking for some attribute of Hinduism, for example, that would explain the merchants' success or failure, or would determine their business choices.

As Machado reported on p. 239, 'There does not appear to have been any Hindu opposition to, or prescription against, the shipping of African slaves.' He at least notices that a moral discussion is missing on this topic. But Machado seems mostly an apologist for the Gujurati merchant traders. He explains 'Slave trafficking had, in other words, become part of the fabric of coastal exchange and was therefore unavoidable as a reality for those conducting business along the coast' (pp. 248-9). The traders had not gone out of their way to seek this kind of trade, circumstances mostly just thrust themselves upon the traders. He also explains that few slaves, maybe only 400-500 yearly, were brought to Asia (p. 252). Indian traders (Hindu and Muslim) began trading African slaves before the Portuguese arrived (p. 213). Machado mentions that there was a 'lively' slave traffic in Porbandar, the city of Mohandas Gandhi's birthplace (p. 256). Also, African slaves were circulated in a trade that included South Asian slaves, usually women and girls; perhaps this is why the demand for African slaves focused on boys (pp. 258-9). Machado also mentions that sometimes African slaves were preferred, especially for domestic work, because lower-caste Indians taken as slaves or servants could 'pollute' their owner in a way that Africans could not (p. 261). Slavery only came to an end due to British pressure which led to its criminalization in 1860 (p. 261). Much of this history of slavery in India could be found in *Slavery and South Asian History* by Indrani Chatterjee (the book which Machado keeps quoting).

The one place that Machado discusses moral issues involved with slavery is on p. 221 where he notes that the Portuguese Viceroy wanted to ensure that Vaniya slave traders brought slaves to Catholic ports (where they could be baptized) and not to Muslim destinations. Machado claims that the Portuguese were actually worried about competition from Muslim merchants (and not sincere in their seeming moral concern). He notes that Hindus were not allowed to convert Africans since their religion was not one that proselytized (p. 220). In Machado's coverage of Hindu traders' involvement in the slave trade, he says, 'Slave trafficking had, in other words, become part of the fabric of coastal exchange and was therefore unavoidable as a reality for those conducting business along the coast' (pp. 248-9). So, since they wanted to sell cloth, and get silver, they had to involve themselves in the slave trade. There is a need for more detail on this topic. It would be good to know more about the conditions of slaves, both on the boats and when they arrived at their destinations and were sold.

But one area that Machado has covered in detail is the organization of the Indian spinners, weavers, and designers. Machado explains that this whole chain of production in India was self-governing, without the influence of Europeans, until finally the Portuguese insisted on imposing themselves directly on this chain of supply (in an effort to cut out Hindu middlemen). One could wish that he told the gender story of the spinners and weavers in a little more detail, so that readers could get a better glimpse into the life of women in the region. Machado also excels in telling the story of how traders conveyed African customer preferences back to India and directly influenced the production of cloth. No one book can tell an entire story. The world is so interrelated, at a certain point one has no choice but to drop the story line and leave parts to others. But Machado's book fills an important gap. We learn about the Hindu Vaniya traders, the bankers and financiers of Surat, and the Daman ship builders, and their relationships with the traders and customers of Southeast Africa, to an extent heretofore not covered by other authors.

And now, at last, our attention can turn to the animals and the question of animal rights. The topic absent in Machado's book is the discussion of the morality of the ivory trade, from the perspective of the merchants themselves as practicing Hindus. Machado says that estimates are that 26,000 to 31,000 elephants were killed from the 1750s to 1760s (p. 207), so imagine over the course of one hundred years how many elephants had been killed. He had made a big point of the fact that the hunters were Hindu, and not Muslim (p. 71). He doesn't comment once about any possible moral questions regarding killing elephants in pursuit of (meat and) ivory. Not only were the merchants Hindu, but, the area of Gujarat which was the focus of his study was a center of Jainism, an even more strict religion of non-violence, where all living beings are treated as equal, and where caste was not practiced. At least, Jainism did not practice caste (at least in its early days near its founding), although over time they have practiced it (some said it was the influence of Hinduism). Machado notes that elephants were not killed in India for their ivory because they were too valuable as beasts of burden (p. 169). Machado's book may not be able to cover all topics from all angles, but the depth in which he delves to uncover the history of Hindu merchants on the Indian Ocean is formidable, and very helpful to scholars.

REFERENCES

Chatterjee, Indrani and Richard M. Eaton (eds.), *Slavery and South Asian History*, Bloomington and Indianapolis: Indiana University Press, 2006.

Eaton, Richard M., 'Introduction', in Indrani Chatterjee and Richard M. Eaton (eds.), *Slavery and South Asian History*, Bloomington and Indianapolis: Indiana University Press, 2006, pp. 1-16.

Kopytoff, Igor, 'The Cultural Biography of Things: Commoditization as Process', in *The Social Life of Things: Commodities in Cultural Perspective*, ed. Arjun Appadurai, Cambridge: Cambridge University Press, 1986, pp. 64-94.

Machado, Pedro, *Oceans of Trade: South Asian Merchants, Africa and the Indian Ocean, c. 1750-1850*, Cambridge: Cambridge University Press, 2014.

Manning, Patrick, *Navigating World History: Historians Create a Global Past*, New York: Palgrave MacMillan, 2003.

Mintz, Sidney, *Sweetness and Power: The Place of Sugar in Modern History*, New York: Penguin, 1985.

Rediker, Marcus, *The Slave Ship: A Human History*, New York: Penguin, 2007.

Wolf, Eric R., *Europe and the People Without History*, Berkeley: University of California Press, 2010.

CHAPTER 10

Zee TV and the Reinforcement of Ganesha Worship among People of North-Indian Origin in Durban

ANAND SINGH

INTRODUCTION

When Hindi and Bhojpuri[1] speaking Hindus from the north of India first arrived in South Africa as indentured labourers they especially carried with them two of their most popular epic scriptures, viz., the *Ramacaritamanas* (*Ramayan*) and the *Bhagavad Gita*. In the absence of temples (focusing mainly on rituals) and *ashrams* (institutes of higher philosophical learning), they gathered under shady trees on Sunday afternoons to recite and keep alive their normative patterns of prayer from these scriptures. The deities were mainly Rama and Krishna, although other deities such as Ganesha did feature among them. The situation with Hindus in those early stages of their settlement in South Africa was confused and lacking in any form of organized religion. Fatima Meer (19) pointed out that the diversity among Hindus and the absence of a central controlling body on religious affairs had initially failed to bring about some measure of consistency in their beliefs and major observances. And Usha Shukla, with reference to the Hindi-speaking community among the broader population of indentured labourers in South Africa wrote that:

> Many of them also brought along with them the Ramacaritamanasa of Tulsidasa and a few also carried the Bhagavad Gita and other scriptures. . . . Amongst them were mendicant bards who could in fact read and also knew large

portions of the great stories of Hinduism, especially the Ramayana, the Mahabharata and the Gita by heart. (Shukla 2002: 106-7).

It is evident from this statement that Ganesha and the texts associated with him did not feature as prominently then.

In India too Ganesha appears 'late' in the popular literature, and belief among academics and researchers is that propitiation of him only began around two thousand years ago. Yet there are references to him in Hinduism's oldest epic, viz., the *Rigveda*, a date for which there is no accuracy. The earliest possible reference to Ganesha appears in the second book of the *Rigveda*, in the *rik* starting with *Gananamtva Ganapatigum Havamahe* (RV 2.23.1), where he is viewed by many as *Ganapathi*.[2] Praise abounds for him in the invocation, as the Chief and leader of the group of *ganas* ('army' of enlightened souls) because he ranked among as the highest seer among seers of the truth (cosmic creation), and the lord of the *mantras* (holy Sanskrit verses). In boisterous Sanskritic style Ganesha is ululated as *Jyeshta Rajam Brahmanam*, or Brahmanaspathi, a Vedic divinity of the highest order, the leader of the heavenly bands and a sage (*kavi*) among sages. Literature on Ganesha is replete with praises that are akin to him being the creator of the universe, with an omniscient omnipresence that goes beyond his unique form. Yet his emergence into this world is a based on a story that remains unconvincing to the critical, if not cynical Western writers. Jayaram (n.d.) for instance stated that 'Looking at his form, a foreigner who is not familiar with the tenets of Hinduism, would perhaps draw wrong conclusions about Ganesha and about Hinduism'. Ganesha's origins, as described in the epic scriptures, are what are responsible for the cynicism in which so many Western scholars have written about him and epic characters that are central and deterministic in moulding the cosmological and moralistic approach to life that Hindus all over the world cherish. Ganesha is a creation of his mother Parvati, who, after using her divine powers, created him as a reaction to Shiva's preoccupation with long periods of meditation and not wanting to have any children. Ganesha was appointed by Parvati as a 'doorkeeper' while she proceeded with cleansing herself in the privacy of her bathroom. When Shiva returned he was stopped by Ganesha from entering the abode since neither of them of them knew of each other. In a violent struggle Shiva decapitated Ganesha, only to find out after the event about who he was. Upon hearing of this calamity Parvati instructed Shiva to replace the head of Ganesha with that of the very first living entity that he came across. It was an elephant that he first saw and acted with speed to cut off its head to compensate the beheaded child with it. After connecting the head of the elephant to Ganesha, Shiva's instruction to Parvati and hence to all devotees subsequent to this, was to venerate Ganesha at the beginning of every ritual event, irrespective of whichever deity is being worshipped. Among the conservative followers of Sanatana Dharma (wisdom of the eternal truth), the practice still prevails (Courtwright 1985; Rocher 1991; Jayaram 2015).

Finding support in the work of Lawrence Cohen, Robert Brown (1991: 4) refers to Ganesha's celibate status as a characterization that emanates from south India. But Brown goes on to make a provocative statement that demonstrates more of a patronising attitude than a respectful one towards Hindus and their substantial scientific and economic achievements that rested significantly upon the belief systems to which he mockingly refers: 'It is true that Ganesha is not a womaniser as is his father, Shiva, or as is Visnu in his avatara Krsna'.

Brown's reference to 'Western realism' and the 'myths' of Ganesha must by its very content suggest that Hindu belief in Ganesha is unreal. And to refer to Shiva and Krishna, two deities who are so integral to the Hindu pantheon as 'womanizers' demonstrates in him an academic hollowness and a serious lack of sensitivity that goes beyond the bounds of 'freedom of expression'. Further flaws in Brown's analysis of Ganesha is demonstrated in his acknowledgement that Shiva had to act expeditiously to replace the severed head of Parvati's child from the very first sight of whatever living entity he encountered. Yet he goes on to suggest confusion on the instruction from Parvati about why it was the head of an elephant and not any other animal or human head. Couple these issues with Brown's failure to define the context in which he uses the word 'myth', and it tells a story about how patronising Brown is towards Hindu epics and their followers.

While there has been a tendency to reduce Ganesha worship to a cult-cum-tribalistic practice, its prevalence across the Asian continent precluded scholarship to reduce it to that level. Ganesha worship has spread across India, with its popularity especially among seafaring traders. It was the basis of their entrepreneurial ventures into Middle and Far Eastern countries. As the remover of obstacles Ganesha also became known as the God of success and knowledge. By removing obstacles from their paths towards positive outcomes to their businesses he endows them with the knowledge on how to conduct their businesses, consequently translating into a deity of success. Sea-faring traders from within and outside India had cottoned on to his veneration as well, but through the practice of Buddhism rather than Hinduism. In both religions Ganesha is known as 'Vinayaka' and in some places he is depicted as a dancing deity, a form often referred to in north India and Nepal as Nrtta Ganapati, and appears in a similar form in the Malayan archipelago's temple of Candi Sukuh. But the predominant emphasis on Ganesha is about him being a liberator of worldly attachments through an enlightenment that transcends the mundane and the materialistic, viz., Nityabuddha: eternal enlightenment. Ganesha worship spread to China from India, and from China to Japan around AD 806. In Japan Ganesha worship flourished under the Shingon sect, who referred to him as Kangiten. Since then more than 30 forms of Ganesha appear in Japanese style iconography (James Sanford 1991). But crucial to these forms were the allegorical messages that he was understood to represent, appoint that Brown (1991) and Courtwright (1985) also recognized.

THE RELEVANCE OF GANESHA WORSHIP IN HINDU RITUALISM

Courtwright (1985) had brought out the allegory in Ganesha worship more than Brown had done, especially in his recognition that although at the outset it might seem too esoteric to appreciate, a closer examination of the philosophy does 'add up in the end'. He mentions that beyond the esoteric dualistic form that he assumes Ganesha is viewed as the progenitor of the five basic elements, viz., earth, water, fire, air and ether, a point that is central to the *Ganesha Purana* (holy text). There is continuity in subsequent manifestations in scriptural texts to those who are regarded as *avatars* (God reincarnated in human form). A very similar utterance appears in Hinduism's major contemporary scriptural text, the *Bhagavad Gita.* In chapter 7, verse 4, Krishna[3] explains to Arjuna (the recipient of his message), that he is 'earth, water, fire, air, ether, mind, intellect and egoism: thus is my prakriti divided eightfold (*bhumirapo 'nalo vayuhkhammanorbuddhireva ca; ahamkaraiti yam me bhinnaprakrtirasthadha*) Swami Chidbavananda 1971: 417). Such multitudinous features are known to characterize Krishna which has given rise to an equal number of names and references.

In similar fashion, there are several names that are attributed to Ganesha too, viz., Ganesh, Ganapati, Vinayaka, Mahotkata, Gajanana, Ekadanta and Bapu, among others—often dependent upon region and levels of affection that devotees demonstrate towards the deity. Characterized by an elephant head, inflated stomach and a mouse as a vehicle, Ganesha enjoys a popular place in ritualism throughout the near and far east. Ritualism in Hinduism, especially in the Sanatanist tradition, is characterized by variation in form and ascendency in deity worship that often reflects the purpose, period and practice among followers of a particular deity. Ganesha's image is found throughout the neighbouring regions, including India, Nepal, Sri Lanka as well as Far eastern countries such as Thailand, Singapore, Indonesia, Bali, Taiwan and the Peoples' Republic of China. Each of the countries have adopted and adapted Ganesha worship according to localized understanding and economic and personal needs. While there is a common acceptance of his worship emanating from India, there is wide variation in the manner and means through which he is worshipped. Whatever form of worship of Ganesha takes, it is his popularity across class, caste and region that is axiomatic to the prevalent international academic scrutiny.

India's commercial and intellectual links with neighbouring and distant countries carried with it forms of worship that gradually grafted unto to the communities that were receptive to traders and scholars. Inclement weather conditions and the dangers associated with it, as well as the propensity to succeed in trade and intellectual exchanges, thrust forth Ganesha as a deity of choice for the varying qualities that are alleged to manifest from within him. In history's twists of irony, while Jainism and Buddhism, preached against elaborate forms of ritualism and deity worship, neither of these off-shoots from Hinduism have been able to ignore the popularity of Ganesha worship. The curiosity, persuasiveness and somewhat compelling attraction for a deity so strange, yet so appealing has presented itself as an unavoidable object of worship. While principally known as the 'Remover of obstacles', he is also honoured as the patron of arts and sciences and the deliverer of wisdom and intellect. In every human endeavour, according to believers in Ganesha worship, obstacles in some form, either expected or unexpected, are bound to appear. They can range from common expectations to unexpected hurdles that could render a project irrelevant and a loss of investment in time, money and energy. It is in these processes that believers tend to see a need to either offer a prayer or embark on a ritual that propitiates Ganesha in ways that hopefully wins his favour as remover of the obstacles that could otherwise render the task/s useless. There are several scriptural texts written in his honour and expounded in ways that that make his relevance and existence as realistic as any other prophet or deity of the major religions in the world. At least three principle texts that are dedicated to Ganesha depicts him in ways that are equivalent to a supremacy that is second to none. For instance, the *Ganesha Purana*, the *Mudgala Purana* and the *Ganapathi, Atharvashirsa* view Ganesha as an authentic manifestation of the absolute power we call 'God' and as the source of creation. In terms of Hindu scriptural discourses, life and time itself is periodized as four *yugas,* which are the cosmic eras that degenerate over time until the world finally dissipates due to human failures in morality and spiritual commitments. In each of these *yugas* Ganesha manifests in part animal-part anthropomorphic forms that are intended to guide humankind out of the quagmires of evil and confusion into forms of allegorical existences. The scriptures associated with him abound with his deeds of righteousness and with his abilities to guide and protect those who seek his guidance and protection, albeit in metaphysical contexts (Dhavalikar 1991; Narain 1991).

While Ganesha is seen by scholars as an important deity among the pantheon of Hindu deities there is more to what he represents. In the physical form that he is known, single tusked with an elephant head, and human body with a bloated yet pleasantly appealing belly, a philosophy of wider cosmic dimensions prevail. There are at least three dimensions from which belief in him has been sustained over the generations. The first is that as a remover of obstacles he is inclined to serve as a source of inspiration and protector to those who function on the mundane level of aspirations and materialistic goal setting. In this category of worshippers the limits are about faith and acquisition of material benefits in whatever endeavours individuals, families or businesses may embark upon. A positive end result is often a confirmation of faith and reinforcement of belief. The second is about philosophical inquiries that go beyond the form in which he is presented to humankind. The fact that he is an incarnate in various forms over different *yugas* demonstrates a manifest power that is beyond earthly understanding. In pursuit of knowledge about such forms and manifest powers, the goals are to study and learn about what they mean in terms of cosmic creation and what can be achieved outside of the mundane norms of ambition and materialistic needs. To this extent a personalized attempt is made to connect with the manifest power that has given rise to Ganesha rather than to identify with him in name and form. These attempts provide a basis for non-attachment to personal ambition and achievements with a goal to interrogate and understand what lies beyond observable criteria. The third is about renunciation of the world, where the first two criteria are surpassed through attainment of a higher form of detachment from name, form, ambition and material desires. Association with Ganesha at this level is about going beyond both the observable and experiential, to identify with that creative force that manifested as Ganesha and his different forms over the *yugas.*

ZEE TV AND THE PROJECTION OF GANESHA WORSHIP

Digital television services in South Africa is a recent phenomenon and Zee TV, was introduced several years after it. It is a station that has its productions made in Mumbai and beams them to numerous countries in the world, especially where there are segments of the Indian Diaspora. Against the background of the Hindu pantheon, the vastness of the country and diversity of worship patterns, it would be appropriate to briefly highlight at least some aspects about Hinduism in India and the diversity that characterizes it. While worship of Ganesha is near standard practice in Hindu ritualism throughout India, he is not the deity that reigns supreme throughout the country. Among the millions of manifestations that are believed to emanate from the one God, each region has entrenched preferences in the manifestation that they choose to worship. The levels of belief and worship are contingent upon individual levels of consciousness that shapes and determines how each relates to the relevant deity and what materialistic or spiritual benefit can be derived from such association. In northern India, especially in Uttar Pradesh and Bihar, the deities Ram and Krishna are most venerated, while in the eastern state of West Bengal Kali and Durga (female manifestations of God), are preferred deities. In the western state of Gujarat, God in female manifestation is equally significant, although here she is referred to as Ambe Ma and Santoshi Ma.

Mumbai, the capital of the western state of Maharashtra (south of Gujarat), is often projected as the epicentre of Ganesha worship in India. The state is renowned for the worship of Ganesha and his celestial father Bhagawan (Lord) Shiva. Worshippers of Shiva are referred to as 'Shaivaites' or followers of Shaivism. Propitiation of Ganesha is central to Shaivism although the worship of Ganesha is often conducted independently of Shiva. In Zee TV, a Hindi digital channel, deity propitiation on screen is usually Ganesha, affectionately referred to as *Bappa.* Several factors contribute towards viewer appreciation of Ganesha, if not enhancement in belief. Each of these factors is a form of persuasive curiosity that enlivens the belief in the deity, especially when prayers are done in the form of a strong appeal for either from an affliction or for material benefit of some sort. Three issues are highlighted here to demonstrate such persuasiveness and the impact that television programmes can have on viewers, viz., the architecture and layout of temples, actors' sincerity in prayer and almost immediate 'reward' to the prayer, and the familial socialization that is an integral part of the ritual process. Each of these issues are amplified below.

In the Zee TV entertainment episodes, temples dedicated to Ganesha are almost always situated on hill tops that require climbing stairs before reaching the shrine. The symbologies in the process of reaching the shrine and the architecture of the temples themselves extend beyond mere decorative designs or want of aesthetic creations. The arduous process of climbing stairs to reach the shrine is symbolic of the gradual process that is needed to acquire true devotion and knowledge of Ganesha. While Ganesha is viewed to be the creator and remover of obstacles in the paths towards success and stability in peoples' lives, there is a deeper metaphysical side towards belief in him. His physical form and sites of worship are no more than intermediaries towards a higher vision and goal of life, to which there is neither a beginning nor an end. The domes on the roofs of the temple and their pillars are symbolic of this timeless message. Ardent followers of Ganesha place no less emphasis on what he represents than the more popularly propitiated deities such as Krishna and Rama. For instance, in the *Bhagavad Gita*, Krishna refers to himself as an 'entity' beyond observable phenomena. Ganesha too is viewed in a similar vein:

> You are the visible: 'That Thou Art' (*tatvamasi*). You indeed produce the universe. You indeed sustain it. You indeed destroy it. You indeed are the all-pervading reality. You are the manifestation of the eternal self. The entire world is born from you. Through you the entire world is maintained. Through you the entire world is dissolved. The entire world returns to you again. You are earth, water, fire, air and space. (Courtright 1985: 252)

Acting and actors not only portray a story for the sake of entertainment, but they also convey social messages that have either intended or unintended consequences. Some of the images in fictional episodes that are purely for entertainment can carry in them profound messages that can serve as life-altering lessons for viewers. Acting is intended to convey to the viewership ordinary situations with an intensity that is convincing and persuasive to the point of making it emulative. In Zee TV programmes actors often take refuge in Ganesha, with positive results to earnesty earnings for solutions to problems. Going to temples and offerings of prayers in Zee TV programmes is almost always at a Ganesha Temple. At least two aspects in most programmes tend to surface, viz., the good characters making the appeal in deep conversational tones and the results inevitably positive, after measures of prolonged perseverance against evil characters. The home is always the site of action, the family is always at the centre of what prevails, and if they are about Hindu family dynamics, the deity is usually Ganesha. The moral of each episode is almost always the triumph of good over evil and the role of family and faith in resolving issues of personal differences and evil deeds and intentions.

Ritualism in most situations in the world is always about a sense of community as well national and ideological identity when a majority population observes such rituals. But in India it first emphasizes family in the broadest possible ways, especially the extended family in the sense of it being a three generation household that is genealogically related, characterized by a paternalistic hierarchal order. While Ganesha worship is about family bonding time, it is also to use the household as a platform to pray for familial success in education, entrepreneurial activities, peace within the home, staying together as a united extended family (*kutumb/parivar*) and being healed from sickness. As the programmes are played out over television, the fervour of family and togetherness is entrenched in ways that serve to reinforce the normative existence of extended families. Joint families too are a feature when parents are no longer alive. As two generation households where siblings, especially brothers reside under one roof, there is an equal sense of co-responsibility over each other and their respective nuclear families. Often the residence is an inheritance from parents whose expectations are not only about living together to demonstrate family unity, but to use the household as an institution to enculturate future generations into the entrenched practices of family traditions. In the state of Maharashtra Ganesha worship is a normative practice, and in Sanatanist Hindu households, Ganesha worship is always in the introductory part of every family and community ritual. Yet historically, there has been among the South African Indian diaspora a complacency to go beyond viewing him as 'remover of obstacles' to delve deeper into the philosophical messages that underpin his existence. The deities Rama and Krishna as creators of the Universe reigned supreme since the arrival of Indians in South Africa in 1860. Their philosophies of the impermanence of the body against the permanency of the soul, and love of God in the context of non-injury to others and strict discipline, especially in respect of mind control, has not as yet been popularly associated with Ganesha. Yet those who have adopted him as a representation of the manifest world view him as being bestowed with the purpose of conveying serious worshippers beyond the phenomenal world of materiality and duality. Ganesha to such worshippers is no less a deity than the more popular figures Rama and Krishna in the major epics of the *Ramayana* and *Mahabharata.*

SOME VIEWS AND RESPONSES FROM WORSHIPPERS OF GANESHA

While it is always been mandatory for the officiating priests in the Sanatan tradition to begin with obeisance to Ganesha, as the *Shiva Purana* suggests to devotees, there is still a tendency to view Ganesha in a restrictive sense. Yet among the more informed he is known to represent that primordial creative force for which both Rama and Krishna have become universally known. In an incident in the year 1990 I was witness to an astounding response to a question put to a Hindu monk by a specialist medical practitioner. It was common practice on a Sunday evening for close devotees of the religious institution to gather around the monk when the larger congregation took leave of the ashram after the weekly public service. The question to the monk was: 'Swamiji, what is the Hindu view on heart transplants'? An immediate spontaneous response emanated from his lips almost like a 'bolt of lightning', in a sharp and determined voice, that sent the group sitting around him into a stunned silence: 'Why is a heart transplant being made into such a big issue. We Hindus have already carried out a head transplant. Don't you believe in Ganesha? If you pray to him you must believe in him!' It was not just his authoritative voice that commanded a submission to his reply, but the conviction and seriousness with which he said it. It was for the first time that many who sat around him on a frequent basis got thinking about Ganesha on a more serious level than they ever did. None dared to ask a follow-up questions butcontinued to sit cross-legged in a manner of total submission. It was an awe-inspiring moment that somewhat re-confirmed the authenticity with which their spiritual *guru* spoke. It was from this point onwards that my curiosity in Ganesha grew and engendered within me a comparative urge to view the enthusiasm that devotees worshipped him and other deities.

The respective religious institution has the distinction of being an *ashram*, distinguishing it from a temple in that *ashrams* are centres for higher learning (of scriptural texts), while the former is a centre for ritual worship. Since the rise of *ashrams* in Durban in the 1950s, with the Ramakrishna Centre of South Africa being the first, the philosophical traditions associated with each deity was being ushered in at a significantly different level. Through the appointment of resident monks (*swamis*), the ritualism around deity worship on their respective days in the year is now by public services (mass) with discourses that transcend the narrow perceptions that prayer is for materialistic gains alone. In Durban, at least two other renowned centres, viz., the Divine Life Society and the Chinmayananda Mission observe Ganesh Chaturthi, i.e. the birthday of Ganesha, in the Hindu month of Bhadra, which falls between mid-August and mid-September. It is a period of fasting and rejoicing over a ten-day period that ends on Ananta-Chaturdasi, when specially constructed idols that serve as a medium of worship are immersed into the closest mass of water—either the sea, rivers or dams. As the most popular deity of the western Indian state of Maharashtra, Ganesha worship takes on the pomp and splendour that Christmas assumes on in predominantly Christianity countries, or Eid-ul-Fitr in Muslim countries. It remains their main festival of the year, overshadowed only by the festival of lights (Diwali: the celebration of light over darkness/good over evil), which has assumed wider national and international popularity.

The worship of Ganesha in major centres of worship assume on a specific framework in Durban—that is through mass services.

Since *ashrams* and their resident monks have reintroduced the higher philosophical aspects to their worship of Ganesha, temples too have begun to follow suit, especially since the 1990s. Mass services are constituted of *bhajans* and *kirtans* (religious songs of praise) including discourses that bring out both the relevance of prayer that addresses the afflictions and anxieties of people in their pursuits for a better life, as well as the benefits of a life of detachment and discipline for aspirants who have higher spiritual goals in life. While Ganesha is significant in the Hindu pantheon, his glorification is only beginning to take on a more widespread and popular appeal than it used to in Durban. In this instance Zee TV, largely among the middle classes that can afford digital satellite television, is playing a key role in popularizing the worship of Ganesha. In the course of talking to people about his worship, at least some of the statements serve to demonstrate the appeal he has among his followers and the meaning they attach to their belief in him:

> There is a quaint yet positive vibe about the name and form of Ganesha. Although unusual and possibly unacceptable as a real form for a deity, it is hard to ignore him, especially when you view so many millions of people throughout the world worshipping him. He is not only worshipped by Hindus in India, but also by Buddhists and Jains in other eastern countries. While the head of an elephant and the body of a man might not be convincing to the non-Hindu mind, there is an appeal to his composure, to the philosophy that has become known through him, and the temples that are dedicated to him. Ganesha is alive for me as any other living God in this world. I believe in him.
>
> Although we know about Ganesha prayers and the fact that we start all prayers by reciting holy verses to him, we never really took him as real as we do now. I think watching Zee TV has made us realize his importance to us as Hindus. When we watch these Bollywood soapies and how sincerely the actors pray to Ganesha, they make it look so real . . . Of course we know that soapies are only entertainment, but then they do have lessons to teach us too! But above all Ganesha is a real God to us Hindus. He is being made all the more real on television . . . and it is a real pleasure to watch how he is worshipped on screen. . . . It has had a definite influence on me and my family for sure . . . I now believe in him even more than I used to.
>
> Ganesha is more than that dualistic form that you see in pictures and

sculptures. Not only is his half elephant and half man formation a miracle of the Almighty, but he is also a remover of the obstacles towards God realization. People think too often of Ganesha as a remover of obstacles for material benefit only. But he is just as much a path to the ultimate realty as Lord Rama or Lord Krishna is. People will see in Ganesha whatever they wish to see in him . . . yes his name and form is an easy target for those who want to find fault with what Hindus believe in. But he is God almighty manifest, and he is ultimately beyond name, form and consciousness. God takes whatever form he wishes to take, and Ganesha is one of them. One can get out of Ganesha whatever they want, but they must have faith in him first . . . Hindus in South Africa are beginning to realize who and what he really is.

Each of the responses above is not only distinctly favourable towards Ganesha worship, but they bring out a significant amount of information that contributes towards an extensive and intensive insight into the practice in Durban. The responses are only 3 out of 20 recorded interviews. While the veracity of the information might be contested the fact that they were random interviews and the responses were spontaneous, indicates a fair measure of how worshippers of Ganesha view their beliefs in him. There were two significant aspects of the information that is recorded above. First, all three of the respondents were professionals: one a teacher, one a medical specialist, and one a civil engineer. And second, they spoke about a form of worship that would be either rather esoteric or unacceptable to people who are generally critical about something that would fall out of their realm of worship, or about what modern science cannot verify. At least three issues emerge out of the responses, viz., that Ganesha worship is not restricted either to India or its diaspora only, in that he is worshipped throughout the far-eastern countries as well; that despite his form with an elephant head and a human body, he still commands an appeal that cuts across class and caste barriers; and that the form that he appears in is not the end-all of what he represents. The philosophy that embraces his being is no less metaphysical than what the other major Hindu scriptures have to offer. There was belief and acceptance in his existence as well as in the spiritual lessons that his form and teachings has to offer. Beyond the three responses above, each of the twenty respondents were emphatic about their belief in Ganesha, albeit in terms of their levels of consciousness.

At least six of the twenty respondents saw Ganesha strictly in terms of him being a remover of obstacles in their pursuits for their children's education, family businesses and sickness within the household. Their beliefs were distinctively restricted to the mundane and materialistic, and devoid of the metaphysical plane at which the more discerning devotees had ventured to learn about him. To the six respondents obeisance to Ganesha was largely about their venerating him on Ganesh Chaturthi and remembering him for how he rewards devotees in their prayers to him. The prevalence of a higher philosophy was immaterial and literally unknown to them. In their quest for personal and family upliftment, Ganesha is there 'for the asking', and as vulnerable, defenceless human beings, can only remain meek and humble devotees. Grasping that metaphysical reality beyond his anthropomorphic dimensions was often articulated as beyond the boundaries of their cognitive and mental planes. He was to be understood simply as a 'giver of boons' and one whose greatness is not fathomable. There is the common view that against the uncertainties and risks that prevail in the world Ganesha remains as a protector through a divinity that transcends the limits of human understanding.

CONCLUSION

There are at least three issues that emerge from the discussion above: the seriousness and ambiguities of academic scholarship on Ganesha worship, the spread of a deity across countries in Asia, and the role that television can play in enhancing the meaning of worship of a deity who would otherwise be kept a secretive affair because it is so indefensible to the lay person. On the first issue, viz. the seriousness and ambiguities of scholarship on Ganesha, a major factor here is the ethos of Western education and the impact that scientific inquiry has on people's ability to relate to what is observable and believable, and what is esoteric and mythical to irrational. While Courtwright wrote on Ganesha in an allegedly offensive way, he responded to those who threatened him subsequent to his book being published in ways that could be almost humbling. By stating that the furtherance of scholarship on Ganesha is guided by him standing at the door of learning and blocking the obstacles to freedom of inquiry could be understood as an attempt at endearment towards people who worship Ganesha. But it could also be a subtle form of patronizing. The ambiguity here is taken further when Brown labels Shiva and Krishna as 'womanizers'—a term that could have him charged for blasphemy and possibly a price on his life if it were hurled at another religion.

But religions of the East are reputed to deal with criticism and blasphemous taunting with a greater degree of understanding and patience than religions from other parts of the world. This is why defending belief in Ganesha through threats of violence was restricted to an insignificant minority. And it is also the reason why (on the second issue) the spread of Ganesha worship throughout Asia, had an appeal. It is strange and unconvincing on the one hand, yet laden with curiosity and appeal on the other hand. It is for this reason that almost every country in South and Southeast Asia has taken to his veneration. These are countries that once dominated world trade, sank into relegated positions in the global economy and are beginning to resurface as major world players in significant ways, almost to the point of displacing contemporary Western hegemonic forces. Many in Asia who choose to remain as Ganesha worshippers believe that their ascendancy towards more successful business with the outside world is dependent upon their propitiation of and faith in him.

The third issue is about the role of television in enhancing what people believe in and reshaping their public responses to it. The interviews with Hindus in Durban provide a glimpse into the role that a channel such as Zee TV in reaffirming public belief in a deity that is too unnatural for the non-Hindu or scientific mind to accept as real. Hindus in South Africa have come long way since their early days of disorganization as indentured labourers and passenger Indians. The rise or organized religion among Hindus has brought about a commendable level of coherence in and stability in the paths that each individual wishes to choose. In promoting Ganesha as a key deity in most of its entertainment programmes Zee TV is indirectly reinforcing belief and propitiation of a deity that would otherwise not surface in ways that they are now surfacing. In Durban Ganesha worship is increasing to the level that other scriptural texts such as the *Ramayana* and the *Bhagavad Gita* currently enjoy prominence. If it does acquire a similar status in South Africa among Hindus then popular entertainment through Zee TV would have played a significant role in that.

NOTES

1. Bhojpuri is a dialect of Hindi. Most indentured labourers who came to South Africa were of south Indian background.
2. The term could have been easily with reference to Rudra who often led the armies of the gods. So, caution is needed with such comments.
3. More affectionately known as Lord/'Bhagawan Sri' Krishna.

REFERENCES

Brown, Robert L., 'Introduction', in Robert L. Brown (ed.), *Ganesha: Studies of an Asian God,* New York: State University of New York Press, 1991.

Cohen Lawrence, 'The Wives of Ganesha', in Brown (ed.), *Ganesha: Studies of an Asian God,* ibid., pp. 115-40.

Courtright, Paul B., *Ganesha: Lord of Obstacles, Lord of Beginnings,* Oxford: Oxford University Press, 1985.

Dhavalikar M.K., 'Ganesha: Myth And Reality', in Brown (ed.), *Ganesha: Studies of an Asian God,* op. cit., pp. 49-68.

Jayaram, V. Ganesha, http://www.hinduwebsite.com/hinduism/ganesha.asp (on accessed 26 June 2015).

Lancaster Lewis L., 'Ganesha in China: Methods of Transforming the Demonic', in Brown (ed.), *Ganesha: Studies of an Asian God,* op. cit., pp. 277-86.

Ludo Rocher, 'Ganesha's Rise to Prominence in Sanskritic Literature', in Brown (ed.), *Ganesha: Studies of an Asian God,* op. cit., pp. 69-84.

Narain, A.K., 'Ganesha: A Protohistory of the Idwa and the Icon', in Brown (ed.), *Ganesha: Studies of an Asian God,* op. cit., pp. 19-48.

Sanford James L., 'Literary Aspects of Japan's Dual-Ganesha Cult', in Brown (ed.), *Ganesha:* Studies of an *Asian God,* op. cit., pp. 287-336.

Swami Chidbhavananda, *The Bhagavad Gita,* Sri Ramakrishna Tapovan (Publication Section). Madras State, 1971.

CHAPTER 11

The Contributions of Pandit Nardev Vedalankar to Hinduism in South Africa

KALPANA HIRALAL

INTRODUCTION

The arrival of indentured and later free or 'passenger' Indians inevitably laid the foundations of permanent settlement of Indians in South Africa. Both indentured and free Indians were heterogeneous in terms of their language, ethnic groups and religion. The indentured immigrants were predominantly Hindus, who constituted 90 per cent of the labouring immigrants. Migration did not deter some immigrants from practising their religion. This often took the form of customary worship by building small temples and shrines (Maxwell, Diesel and Naidoo 1995: 179). However, Hinduism was far from structured and lacked a sense of coherency in beliefs and rituals. Hindu missionaries from India played a pivotal role in instilling renewed faith in Hinduism amongst the Indians in South Africa at the turn of the last century. In South African Indian historiography, the contribution of Hindu missionaries to Hinduism has received scant attention, in particular the role of Pandit Nardev Vedalankar. Existing studies have sought to locate their discussions within a historical and contemporary perspective in the context of identity, ethnicity, rituals and beliefs (Kuper 1960; Diesel 1992; Naidoo 1992; Diesel and Maxwell 1993; Kumar 2013). Diesel and Maxwell (1983) in their study on Hinduism in South Africa focus on the beliefs and practices common to all Hindus, and those aspects which distinguish the main groups thus providing a deeper insight into the practice of the religion. Kumar (2013) maps out how Hinduism flourished within the last 150 years in South Africa, and how Hindu beliefs and practices were shaped by socio-economic and political conditions. The study also documents the survival mechanism of immigrants and their descendants in the migration process. Naidoo (1992) examines the structure and functions of the Arya Samaj movement in South Africa in the context of Swami Dayanand. His work is significant because it sheds light on the role of Hindu missionaries and their strong influence in religious propagation in South Africa. While the above studies are significant in understanding the complex nature of Hinduism both from a historical and contemporary perspective, there have been no biographical accounts of the contributions of Pandit Nardev Vedalankar to Hinduism and his promotion of the Hindi and Gujarati languages in South Africa. This paper maps out the contributions of Pandit Nardev Vedalankar, one of the pioneers of Hinduism in South Africa. Hindu religion at the turn of the century was promoted and spearheaded by several leading teachers and scholars. Pandit Vedalankar was amongst its leading proponents. During his stay in South Africa, the principles of the Arya Samaj and Hinduism became firmly rooted in South Africa. He promoted the Hindu religion and language in South Africa by giving it structure, clarity and meaning. Ordinary Hindus could identify with its tenets and promote their religion within the home. He also sought to promote religious unity amongst the various Hindu ethnic groups. This paper, using a biographical narrative, documents the contributions of Pandit Nardev Vedalankar to Hinduism and argues that Hindu missionaries played a significant role in shaping and defining religiosity in the diaspora.

Religion and diaspora have become significant research themes over the past few decades. Some scholars have highlighted the intersections of religion and diaspora in that it provides an insight into 'general patterns of religious transformation' and assimilation (Vertovec 2000: 8). Ninian Smart has argued that in Hinduism, issues such as yoga, priests, *bhakti* (devotion), pilgrimage, temple rituals and practice of astrology which 'are woven together into the complicated fabric of Hinduism in India', do not travel equally to new environments (Smart 1999: 424 cited in Vertovec 2000: 9). According to Robin Cohen, religions are 'cognate' to diasporas and they 'can provide additional cement to bind a diasporic consciousness' (cited in Vertovec 2000: 10). Vertovec (2000) argues that migration often leads to the modification of social organization and religious practice (2000: 13). This paper locates its discussion within the above theoretical framework and illustrates how Hinduism in South Africa evolved, and the role played by religious scholars (in particular, Pandit Nardev Vedalankar) in shaping and defining early religious identities in South Africa.

RELIGIOUS AWAKENING IN SOUTH AFRICA

Hindu missionaries from India played a significant role in revitalizing Hinduism in the diaspora, particularly in places such as South and East Africa, Mauritius, Fiji, Trinidad, Guyana and Suriname. This was largely through the efforts of the reform movement known as the Arya Samaj (Society of Righteous). According to Kelly (1991), in the late 1920s 'Fiji's Arya Samaj was dynamic, aggressive, accomplished, and promising. It was an effective organizer of counter-Christian school-building projects' (1991: 121). This organization was founded in India at the turn of the last century by Swami Dayananda Sarasvati which sought to revitalise Hindus to Vedic-based teachings. The Samaj commenced its missionary work among its people as early as 1905 in India and abroad. According to van der Veer (2001: 50-2), the Samaj was responding to the challenges of British rule and counteracting Christian influences. The Samaj stressed the importance of the text as opposed to priests, and appealed to the Hindu public regardless of caste distinctions. Among its most notable reformer and educationists was Bhai Parmanand, who arrived in South Africa on 5 August 1905 on behalf of the Arya Samaj and the Dayanand Anglo-Vedic College. He was an eloquent multilingual speaker, fluent in both English and Hindi. During his South African tour, he gave a series of talks and lectures on 'Practical Religion' and 'The Work of the Arya Samaj' in Natal, Cape Town and Johannesburg (*Indian Opinion*, 2 October 1905, 4 November 1905, 11 November 1905; Maxwell, Diesel and Naidoo 1995: 192). In Boksburg in the Transvaal, the local reception committee gave him a warm reception, 'We, the undersigned, on behalf of the reception committee at Boksburg, extend to you a hearty welcome to this town. We are most beholden to you for having spared the time to visit us. We pray that God may long spare you to continue the noble work of self-sacrifice which, in common with the band of other workers in connection with the Arya Samaj, you have commenced' (*Indian Opinion*, 25 November 1905). Bhai Parmanand left South Africa in December 1905. He was followed by Swami Shankeranand in October 1908. *Indian Opinion* reported his arrival as follows, 'The arrival of Swami Shankeranand in South Africa has created a stir among the Hindus in particular and Indians in general. The former rejoice over the fact that renowned religious preacher has travelled to South Africa to impart religious instruction. All the other Indians rejoice to see in their midst a distinguished Indian scholar' (*Indian Opinion*, 10 October 1908). Like Bhai Parmanand, he was a good orator and believed that his duty was to preach the essence of Hinduism. Local European missionaries also attended his lectures. In 1908, at a large gathering of devotees in Durban, there were several European members of the Theosophical Society who were present (*Indian Opinion*, 10 October 1908). During his stay in South Africa he made an indelible contribution to reawakening Hinduism. He delivered discourses on Hindu culture, religion, the importance of education and the vernacular languages. It was largely through their efforts that the Arya Samaj movement became a vibrant institution in South Africa. However, Swami Shankeranand during his visit in South Africa was also subject to discriminatory treatment. In 1909, he boarded a Pietermaritzburg tram car on his way to the railway station. The Swami took a seat inside the car and was later 'rudely ordered out of the car' (*Indian Opinion*, 27 March 1909). During his stay in Natal, the Swami also acted as a peace-maker amongst members of the Tamil community. A dispute arose between the Hindu Young Men's Society—V.K. Sabbah, C. Nulliah, V.R. Pillay, R.S. Pillay, Karappana Moodley, A.S. Padyachee, M.K. Pillay and Mooruga Chetty (*Indian Opinion*, 3 April 1909).

The early religious reformers who arrived in South Africa at the turn of the century can be perceived as long-term and short-term proponents of Hinduism. Bhai Parmanand and Swami Shankeranand, played a significant role in spearheading Hinduism in South Africa, but their stay was temporary. They came for several months or years at a time, but later returned to India. During their stay, they propagated Hinduism via lectures, talks and performing rituals. Others, like Pandit Nardev Vedalankar and Swami Bhawani Dayal, remained in the country for longer periods, and found permanent homes in South Africa. They played a significant role in imparting religious education among the Indians and succeeded in training people to perform religious ceremonies. These missionaries also sought to promote languages such as Hindi, Sanskrit and Gujarati thereby highlighting the importance of mother-tongue languages. Pandit Vedalankar became a household name for many South Africans from the 1950s onwards. His tireless efforts to promote the Hindi and Gujarati languages alongside his teachings of Hinduism earned him both national and international recognition for promoting religious unity (*Veda Jyoti*, 1992: 28-9).

EARLY LIFE

Pandit Vedalankar was born on 17 November 1913 in a village called Tundi in Surat in Gujarat. His childhood name was Nanubhai Narothambhai which changed to Nardevbhai Vedalankar when he graduated at the Gurukul Kangdi, Haridwar, India. He was affectionately called 'Panditji' in South Africa. His co-workers called him 'Bhaiji', and so did his children. His father was Shri Narotambhai Shankarji—a book keeper. His mother, Jamnabhen, died while he was still in school. After his graduation Pandit Nardev enrolled at the Wardha Hindi Prachar Samiti for specialized training in Hindi—an institute established by Gandhi. He later became the *acharya* of the Hindu Pracharak Mandal in Surat, supervising 80 teachers on a part-time basis (*Hindi News*, 2014). In 1944 he married Jaywantibhen, with whom he had seven children. He arrived in South Africa on 24 November 1947 to teach Gujarati to the local Gujarati community. At the time of Pandit Vedalankar's arrival, the political climate of South Africa after the war years was particularly volatile. Rising food prices, low wages, and shortages of food and housing led to worker militancy and radicalism and the politicization of Indian, African and coloured communities. In the 1940s anti-Indianism was rife. In 1946 the Asiatic Land Tenure and Indian Representation Act, dubbed the 'Ghetto Act', as it restricted Indian land purchases in 'controlled' areas which were dominated by whites. Both the Transvaal Indian Congress and the Natal Indian Congress rejected the Act and embarked on passive resistance between 1946 and 1948 (Reddy and Meer 1996: 40-6). It was against this political and social climate that Pandit Nardev Vadalankar sought to promote religious unity and propagate Hinduism. This was certainly no easy task.

By the 1940s, a Gujarati population had already settled in South Africa. Many of the early Gujarati Hindus arrived in the early years of the century. The stringent immigration laws—particularly after 1913 (which affected the free Indians, in particular, the Gujarati-speaking Hindus and Muslims)—forced many of them to bring their families across to Natal from the 1930s onwards (Hiralal 2013). There was a strong desire amongst the local Gujarati population to promote their vernacular language. Some were influenced by Gandhi's philosophy with regard to mother-tongue language,

> It has always been my conviction that Indian parents who train their children to think and talk in English from their infancy betray their children and their country. They deprive them of their social and spiritual heritage of the nation, and render them to that extent unfit for the service of the country. Having these convictions I made a point of always talking to my children in Gujarati. . . . This happened about twenty years ago (1905) and my convictions have only deepened with experience. (Gandhi 1945: 381)

Pandit Vedalankar arrived at the invitation of the Surat Hindu Educational Society. This society was established in 1933 by the Surat Hindu Association with the aim of establishing a Surat Hindu Gujarati School. The Gujarati school was located in central Durban where the vast majority of Gujarati Hindus resided. Pandit Vedalankar formalized the school with a structured syllabi and examination provisions for classes from one to seven (Desai 1997: 122).

On arrival to Natal, Pandit Vedalankar discovered that while Hindi was well known, it was not spoken fluently by the local Indian population. There were no Hindi schools, structured syllabi or trained teachers. However, prior to Pandit Vedalankar's arrival, attempts were made to promote the Hindi language—largely through the efforts of a prominent colonial born Vedic scholar, Swami Bhawani Dayal. Dayal was disillusioned that the local Indians in Natal were more interested in speaking and writing in English rather than Hindi. To counteract this, he decided to promote the Hindi language in the province. He founded a Hindi Pracharini Sabha, a Hindi Night School and a Hindi Football Club in 1914 at Germiston. The Hindi Pracharini Sabha met every Sunday and discussions were held in Hindi. In 1916, he held the first 'Hindi Literacy Conference' in Ladysmith (Agrawal 1939: 162-4). The Arya Patinidhi Sabha (APS) also played an important role in promoting the Hindi language. The APS was one of the main Hindu organizations in Natal at the time. The APS was established on 22 February 1925. Prior to 1925, there were no central organizations coordinating the activities of several Arya Samajes that were established in Natal. The APS became the central Hindu body in Natal that sought to co-ordinate the social and cultural aspects of the Hindus in Natal. The APS sought to promote Hinduism and Vedic culture in South Africa by inviting highly trained scholars and priests from India to visit South Africa. Amongst them was Professor Ralaram from Hoshiarpur, India who arrived in 1931 and gave a series of lectures on Vedic religion in Cape Town, Transvaal and Natal. He was followed by Pandit Mehta Jaimini, a Vedic missionary who arrived in South Africa in 1934 (*Veda Jyoti*, 1992: 29-30). While the visiting scholars and priests played an important role in informing and educating the local Hindus in Vedic culture, Hindi as a spoken language still lagged behind.

Besides the language issue, another challenge facing the Hindu community at the time was the lack of unity among the groups. In the 1940s the various linguistic groups, such as the Gujarati, Hindi, Tamil and Telugus worked and socialized in isolation. Inter-linguistic and inter-caste marriages were largely forbidden. Pandit

Vedalankar on arrival began to associate with the South African Gujarati Maha Sabha and became aware of the visible Hindu divide in the community. However, Pandit Vedalankar was a visionary, his outlook on religion was broad and rational. In order to promote unity amongst the various linguistic groups he used religious discourses to show commonality prevailing in Hinduism. For example, during religious festivals such as Deepavali, Ram Navami and Krishna Jayanti, his lectures highlighted the common tenets of Hinduism and that irrespective of language groupings, all Hindus were equal and united by a common belief. His discourses provided in many ways religious awakening for many Hindu groups in South Africa. Both the Arya Samaj and the Sanatan Dharma organizations—who were often at loggerheads with each other at the time—invited Pandit Vedalankar to address them. He subsequently succeeded in uniting these two groups (*Veda Jyoti*, 1992: 123-4).

One of the key issues he addressed was the declining status of the Hindi language. With the assistance of the APS he organized a Hindi conference between 24 and 25 April 1948. The conference was significant because it culminated in the formation of the Hindi Shiksha Sangh (HSS) in 1948, wherein Pandit Vedalankar was appointed first President. Pandit Vedalankar's sterling work in promoting the Hindi language within the Sangh earned him the title 'Father of Hindi Shiksha Sangh' (*Veda Jyoti*, 1992: 29-31).

FORMATION OF HINDI SHIKSHA SANGH

Under the leadership of Pandit Vedalankar, the HSS played an important role in propagating the Hindi language. Hindi became more centralized and coordinated in the context of syllabi and written examinations. Most Hindi schools at the time lacked a uniform Hindi syllabi, teaching methodologies and examination systems. Pandit Vedalankar sought to rectify this. First, he went on a promotional tour of Natal, urging local Hindus to learn the language, and second, he advocated religious unity by appealing to local Hindu organizations to set aside their differences and work collectively to promote Vedic culture and the Hindi language. Subsequently by 1948, 35 institutions were affiliated with the HSS

(*Veda Jyoti*, 1992: 93). Pandit Vedalankar believed that for Hindi to survive as a language it was imperative that Hindi teachers had a proper training programme that would equip them with the necessary teaching skills. Many teachers at the Hindi schools in Natal at the time were not adequately qualified. To rectify this, Pandit Vedalankar conducted Hindi Teachers Classes with the assistance of Pandit Jugmohan (Vidyarathan). In 1948, 22 of his students wrote the international examination, the Pravesh Examinations set by the Rashtrabhasha Prachar Samiti, Wardha in India (South African Gujarati Maha Parishad: Secretarial Report, SD File 547/126; *Veda Jyoti*, 1992: 93). The HSS prepared a uniform syllabus and examination system at all Hindi schools. By 1983 there were 45 Hindi schools attended by 5-7 per cent school-going children. The HSS also set up its own Examination Board. It conducted examinations from Standard II (*Prathmik* level) up to Standard X (*Kovid*). They were modelled under the Rashtrabhasha Prachar Samiti of India. There were also adult education classes in many areas in Natal. They were conducted for the Rashtrabhasha Prachar Samiti, of India. Since 1948, classes for these examinations were conducted from Std. IV to X level. About 100 men and women wrote these examinations annually. The Std. X examination was called the *Kovid* which was equivalent to the Hindi Matriculation Examination. The *Kovid* entailed four 3-hour papers and also an oral examination. The examination papers were sent to Wardha, India, where they were graded. Certificates from India were awarded to successful candidates. Provision was also made for higher education in Hindi. After the *Kovid* there was the *Rashtra-bhasha Ratna* examination, which was equivalent to a Degree (South African Gujarati Maha Parishad: Secretarial Report, SD File 547/126; *Veda Jyoti*, 1992: 93). By 1983, there were six men and women from South Africa who obtained the *Ratna*, and 51 obtained the *Kovid* examination. A total of 5041 candidates wrote the Wardha examinations at various centres in South Africa since its inception. Pandit Vedalankar also initiated part-time Hindi classes at the ML Sultan Technikon between 1959 and 1980. Other activities of the HSS which sought to popularize Hindi included eisteddfods, speech contests, debates and poetry. In 1950, the HSS launched a Hindi debate competition in memory of Swami Bhawani Dayal and the Hindi Eisteddfod. The latter consisted of play acting, speech-making, Veda, *Gita*, *Ramayana* and poetry recitals, singing and dancing—all aimed at promoting Hindi and Hinduism, particularly among the youth. In 1958, as a means of popularizing Hindi, the HSS embarked on a 17-day tour of Natal and the Transvaal with the play *Raj Tyag*. Other plays staged were *Sita Haran*, *Taimur Ka Haar* and *Bimar Ka Elaaj* (*Veda Jyoti*, 1992: 93).

VEDA NIKETAN

In 1965, Pandit Vedalankar was instrumental in the formation of the Veda Niketan (VN), a sub-committee of the APS. The VN was established to propagate the Vedic religion and philosophy and Pandit Vedalankar was at its helm for 20 years between 1965 and 1985. His passion for the Vedic scriptures, his many publications and lecture talks played an important role in making South Africa a leading proponent of Vedic teachings globally. In 1973, S. Chotai, former president of the Arya Pratinidhi Sabha, stated, 'The success of the Veda Niketan has depended very largely on the inexhaustible fund of energy and the organizational ability with which Pandit Nardev Vedalankar is endowed. His persuasive approach has brought willing and ready response financially from benefactors in the community' (*Veda Jyoti*, 1992: 53). The Veda Niketan promoted Vedic teachings through the publication of literature and conducted religious examinations, both in English and Hindi. Pandit Vedalankar had a passion for reading and writing. His daughter, Jyoti Desai recalls, 'When I was young, I woke up at night to find my dad busy writing at his table. I always wondered what he wrote about all the time. At that time I did not realize that one day I would be studying his great works, *The Spiritual Teachings of Hinduism*, and later, the *Shastra Navanitam*' (*Hindi News*: South Africa: August 2014). Pandit Vedalankar's publications played a significant role in generating awareness about Hinduism. For example, his book *Elementary Teachings of Hinduism* and *Basic Teachings of Hinduism* became very popular both in South Africa and abroad. It was circulated in North America by the Arya Samaj Foundation of

North America. His books explained the Vedic teachings in simple terms, clearly defining and explaining concepts of Hinduism, such as the nature of *Dharma*, God, and the significance of prayer (Khorana 1993: 405-6). Another publication, *Aryan Prayer,* was published in Durban in 1954. It was edited and co-compiled with S. Chotai. A revised edition was printed in 1968 and by 1983 over 60,000 copies were printed and distributed. The prayer book provided Hindus with basic guidelines as to how to conduct *sandhya, hawan* and other rituals. It was multilingual, printed in Hindi, Sanskrit and English, thereby creating greater accessibility to Hindus, unfamiliar with Hindi or Sanskrit as a language. The book was important in that it provided Hindus with uniformity in conducting religious prayers in times of festivals and death. These publications were widely circulated not just in South Africa, but many areas of the Indian diaspora such as Central and East Africa, Fiji, Mauritius, United Kingdom, Trinidad, Guyana, Suriname and the United States of America (*Veda Jyoti,* 1992: 53-4). Another book titled *Religious Awakening in South Africa* provided a historical account of the Hindu religious movement in South Africa between 1901 and 1950. In 1975 Pandit Vedalankar co-authored a book with M. Somera titled *Arya Samaj and Indians Abroad,* mapping the socio-cultural and religious developments of the Indian diaspora (*Veda Jyoti,* 1992: 55). Another milestone publication co-authored by Pandit Vedarachaspati and Dr. Sureshkumar Vidyalankar of India, was the *Concise Study of Hindu Scriptures* (Shastra Navanitam). The book aimed to provide a Vedic perspective of Hinduism in English. Most publications on Hinduism at the time provided a Western-oriented version of Hinduism. This publication was significant because it provided an 'insider's' view of Hinduism. Swami Sahajananda of the Divine Life Society of South Africa commended Pandit Vedalankar for conscientizing the Hindu community in the tenets of the Vedic philosophy, 'Panditji (Nardev Vedalankar) is to be warmly congratulated for his great labour of love in preparing this volume. It should find a place in every Hindu home. Many Westerners are eager to know more about Hinduism. This compilation should fulfil that need' (*Veda Jyoti,* 1992: 55). The book contained 512 pages with extracts from the Vedas, selected texts from the Upanishads, *Bhagavad Gita*, *Ramayana*, *Mahabharata* and *Manusmriti* (*Veda Jyoti*, 1992: 55). Professor G.C. Oosthuizen, a former academic at the University of Durban-Westville stated, 'The intelligent reader, whatever his religious background may be, could benefit from reading this book. One gets to the essence of Hinduism. . . . The material has been well selected and excellently introduced' (*Veda Jyoti*, 1992: 55). Pandit Vedalankar was also instrumental in launching the first edition of the monthly journal *Veda Jyoti* in 1984. He played a key role in its editorial and widespread readership.

FORMATION OF THE ACADEMY OF VEDIC PRIESTS (VEDIC PURHOHIT MANDAL)

Prior to the formation of the Vedic Priest Academy of South Africa there was no uniformity in the manner in which religious ceremonies were conducted. Some priests were not familiar with *mantras* and correct procedures of performing religious rituals. Vedic sacraments and *hawan* ceremonies were initiated by Swami Shankeranand, and later propagated by Swami Bhawani Dayal. However, there was no official body that coordinated the activities of the priests. Pandit Vedalankar realized the importance of formulating a uniform code of religious procedures which all priests affiliated to the APS could follow. He subsequently founded the Vedic Priest Academy in 1952. It trained young men and women seeking to enter priesthood with religious instruction and the correct procedures in conducting religious prayers. Workshops and religious discourses were regularly held. Students were tutored for the 'Siddhanta Ratna' examination based on the syllabus prepared by the Sarvadeshik Arya Pratinidhi Sabha, New Delhi. Students were also given oral examinations for the correct pronunciation of the Vedic *mantras* and a practical test on conducting religious ceremonies. Successful candidates received a certificate and a gown, which became a uniform dress code for any Vedic priest when conducting prayers. The Academy was also open to female priests. In 1975, of the 25 successful candidates, five were women. The first batch of women to become Vedic priests were P. Nanackchand, C. Padarath, D.

Sewpaul, T. Suknundan and D. Sukram (*Veda Jyoti*, 1992: 65-7). By the 1980s the Vedic Priest Academy was the only institution in South Africa that provided theoretical and practical training to Vedic priests (ibid.).

PROMOTING GUJARATI UNITY AND LANGUAGE

Pandit Vedalankar played a key role in promoting unity amongst the Gujarati community. The latter were divided internally along caste, class and regional origins. During the early days there was very little socialization amongst the Gujaratis who originated from Kathiawad and Surat. Hence this division between the Surtis and Kathiawadis was known as the 'Great Gujarati Divide' (Hiralal 2014: 66). Pandit Nardev keen on bridging the divide and forging Gujarati unity called upon members of the community to work towards this goal. Pandit Vedalankar's efforts gave rise to the formation of the South African Gujarati Maha Parishad in 1975, which sought to unite all Gujaratis under one national body to promote their language and culture (Hiralal 2014: 69.) Pandit Vedalankar also played a significant role in the promotion of the Gujarati language. As stated earlier in the paper, Pandit Vedalankar arrived at the invitation of the Surat Hindu Educational Society in 1947. There was a strong desire among the local Gujarati population to promote the Gujarati language in Natal. In fact, it became a 'priority' for the community, and between 1932 and 1960, about 90 per cent of the school-going children in the Gujarati community received mother-tongue education (Desai 1997: 120). Much of the success of the Gujarati schools must be attributed to Pandit Vedalankar. He ran a thriving Gujarati school for many decades at the Bharat Hall, in central Durban, which was the largest of its kind, comparatively to the other mother-tongue languages, such as Tamil and Telugu. This was noticeable in terms of its structured curriculum, teaching and assessment methods. There was at least one India-trained Gujarati teacher in every school. Between 1953 and 1983, approximately 20 teachers from India came from Gujarat (South African Gujarati Maha Parishad, SD File 547/122). Between 1950 and 1962, student enrolment at Gujarati schools averaged 950, and between 1960 and 1965, 80 per cent of school-going children received education in Gujarati (*Veda Jyoti*, 1992: 126; South African Gujarati Maha Parishad, SD File 547/122). In the 1950s, political setbacks did not deter the promotion of the Gujarati language. This was largely due to the initiative and leadership that Pandit Vedalankar provided to the community in Natal. For example, the passing of the Group Areas Act of 1950 by the Nationalist Party created residential segregation among the various racial groups in South Africa. The Gujarati community, many of whom resided in central Durban, were forced to relocate to the outskirts of town in places such as Reservoir Hills, Clare Estate, Effingham Heights and Overport. A similar situation developed in the Transvaal in the period of 1960-75. Hundreds of Indians were forced to leave central Johannesburg and re-settle in Lenasia (South African Gujarati Maha Parishad: Secretarial Report, SD File 547/126) However, Pandit Vedalankar, realizing the implications of residential resettlement on the Gujarati language, called upon the two major Gujarati organizations—Surat Hindu Association and the Kathiawad Hindu Seva Samaj to assist in establishing Gujarati schools in the new areas.

Thus, by the 1970s, all the major centres of Gujarati settlement had their own Gujarati schools. In 1983, there were approximately 25 Gujarati schools existing in South Africa (South African Gujarati Maha Parishad, SD File 547/122). Pandit Vedalankar also founded the Gujarati National Eisteddfod under the aegis of the South African Gujarati Parishad. It was an important platform to promote and nurture the Gujarati language and cultural identity (Desai 1997: 134; *Fiat Lux* 1983: 30; *Samachar* 1980: 6; South African Gujarati Maha Parishad, SD File 547/122; *Samarpan,* Pandit Nardev Vedalankar, November, 1988: 37). Pandit Vedalankar also promoted Gujarati language at tertiary institutions. He taught Gujarati classes at undergraduate and postgraduate levels at the former University of Durban-Westville. In 1983, there were 19 Gujarati students, 11 of whom majored in the subject (South African Gujarati Maha Parishad, SD File 547/122).

PROMOTION OF HINDUISM AMONGST NON-HINDUS

Pandit Vedalankar was a firm believer in non-racialism. He believed that religion could play a key role in building and promoting tolerance and peace within a multi-racial society. He was keen on promoting and spreading Hinduism amongst non-Hindus, particularly amongst the African community. He stated,

> We live in this country so we are South Africans and we have an Indian culture and religion. But we have not introduced these to the people of South Africa. We do not find any of our religious books in Zulu, Xhosa, Afrikaans or other local languages so we can't get interest and sympathy. We haven't given them any idea of our culture, religion, history and the like. If we want to work with them we must adjust to these conditions and prove that we can walk shoulder to shoulder in any field. (*The Graphic* 10 August 1979, 28(32): 2)

In the 1980s books on Hinduism were published into the following languages: Zulu, Xhosa, and Sotho. Pandit Vedalankar believed that the translated Hindu books would provide the African community with a deeper insight into Hinduism (*Veda Jyoti*, 1992: 127).

CONCLUSION

Pandit Nardev Vedalankar's contributions to Hinduism shaped and defined the Hindu religion in South Africa. Ashwin Trikamjee, a member of the South African Hindu Maha Sabha, stated, 'Panditji had a remarkable influence in my life that resulted in my commitment to the cause of *Hindu Dharma*' (*Hindi* News, August 2014). I.C. Meer, the late historian and former columnist of *The Leader*, wrote,

> I also found the work of Pandit Nardev Vedalankar in the fifties most interesting. In 1954 his lecture on *Our Spiritual Heritage* was an interesting exposition of the Vedic philosophy. I admired the work he put into the Gujarati Eisteddfod, where I remember one of his pupils spoke on the life of Hazrat Omar, the second Caliph of Islam, whose just rule was extolled by this

little boy. It was most inspiring to have such unity in thought and action. (*The Leader* 26 May 1989).

The ultimate success of Pandit Vedalankar was his ability to bring the ideals of Hinduism and Vedic teachings to the layman, thereby being true proponents of Hinduism. This is largely an exploratory study and seeks to document the life and contributions of one of the early pioneers of Hinduism in South Africa. There are many, many other unknown religious pioneers whose histories have yet to be documented. Future studies on religious pioneers in South Africa will certainly add to the historiography on religion and identity in the diaspora.

ACKNOWLEDGEMENTS

This work is based on research supported by the National Research Foundation (NRF) of South Africa. Any opinion, findings expressed in this material is that of the author(s) and the NRF does not accept any liability in this regard. My sincere thanks to the Vedalankar family for comments on an earlier draft on this paper.

REFERENCES

Agrawal, Prem Narain, *Bhawani Dayal Sannyasi: A Public Worker of South Africa.* Ajmer: The Fine Art Printing Press, 1939.

Desai, Usha, 'An Investigation of Factors Influencing Maintenance and Shift of the Gujarati Language in South Africa', Ph.D. Thesis, Unpublished, Durban: University of Durban-Westville, 1997.

Diesel, Alleyn and Patrick Maxwell, *Hindusim in Natal: A Brief Guide*, Pietermaritzburg, University of Natal Press, 1993.

Diesel, A., 'The Worship and Iconography of the Hindu Folk Goddesses in Natal', *Journal for the Study of Religion*, (1992), 5(2): 3-30.

Fiat Lux, January/February 1983.

Fiat Lux, May (1983), 8(4): 30.

Forbes, Richard Huntington, 'Arya Samaj in Trinidad: An Historical Study Of Hindu Organizational Process in Acculturative Conditions (Caribbean)', *Dissertations from ProQuest*, 1984, Paper 1454. http://scholarly repository. miami.edu/dissertations/1454.

Gandhi, M.K., *My Experiments with Truth*, Navajivan Press: Ahmedabad, 1944.
Hindi News, 2014.
The Graphic 10 August 1979.
Hiralal, K., 'Mapping free Indian migration to Natal Through a Biographical Lens, 1880-1930', *New Contree* (2013), 66: 97-120.
Hiralal, K. 'Forging a Gujarati Hindu Identity in South Africa: A History of Gujarati Hindu Organisations in South Africa 1900-1983', *Nidan*, 2014, 26 (2): 2014, 60-82.
Indian Opinion, 11 November 1905.
Indian Opinion, 4 November 1905.
Indian Opinion, 3 April 1909.
Indian Opinion, 10 October 1908.
Indian Opinion, 2 October 1905.
Indian Opinion, 25 November 1905.
Indian Opinion, 27 March 1909.
'Karma Yogi', *Veda Jyoti*, Souveneir Brochure, September-October 1992.
Kelly, John D., 'A Politics of Virtue: Hinduism, Sexuality and Counter-colonial Discourse in Fiji', Chicago: University of Chicago Press, 1991.
Khorana, Meena G., 'Break Your Silence: A Call to Asian Indian Children's Writers', *Library Trends* (1993), 41(3): 393-413.
Kumar, Pratap P., *Hinduism and the Diaspora : A South Africa Narrative*, Jaipur: Rawat Publications, 2013.
Kuper, H., *Indian People in South Africa*, Pietermaritzburg: Natal University Press, 1960.
Maxwell, P., A. Diesel and T. Naidoo, 'Hinduism in South Africa' in Martin Prozesky, and John de Gruchy (eds.), *Living Faiths in South Africa*, Cape Town: Clyson Printers, 1995, pp. 177-202.
Naidoo, Thillayvel, *The Arya Samaj Movement in South Africa*, New Delhi: Motilal Banarsidass, 1992.
Nardev, Vidhulekha, 'Bhaiji: My father', *Hindi News:* South Africa: August 2014, Issue 12 https://www.facebook.com/207349612732546/photos/a.518847691582735.1073741856.207349612732546/518848258249345/?type=3&theater (accessed on 24 August 2015).
Reddy, Enuga and Meer Fatima, *Passive Resistance 1946 : A Selection of Documents.* Durban: Madiba Publishers/Institute for Black Research, 1996.
Samachar, June-July, vol. 3, 1980.
Samarpan, 1988.
South African Gujarati Maha Parishad: Secretarial Report, SD File 547/126.
The Leader, 26 May 1989.
Trikamjee, Ashwin, 'The Epitome of Humility Pandit Nardevji Vedalankar',

Hindi News: South Africa: August 2014, Issue 12 https://www.facebook.com/207349612732546/photos/a.518847691582735. 1073741856.207349612732546/518848258249345/?type=3&theater (accessed on 24 August 2015), 2014.

van der Veer, Peter, *Imperial Encounters: Religion and Modernity in India and Britain,* New Jersey: Princeton University Press, 2001.

Vertovec, S. 'Religion and Diaspora', Paper presented at the conference on 'New Landscapes of Religion in the West', School of Geography and the Environment, University of Oxford, 27-9 September 2000, pp. 1-45.

Contributors

KALPANA HIRALAL is an Associate Professor of History at the University of KwaZulu-Natal, South Africa. She teaches both undergraduate and graduate level modules on global history, women, gender and politics in Africa. Her PhD dissertation focused on the South Asian Diaspora to Africa in the context of settlement, trade and identity formation. Her current research focus is on African and South Asian Diaspora and gender and politics in South Africa. She has published in several local and international academic journals in the context of gender, identity and agency.

USHA SHUKLA (PhD, Hindi) is an academic in the Department of Languages, Linguistics & Academic Literacy in the School of Arts at University of KwaZulu-Natal. She is President of the Hindi Shiksha Sangh, South Africa (The Hindi Language Institute, South Africa). Her publications include the *Ramacaritamanasa in South Africa* (2002) and *Ramcharitmanas in the Diaspora: Trinidad, Mauritius and South Africa* (2011). Her research focuses on Hindi Language & Literature; Hindu Religion & Culture; Hindi Diaspora Studies.

KUMAR MAHABIR is an Assistant Professor in the Centre for Education Programmes at the University of Trinidad and Tobago (UTT). He obtained his PhD in Anthropology from the University of Florida. For over four decades, he has been conducting research on East Indians/South Asians in Trinidad, Suriname, Guadeloupe, Jamaica, St. Kitts, St Lucia, St Vincent, Grenada, Belize and French Guiana. He has published twelve books and numerous book-chapters, and journal and magazine articles. Mahabir is also the CEO of Chakra Publishing House and Vice-Chairman of the Indian Caribbean Museum.

SUSAN CHAND is currently a Professor of Anthropology in the School of Social Sciences, and Director for Research and Innovation at the University of the Southern Caribbean (USC), Trinidad. Dr. Chand obtained her PhD in Medical Anthropology from Savitribai Phule University, Pune, India. She has been working in Trinidad since 2005. Dr. Chand supervises research work at the undergraduate, graduate and PhD levels in the areas of sociology, anthropology, counselling psychology, human communication and educational psychology. She has presented papers at numerous national and international conferences on cross-cultural studies, juvenile delinquency, qualitative research methods and ethnomedicine and published articles on ethnographic studies on tribal dances of India. She is also the editor-in-chief of the *USC Journal of Research.*

VASHTI SINGH was awarded a research scholarship by the Indian Council for Cultural Relations (ICCR), Government of India and graduated with a PhD in Sociology of Education from Jawaharlal Nehru University, New Delhi, India in 2006. She is currently Programme Leader in the Centre for Education Programmes at the University of Trinidad and Tobago (UTT) and holds responsibility for coordinating all certificate, graduate and postgraduate programmes. Her research interests include interrogations of historical socio-political issues which have impacted upon education in Caribbean societies and new developments in teacher action research. Vashti Singh has served as chairperson for the Social and Human Sciences Sector Committee in the Trinidad and Tobago National Commission for UNESCO over the four year term 2011-15. She also currently serves as chairperson of the UTT Research Ethics Committee and participated in the Caribbean Network of Research Ethics Committees (CANREC) Workshop convened at Bridgetown, Barbados from 21-23 March 2016.

RUCHI AGARWAL is a senior Lecturer at the Mahidol University International College, Thailand where she teaches different courses in economics and religion. She is also a PhD candidate in Multicultural Studies at Research Institute of Language and Cultures (RILCA) of Mahidol University in Thailand. She received a Bachelors degree in General Management from MUIC and holds two MA degrees (one in Culture and Development from RILCA; and another in International Economics and Finance from Chulalongkorn University). Her articles have appeared in journals such as *Nidan, Silpakorn University Journal of Social Sciences, Humanities, and Arts, Journal of Social Sciences Mahidol University*, and several of her entries related to Hinduism and Buddhism in Southeast Asia have appeared in *Religions in Southeast Asia: An Encyclopedia of Faiths and Cultures*, ABC-CLIO Publishing: California. Her research interest include Hinduism in Southeast Asia, Ganesha cults, and the Economics of Religions.

GERELENE JAGGANATH is a Lecturer in the Department of Anthropology in the School of Social Sciences at the University of KwaZulu-Natal, Durban, South Africa. Her research interests include: migration and diaspora, youth and substance abuse, gender and work, community participatory research and food studies. She teaches undergraduate modules in introductory level Anthropology and Applied Anthropology, and postgraduate modules in Local knowledge and Sustainable development.

SAGIE NARSIAH is a Geographer by training. He received his PhD from Clark University, Massachusetts, USA, while on a Fulbright Scholarship. Dr Narsiah teaches in the Social Policy Programme in the School of Social Sciences, Howard College Campus, Durban. His area of research is primarily in the geography of development focusing on the impact of development policy at various geographical scales and the resistance of communities to neoliberal state interventions. Recently, he has been researching and writing, together with students, on issues pertaining to the social aspects of climate change. Dr Narsiah has published in leading national and international journals. He has on-going interests in the political economy of South Africa; social and critical theory; local government; boundaries and boundary disputes; social movements in general; sustainable livelihoods; and public participation among others.

NAMITA NIMBALKAR is an Associate Professor in the Department of Philosophy, University of Mumbai, India. She also taught at Birla College, Kalyan (affiliated to University of Mumbai) for fifteen years. She received her doctorate in Gandhian Philosophy and specialises in Contemporary Indian Philosophy and Comparative Religion. Her current research interests are: Environmental Ethics, Sufi Philosophy and Plato. She is invited at various national and international seminars/conferences to deliver talks on Gandhian Philosophy. She has published research papers and has participated at several national and international conferences held in India and abroad. She is conferred with the prestigious Heras Tata Fellowship (2015-16) to pursue post doctoral work on 'Culture and Travel: The Differing Perspectives of M.K. Gandhi and Rabindranath Tagore'.

GAIL M. PRESBEY is Professor of Philosophy at University of Detroit Mercy. She engages in interdisciplinary work that involves philosophy, world history, and political theory. Her areas of expertise are philosophy of non-violence and African philosophy, with current studies and research on Africa, Latin America, Mohandas Gandhi's movement, feminism, and pan-Africanism. She has done research in Kenya, South Africa, Ghana, and India, having received two J. William Fulbright Senior Scholar grants. She has four edited books and over fifty articles and book chapters published, as well as republications and translations in German, French, Italian, Spanish, and Chinese. She is currently in a graduate programme in World History at Wayne State University. Her home page can be seen at http://presbegm.faculty.udmercy.edu/

ANAND SINGH is Professor of Anthropology at the University of KwaZulu-Natal, Howard College Campus. His broad interests are Indian Diaspora studies, minority issues, nationalism, and ethnicity. He researched and published widely on the Indian Diaspora, with special reference to Indians in South Africa. His PhD is on Indians in Post-Apartheid South Africa and was published by Concept Publishers, New Delhi. The varying practices of the Hindu religion in Durban, South Africa, and the impact of satellite TV on igniting neo-national interests among Indians in South Africa has been of relevance to him since the early 2000s. His research shows how adherence to conventional customs and practices among a significant number of Indians continue to have an impact on their identities as both South Africans and as descendants of people from India, however, distant their ancestral roots might be for them.

Index